ATHEISM
The Case
Against God

THE SKEPTICS BOOKSHELF

ATHEISM: THE CASE AGAINST GOD
George H. Smith

ANTHOLOGY OF ATHEISM AND RATIONALISM
edited by Gordon Stein

THE BEST OF ROBERT INGERSOLL
edited by Roger E. Greeley

CLASSICS OF FREE THOUGHT (REVISED EDITION)
edited by Paul Blanshard

CRITIQUES OF GOD
edited by Peter Angeles

WHAT ABOUT GODS? (for children)

ATHEISM
The Case Against God

by
George H. Smith

 Prometheus Books
59 John Glenn Drive
Amherst, New York 14228-2197

Published in cooperation with
The American Rationalist

Published 1989 by Prometheus Books

Library of Congress Catalog Number: 79-2726
ISBN-13: 978-087975124-1
ISBN-10: 087975124-X

Printed in the United States of America on acid-free paper

To Diane,
for the tender moments

Contents

Introduction

Does a god exist? This question has undoubtedly been asked, in one form or another, since man has had the ability to communicate. Men have pondered the question, discussed it, argued it, and killed over it. It appears to be a simple question calling for a simple answer, but its simplicity is deceptive. Thousands of volumes have been written on the subject of a god, and the vast majority have answered the question with a resounding "Yes!"

You are about to read a minority viewpoint.

This book is a presentation and defense of atheism. This is not a sympathetic examination or interpretation of religious doctrines; it is a straightforward critique, philosophically and psychologically, of the belief in a god, especially as manifested in Christianity.

The subtitle—*The Case Against God*—has a twofold meaning: first, it refers to the philosophical case against the concept of god; and, secondly, it refers to the psychological case against the belief in a god. As a philosopher, I am continually amazed by the credence given to religious claims in the intellectual community; and, as a human being, I am appalled by the psychological damage caused by religious teachings—damage that often takes years to counteract.

Atheism, even in today's "liberal" atmosphere, is still somewhat unacceptable. Simply being an atheist may be acceptable—if, that is, one keeps it to oneself. What is frequently considered inappropriate is to advertise this fact, or openly to attack religious doctrines. Thus, some excellent critiques of theistic belief have been written by philosophers who, for reasons known best to themselves, refuse to acknowledge that what they are advocating is, in fact, atheism. And we also have the unfortunate spectacle of the philosopher who, after demolishing the idea of god philosophically, goes on to assure his audience, with a gesture of glib modesty, that he has merely presented his own opinion, and that he is not so presumptuous as to suggest that his listeners should abandon their belief in god. Finally, there is the philosopher or psychologist who, while openly admitting the irrationality of theistic belief, actually recommends it as a kind of therapeutic device designed to give emotional aid and comfort to mankind—thus lending support to the myth that the average man is emotionally incapable of facing facts.

It is my firm conviction that man has nothing to gain, emotionally or otherwise, by adhering to a falsehood, regardless of how comfortable or sacred that falsehood may appear. Anyone who claims, on the one hand, that he is concerned with human welfare, and who demands, on the other hand, that man must suspend or renounce the use of his reason, is contradicting himself. There can be no knowledge of what is good for man apart from knowledge of reality and human nature—and there is no manner in which this knowledge can be acquired except through reason. To advocate irrationality is to advocate that which is destructive to human life.

It is not my purpose to convert people to atheism; such efforts are usually futile. It is my purpose, however, to demonstrate that the belief in god is irrational to the point of absurdity; and that this irrationality, when manifested in specific religions such as Christianity, is extremely harmful. In other words, I have attempted to remove the veneer of intellectual and moral respectability that often enshrouds the notion of a god. If a person wishes to continue believing in a god, that is his prerogative, but he can no longer excuse his belief in the name of reason and moral necessity.

Although this book is intended primarily for laymen, it is impossible to avoid some degree of technicality due to the complexity of many religious doctrines. A writer cannot make an issue simpler than it really is; all he can do—and what I have attempted to do—is to present the relevant issues as succinctly and clearly as possible, discussing them in terms of their fundamentals, while remaining fair to the various sides under consideration. It is also impossible, within the scope of one book, to consider every argument ever presented in favor of theistic belief, or to answer every objection that might be raised against atheism, so I have necessarily restricted this discussion to those issues which I consider most important.

This book is divided into four major parts. In Part One, I discuss the nature of theism, atheism and agnosticism, and I present the insurmountable problems and contradictions entailed by the concept of god. In Part Two, I discuss the nature of reason, demonstrating its incompatibility with faith and revelation. In Part Three, I consider the most significant attempts to demonstrate the existence of a supernatural being through an appeal to reason, showing how each alleged proof fails totally to make its case. In Part Four, I discuss the harmful effects of religion in general, and Christianity in particular, upon morality and the attainment of man's happiness and well-being on earth.

My approach to atheism is eclectic in the sense that I draw from many different sources in defense of various positions. In no instance, however, should it be assumed that my use of a source implies an agreement with the atheistic position by that source. Similarly, my use of an author in support of a particular position implies my agreement to that extent only, and in no case should further agreement be assumed.

Also, it is necessary to mention that I employ the term "god" in two different ways. I use it with a lower case "g" (god) to refer to the generic idea of a god, *i. e.*, the general notion of a supernatural being, apart from any specific characteristics. I use the term "God" (with an upper case "G") to refer specifically to the God of Christianity, along with its various attributes, such as omnipotence, omniscience and so forth. This unusual method provides me with a simple means of indicating, in any given context, whether I am referring to the idea of god in general or to the idea of the Christian God in particular.

Finally, I wish to thank the many people who aided in the preparation of this book, who are unfortunately too numerous to be listed individually. I wish, however, to express my appreciation to two people who were especially instrumental in the writing of this book: Roy Childs, without whom the first line would never have been written; and Sylvia Cross, my editor, without whom the last line would never have been written.

George H. Smith
April 1973
Los Angeles

PART ONE:
ATHEISM AND GOD

I put the following work under your protection. It contains my opinion upon religion. You will do me the justice to remember, that I have always strenuously supported the right of every man to his opinion, however different that opinion might be to mine. He who denies to another this right, makes a slave of himself to his present opinion, because he precludes himself the right of changing it.

The most formidable weapon against errors of every kind is reason. I have never used any other, and I trust I never shall.

—Thomas Paine
Age of Reason

1.
The Scope of Atheism

The Myths of Atheism

The fool says in his heart, "There is no God." They are corrupt, they do abominable deeds, there is none that does good. (Psalms 14. 1)*

This frequently quoted passage captures the essence of how the average religious person views atheism. Atheism is probably the least popular—and least understood—philosophical position in America today. It is often approached with fear and mistrust, as if one were about to investigate a doctrine that advocates a wide assortment of evils—from immorality, pessimism and communism to outright nihilism.

Atheism is commonly considered to be a threat to the individual and society. It is "science divorced from wisdom and the fear of God," writes one philosopher, "which the world has directly to thank for the worst evils of 'modern war'. . . ."[1] In a

---

*Unless otherwise noted, all biblical quotations in this book are from the Revised Standard Version (1952).

recent critique of atheism, Vincent P. Miceli claims that "every form of atheism, even the initially well intentioned, constricts, shrinks, enslaves the individual atheist within and against him- self and, eventually, as atheism reaches plague proportions among men, goes on to enslave and murder society."[2]

Through similar representations of atheism as an evil, destruc- tive force, religionists throughout history have prescribed various forms of punishment for atheists. Plato, in his con- struction of the ideal state, made "impiety" a crime punishable by five years imprisonment for the first offense and death upon a second conviction.[3] Jesus, who is offered as the paradigm of love and compassion, threatened that nonbelievers will be thrown "into the furnace of fire" where "men will weep and gnash their teeth," just as "the weeds are gathered and burned with fire. . . ." (Matthew 13. 40-42). Thomas Aquinas, the great medieval theologian, taught that "the sin of unbelief is greater than any sin that occurs in the perversion of morals,"[4] and he recommended that the heretic "be exterminated from the world by death" after the third offense.[5]

Although the atheist now enjoys a comparative amount of freedom in the United States, the struggle for the legal rights of the atheist has been a difficult, continuous battle. For example, until the early part of this century, many states would not permit an atheist to testify in court, which meant that an atheist could not effectively file civil and criminal charges. The reasoning behind this prohibition was that, since the atheist does not believe in rewards and punishments after death, he will not feel morally obligated to tell the truth in a court of law. In 1871, the Supreme Court of Tennessee published this remark- able statement:

> The man who has the hardihood to avow that he does not believe in a God, shows a recklessness of moral character and utter want of moral responsibility, such as very little entitles him to be heard or believed in a court of justice in a country designated as Christian.[6]

Here we have the stereotype of the atheist as an insensitive, amoral cynic—a portrayal that remains widespread in our own time. Atheism, it is charged, is nothing but pure negativism: it destroys but does not rebuild. The atheist is pitted against morality itself, and the struggle between belief in a god and godlessness is viewed as a struggle between good and evil. If true, atheism is claimed to have ominous implications on a cosmic scale. A. E. Taylor expresses the fear of many theists when he writes:

> ... even in our hours of most complete and serenest intellectual detachment we cannot escape facing the question whether God can be eliminated from either the natural or the moral world without converting both into an incoherent nightmare.[7]

This image of a godless world is only one among many. Atheism has become so enshrouded with myths and misconceptions that many supposed critiques of atheism are notable for their complete irrelevancy. Some religious critics prefer to attack the unpopular ideas associated with atheism rather than face the challenge of atheism directly. Indeed, it is not uncommon to find entire books with the expressed intent of demolishing atheism, but which fail to discuss such basic issues as why one should believe in a god at all. These books are content to identify atheism with specific personalities (such as Nietzsche, Marx, Camus and Sartre) and, by criticizing the views of these individuals, the religionist author fancies himself to have destroyed atheism. In most cases, however, the critic has not even discussed atheism.

Presenting the atheistic point of view is a difficult, frustrating endeavor. The atheist must penetrate the barrier of fear and suspicion that confronts him, and he must convince the listener that atheism represents, not a degeneration, but a step forward. This often requires the atheist to take a defensive position to explain why atheism does not lead to disastrous consequences. The atheist is expected to answer a barrage of questions, of which the following are typical.

Without god, what is left of morality? Without god, what purpose is there in man's life? If we do not believe in god, how can we be certain of anything? If god does not exist, whom can we turn to in a time of crisis? If there is no afterlife, who will reward virtue and punish injustice? Without god, how can we resist the onslaught of atheistic communism? If god does not exist, what becomes of the worth and dignity of each person? Without god, how can man achieve happiness?

These and similar questions reflect an intimate connection between religion and values in the minds of many people. As a result, the question of god's existence becomes more than a simple philosophical problem—and atheism, since it is interpreted as an attack on these values, assumes a significance far beyond its actual meaning. Defenses of religion are frequently saturated with emotional outbursts, and the atheist finds himself morally condemned, diagnosed as a confused, unhappy man, and threatened with a variety of future punishments. Meanwhile, the atheist's frustration increases as he discovers that his arguments for atheism are futile, that the average believer—who was persuaded to believe for emotional, not intellectual, reasons—is impervious to arguments against the existence of a supernatural being, regardless of how meticulous and carefully reasoned these arguments may be. There is too much at stake: if the choice must be made between the comfort of religion and the truth of atheism, many people will sacrifice the latter without hesitation. From their perspective, there is much more to the issue of god's existence than whether he exists or not.

Where does this leave the atheist? Must he offer atheism as an alternative way of life to religion, complete with its own set of values? Is atheism a substitute for religion? Can atheism fulfill the moral and emotional needs of man? Must the atheist defend himself against every accusation of immorality and pessimism? Does atheism offer any positive values? These questions are not as complex as they may appear. Atheism is a straightforward,

6

easily definable position, and it is a simple task to outline what atheism can and cannot accomplish. In order to understand the scope of atheism, however, we must remove the wall of myths surrounding it—with the hope that the fears and prejudices against atheism will collapse as well. To accomplish this goal, we must determine what atheism is and what atheism is not.

II
The Meaning of Atheism

"Theism" is defined as the "belief in a god or gods." The term "theism" is sometimes used to designate the belief in a particular kind of god—the personal god of monotheism—but as used throughout this book, "theism" signifies the belief in any god or number of gods. The prefix "a" means "without," so the term *"a*-theism" literally means "without theism," or without belief in a god or gods. *Atheism, therefore, is the absence of theistic belief.* One who does not believe in the existence of a god or supernatural being is properly designated as an atheist.

Atheism is sometimes defined as "the belief that there is no God of any kind,"[8] or the claim that a god cannot exist. While these are categories of atheism, they do not exhaust the meaning of atheism—and they are somewhat misleading with respect to the basic nature of atheism. *Atheism, in its basic form, is not a belief: it is the absence of belief.* An atheist is not primarily a person who *believes* that a god does *not* exist; rather, he does *not believe* in the existence of a god.

As here defined, the term "atheism" has a wider scope than the meanings usually attached to it. The two most common usages are described by Paul Edwards as follows:

> First, there is the familiar sense in which a person is an atheist if he maintains that there is no God, where this is taken to mean that "God exists" expresses a *false* proposition. Secondly, there is also a broader sense in which a person is an atheist if he *rejects*

7

belief in God, regardless of whether his rejection is based on the view that belief in God is *false*.[9]

Both of these meanings are important kinds of atheism, but neither does justice to atheism in its widest sense. "Atheism" is a privative term, a term of negation, indicating the opposite of theism. If we use the phrase "belief-in-god" as a substitute for theism, we see that its negation is "no-belief-in-god"—or, in other words, "a-theism." This is simply another way of stating "without theism" or the absence of belief in god.

"Theism" and "atheism" are descriptive terms: they specify the presence or absence of a belief in god. If a person is designated as a theist, this tells us that he believes in a god, not why he believes. If a person is designated as an atheist, this tells us that he does not believe in a god, not why he does not believe.

There are many reasons why one may not believe in the existence of a god: one may have never encountered the concept of god before, or one may consider the idea of a supernatural being to be absurd, or one may think that there is no evidence to support the belief in a god. But regardless of the reason, if one does not believe in the existence of a god, one is an atheist; *i.e.*, one is without theistic belief.

In this context, theism and atheism exhaust all possible alternatives with regard to the belief in a god: one is either a theist or an atheist; there is no other choice. One either accepts the proposition "god exists" as true, or one does not. One either believes in a supernatural being, or one does not. There is no third option or middle ground. This immediately raises the question of agnosticism, which has traditionally been offered as a third alternative to theism and atheism.

III
Agnosticism

The term "agnostic" was coined by Thomas Huxley in 1869. "When I reached intellectual maturity," reports Huxley, "and began to ask myself whether I was an atheist, a theist, or a pantheist . . . I found that the more I learned and reflected, the less ready was the answer." According to Huxley, exponents of these doctrines, despite their obvious differences, share a common assumption, an assumption with which he disagrees:

> They were quite sure they had attained a certain "gnosis,"—had, more or less successfully, solved the problem of existence; while I was quite sure I had not, and had a pretty strong conviction that the problem was insoluble.[10]

When Huxley joined the Metaphysical Society, he found that the various beliefs represented there had names: "most of my colleagues were -*ists* of one sort or another." Huxley, lacking a name for his uncertainty, was "without a rag of a label to cover himself with." He was a fox without a tail—so he gave himself a tail by assigning the term "agnostic" to himself. It seems that Huxley originally meant this term as somewhat of a joke. He selected the early religious sect known as "Gnostics" as a prime example of men who claim knowledge of the supernatural without justification; and he distinguished himself as an "a-gnostic" by stipulating that the supernatural, even if it exists, lies beyond the scope of human knowledge. We cannot say if it does or does not exist, so we must suspend judgment.

Since Huxley's time, "agnosticism" has acquired a number of different applications based on its etymological derivation from the negative "a" and the Greek root *gnosis* ("to know"). Agnosticism, as a general term, now signifies the impossibility of knowledge in a given area. An agnostic is a person who believes that something is inherently unknowable by the human mind. When applied to the sphere of theistic belief, an agnostic is one who maintains that some aspect of the supernatural is forever closed to human knowledge.

Properly considered, agnosticism is not a third alternative to theism and atheism because it is concerned with a different aspect of religious belief. Theism and atheism refer to the presence or absence of belief in a god; agnosticism refers to the

9

impossibility of knowledge with regard to a god or supernatural being.

The term "agnostic" does not, in itself, indicate whether or not one believes in a god. Agnosticism can be either theistic or atheistic.

The agnostic *theist* believes in the existence of god, but maintains that the *nature* of god is unknowable. The medieval Jewish philosopher, Maimonides, is an example of this position. He believed in god, but refused to ascribe positive attributes to this god on the basis that these attributes would introduce plurality into the divine nature—a procedure that would, Maimonides believed, lead to polytheism. [11] According to the religious agnostic, we can state *that* god is, but—due to the unknowable nature of the supernatural—we cannot state *what* god is.

Like his theistic cousin, the agnostic *atheist* maintains that any supernatural realm is inherently unknowable by the human mind, but this agnostic suspends his judgment one step further back. For the agnostic atheist, not only is the nature of any supernatural being unknowable, but the *existence* of any supernatural being is unknowable as well. We cannot have knowledge of the unknowable; therefore, concludes this agnostic, we cannot have knowledge of god's existence. Because this variety of agnostic does not subscribe to theistic belief, he qualifies as a kind of atheist.

Various defenses have been offered for this position, but it usually stems from a strict empiricism, *i.e.*, the doctrine that man must gain all of his knowledge entirely through sense experience. Since a supernatural being falls beyond the scope of sensory evidence, we can neither assert nor deny the existence of a god; to do either, according to the agnostic atheist, is to transgress the boundaries of human understanding. While this agnostic affirms the theoretical possibility of supernatural existence, he believes that the issue must ultimately remain undecided and uncertain. Thus, for the agnostic atheist, the proper answer to the question, "Does a god exist?" is "I don't know"—or, more specifically—"I cannot know."

Whether this account represents the exact position of Thomas Huxley is not entirely clear. At times, as we have seen, he seems to indicate that the existence of the supernatural, while possible, is unknowable. Elsewhere, however, he writes that "I do not very much care to speak of anything as 'unknowable.' "[12]   And in summarizing the fundamentals of agnosticism, Huxley does not refer to anything as unknowable or "insoluble."

> ... it is wrong for a man to say that he is certain of the objective truth of any proposition unless he can produce evidence which logically justifies that certainty. This is what Agnosticism asserts; and, in my opinion, it is all that is essential to Agnosticism. ... the application of the principle results in the denial of, or the suspension of judgment concerning, a number of propositions respecting which our contemporary ecclesiastical "gnostics" profess entire certainty.[13]

This passage suggests that, in Huxley's opinion, there is not sufficient evidence to justify the belief in a god, so one should suspend judgment on this matter. In discussing whether the existence of a god is unknowable in principle or simply unknown at the present time, he writes:

> What I am sure about is that there are many topics about which I know nothing; and which, so far as I can see, are out of reach of my faculties. But whether these things are knowable by anyone else is exactly one of those matters which is beyond my knowledge, though I may have a tolerably strong opinion as to the probabilities of the case.[14]

Huxley is reluctant to uphold the absolute unknowability of the supernatural, and he wishes to maintain instead that, *as far as he knows*, knowledge of the supernatural lies beyond the

11

power of man's faculties. It would not be stretching the point to say that, in Huxley's view, the knowability of the super-natural is itself an issue which is unknowable.

Because of the ambiguity in the traditional agnostic position, the term "agnostic" has been employed in a variety of ways. It is commonly used to designate one who refuses either to affirm or deny the existence of a god, and because atheism is fre-quently associated with the outright denial of theism, agnos-ticism is offered as a third alternative. Here is a typical explanation found in the *Catholic Encyclopedia:*

> An agnostic is not an atheist. An atheist denies the existence of God; an agnostic professes ignorance about His existence. For the latter, God may exist, but reason can neither prove nor disprove it.[15]

Notice that agnosticism emerges as a third alternative only if atheism is narrowly defined as the denial of theism. We have seen, however, that atheism, in its widest sense, refers basically to the absence of a belief in god and need not entail the denial of god. Any person who does not believe in god, for whatever reason, is without theistic belief and therefore qualifies as an atheist.

While the agnostic of the Huxley variety may refuse to state whether theism is true or false—thus "suspending" his judgment—he does not believe in the existence of a god. (If he did believe, he would be a theist.) Since this agnostic does not accept the existence of a god as true, he is without theistic belief; he is atheistic—and Huxley's agnosticism emerges as a form of atheism.

Thus, as previously indicated, agnosticism is not an indepen-dent position or a middle way between theism and atheism, because it classifies according to different criteria. Theism and atheism separate those who believe in a god from those who do not. Agnosticism separates those who believe that reason cannot penetrate the supernatural realm from those who defend the capability of reason to affirm *or* deny the truth of theistic belief.

The agnostic theist encounters opposition, not just from atheists, but also from other theists who believe that god's nature can be known (at least to some extent) by the human mind. Likewise, the agnostic atheist encounters opposition from other atheists who refuse to acknowledge the theoretical possibility of supernatural existence, or who argue that reason can effectively show theism to be false or nonsensical.

The agnostic positions have been harshly criticized by believers and nonbelievers, and we shall examine the objections to agnosticism at a later time. Our purpose here is to clarify agnosticism's relation to theism and atheism so that future misunderstandings may be avoided. Agnosticism is commonly used as a refuge for those who wish to escape the stigma of atheism, and its vagueness has earned it the status of an intellectually respectable form of dissent from religion. In many cases, however, the term "agnostic" is misapplied.

Agnosticism is a legitimate philosophical position (although, in my opinion, it is mistaken), but it is not a third alternative or a halfway house between theism and atheism. Instead, it is a variation of either theism or atheism. The self-proclaimed agnostic must still designate whether he does or does not believe in a god—and, in so doing, he commits himself to theism or he commits himself to atheism. *But he does commit himself.* Agnosticism is not the escape clause that it is commonly thought to be.

IV

The Varieties of Atheism

The term "atheism" has been used thus far to cover every case of nonbelief in a god or gods. We shall now briefly analyze atheism's various manifestations.

Atheism may be divided into two broad categories: implicit and explicit. (a) Implicit atheism is the absence of theistic belief without a conscious rejection of it. (b) Explicit atheism is the absence of theistic belief due to a conscious rejection of it.

(a) An *implicit* atheist is a person who does not believe in a

13

god, but who has not explicitly rejected or denied the truth of theism. Implicit atheism does not require familiarity with the idea of a god.

For example, a person who has no knowledge of theistic belief does not believe in a god, nor does he deny the existence of such a being. Denial presupposes something to deny, and one cannot deny the truth of theism without first knowing what theism is. Man is not born with innate knowledge of the supernatural; until he is introduced to this idea or thinks of it himself, he is unable to affirm or deny its truth—or even to "suspend" his judgment.

This person poses a problem for the traditional classifications. He does not believe in a god, so he is not a theist. He does not reject the existence of a god, so, according to this meaning which is commonly attached to atheism, he is not an atheist. Nor does this person state that the existence of a supernatural being is unknown or unknowable, so he is not an agnostic. The failure of the traditional labels to include this possibility indicates their lack of comprehensiveness.

As defined in this chapter, the man who is unacquainted with theism is an atheist because he does not believe in a god. This category would also include the child with the conceptual capacity to grasp the issues involved, but who is still unaware of those issues. The fact that this child does not believe in god qualifies him as an atheist. Since these instances of nonbelief are not the result of conscious rejection, they are best designated as implicit atheism.

At this point, objections may be raised in protest against using the word "atheism" so that it includes uninformed children. Some religionists will undoubtedly charge that this is a cheap victory for atheism accomplished by means of an arbitrary definition. In response to this, we must note that the definition of atheism as the absence of belief in a god or gods is not arbitrary. Although this is a broader meaning than is usually accepted, it has a justification in the meaning of "theism" and the prefix "a." Also, as previously argued, this definition of atheism has the virtue of representing the antithesis of theism, so that "theism" and "atheism" describe all possibilities of belief and nonbelief.

Upon close examination, it is likely that the objections to calling the uninformed child an atheist will stem from the assumption that atheism entails some degree of moral degeneracy. How dare I call innocent children atheists! Surely it is unfair to degrade them in this manner.

If the religionist is bothered by the moral implications of calling the uninformed child an atheist, the fault lies with these moral implications, not with the definition of atheism. Recognizing this child as an atheist is a major step in removing the moral stigma attached to atheism, because it forces the theist to either abandon his stereotypes of atheism or to extend them where they are patently absurd. If he refuses to discard his favorite myths, if he continues to condemn nonbelievers per se as immoral, consistency demands that he condemn the innocent child as well. And, unless this theist happens to be an ardent follower of Calvin, he will recognize his sweeping moral disapproval of atheism for what it is: nonsense.

The category of implicit atheism also applies to the person who is familiar with theistic beliefs and does not assent to them, but who has not explicitly rejected belief in a god. By refusing to commit himself, this person may be undecided or indifferent, but the fact remains that he does not believe in a god. Therefore, he is also an implicit atheist.

Implicit atheism is conveniently ignored by those theists who represent atheism as a positive belief rather than the absence of belief. While this may appear to be a subtle distinction, it has important consequences.

If one presents a positive belief (i.e., an assertion which one claims to be true), one has the obligation to present evidence in its favor. The burden of proof lies with the person who asserts the truth of a proposition. If the evidence is not forthcoming, if there are not sufficient grounds for accepting the proposition, it should not be believed. The theist who asserts the existence of a

15

god assumes the responsibility of demonstrating the truth of this assertion; if he fails in this task, theism should not be accepted as true.

Some believers attempt to escape the responsibility of providing evidence by shifting this responsibility onto atheism. Atheism, which is represented as a rival belief to theism, allegedly cannot demonstrate the nonexistence of a god, so it is claimed that the atheist is no better off than the theist. This is also the favorite argument of the agnostic, who claims to reject theism and atheism on the basis that neither position can provide demonstration.

When atheism is recognized as the absence of theism, the preceding maneuver falls to the ground. Proof is applicable only in the case of a positive belief. To demand proof of the atheist, the religionist must represent atheism as a positive belief requiring substantiation. When the atheist is seen as a person who lacks belief in a god, it becomes clear that he is not obligated to "prove" anything. The atheist *qua* atheist does not believe anything requiring demonstration; the designation of "atheist" tells us, not what he believes to be true, but what he does *not* believe to be true. If others wish for him to accept the existence of a god, it is their responsibility to argue for the truth of theism—but the atheist is not similarly required to argue for the truth of atheism.

It is crucial to distinguish between atheism as such and the many beliefs which an atheist may hold. All atheists do adopt some positive beliefs, but the concept of atheism does not encompass these beliefs. Atheism refers only to the element of nonbelief in a god, and since there is no content here, no positive beliefs, the demand for proof cannot apply.

Atheism is not necessarily the end product of a chain of reasoning. The term "atheist" tells us that one does not believe in a god, but it does not specify why. Regardless of the cause of one's nonbelief, if one does not believe in a god, one is atheistic.

Theism must be learned and accepted. If it is never learned, it cannot be accepted—and man will remain implicitly atheistic. If theism is learned but rejected anyway, man will be explicitly atheistic—which brings us to the second kind of atheism.

16

(b) An explicit atheist is one who *rejects* belief in a god. This deliberate rejection of theism presupposes familiarity with theistic beliefs and is sometimes characterized as *anti*-theism.

There are many motivations for explicit atheism, some rational and some not. Explicit atheism may be motivated by psychological factors. A man may disbelieve in god because he hates his religious parents, or because his wife deserted him for the neighborhood minister. Or, on a more sophisticated level, one may feel that life is futile and helpless, and that there is no emotional room for god in a tragic universe. Motivations such as these may be of psychological interest, but they are philosophically irrelevant. They are not rational grounds for atheism, and we shall not consider them here.

The most significant variety of atheism is explicit atheism of a philosophical nature. This atheism contends that the belief in god is irrational and should therefore be rejected. Since this version of explicit atheism rests on a criticism of theistic beliefs, it is best described as *critical atheism*.

Critical atheism presents itself in various forms. It is often expressed by the statement, "I do not believe in the existence of a god or supernatural being." This profession of nonbelief often derives from the failure of theism to provide sufficient evidence in its favor. Faced with a lack of evidence, this explicit atheist sees no reason whatsoever for believing in a supernatural being.

Critical atheism also assumes stronger forms, such as, "God does not exist" or, "The existence of a god is impossible." These assertions are usually made after a particular concept of god, such as the God of Christianity, is judged to be absurd or contradictory. Just as we are entitled to say that a "square-circle" does not and cannot possibly exist, so we are entitled to say that the concept of god, if it entails a contradiction, does not and cannot possibly exist.

Finally, there is the critical atheist who refuses to discuss the existence or nonexistence of a god because he believes that the concept of "god" is unintelligible. We cannot, for example, reasonably discuss the existence of an "unie" until we know what an "unie" is. If no intelligible description is forthcoming, the conversation must stop. Likewise, if no intelligible description of "god" is forthcoming, the conversation must stop. This critical atheist thus says, "The word 'god' makes no sense to me, so I have no idea what it means to state that 'god' does or does not exist."

These varieties of critical atheism are identical in one important respect: they are essentially negative in character. The atheist *qua* atheist, whether implicit or explicit, does not assert the existence of anything; he makes no positive statement. If the absence of belief is the result of unfamiliarity, this nonbelief is implicit. If the absence of belief is the result of critical deliberation, this nonbelief is explicit. In either case, the lack of theistic belief is the core of atheism. The various atheistic positions differ only with respect to their different causes of nonbelief.

This book is written from the perspective of critical atheism. Its basic thesis is that the belief in god is entirely unsupported—and, further, that there are many reasons for not believing in a god. If theism is destroyed intellectually, the grounds for believing in a god collapse, and one is rationally obliged not to believe in a god—or, in other words, one is obliged to be atheistic.

This book is not a critique of theism plus a defense of atheism: the critique of theism *is* the defense of atheism. Atheism is not the absence of belief in god plus certain positive beliefs: atheism *is* the absence of belief in god. If we can show theism to be unsupported, false or nonsensical, then we have simultaneously established the validity of atheism. This is why the case for atheism is *The Case Against God*.

V

Jacques Maritain and the Slander of Atheism

The preceding divisions of atheism are simple and impartial. They do not prejudice the case for or against atheism by suggesting moral implications. Similarly, we may also list the varieties of theism, such as monotheism and polytheism, without suggesting any moral overtones. Unfortunately, though, when discussing a position of which one radically disapproves, the spirit of objectivity is sometimes sacrificed for prejudice and emotionalism. This is nowhere more evident than in the writing of Jacques Maritain, a prominent Catholic philosopher.

In *The Range of Reason,* Maritain devotes more than one dozen pages to the varieties of atheism, and since his classifications are widely used by other Christian sources (such as the *Catholic Encyclopedia*), it is instructive to examine his approach. Maritain typifies the unfair treatment that atheism has received at the hands of theologians and religious philosophers. Although Maritain presumably intends his classifications to be fair and impartial, they wreak of his personal dislike for atheism. Under the guise of categorizing, Maritain stacks the cards against atheism by assigning to it an inferior moral and psychological status.

Consider the case of what Maritain calls "practical atheism." Practical atheists "believe that they believe in God (and . . . perhaps believe in Him in their brains) but . . . in reality deny His existence by each one of their deeds."[16]

To state that men believe "in their brains" is a confusing way to acknowledge that they do, in fact, accept the existence of a supernatural being. By any rational conception of theism, such persons are theists, pure and simple. They may be hypocritical theists, they may profess to be Christians while ignoring Christian morality—but if these men actually believe in god "in their brains" (meaning: as an intellectual issue), then they are theists, regardless of their conduct or moral beliefs.

But the idea of a hypocritical Christian offends Maritain's sensibilities. The belief in god is morally good, and the theist who does not measure up to certain moral standards then somehow does not *really* believe in god. As to how one can become an atheist through one's actions, Maritain provides a simple answer: if one is sufficiently immoral or hypocritical, one deserves to be called an atheist. Under the cloak of classifying, Maritain purifies theism by pushing its undesirables into the atheistic camp, where he has no difficulty accepting their

19

deviant behavior. After all, what more can one expect from a godless man?

By reason of immorality, hypocrisy and possibly other repugnant traits, Maritain brands the condemned as an atheist—a "practical atheist," but an atheist nonetheless. Practical atheism, as defined by Maritain, is a conceptual garbage dump for theistic rejects; in actuality, it is a personal whim elevated to the status of a philosophical category. If deviousness is also incompatible with theism, then Maritain himself qualifies as a "practical atheist."

The other major form of atheism, according to Maritain, is "absolute atheism." Absolute atheists "actually deny the existence of the very God in Whom the believers believe and . . . are bound to change entirely their own scale of values and to destroy in themselves everything that connotes His name."[17]

We already have a hint that absolute atheism, like practical atheism, will involve moral distinctions. The absolute atheist changes his own values and sets out to destroy everything that reminds him of god. And what reminds us of god? If we take Maritain's word, god is associated with everything good and decent—which, unsurprisingly, leads to the conclusion that the absolute atheist is waging a war against goodness. Maritain thus concludes that "absolute atheism is in no way a mere absence of belief in God. It is rather a refusal of God, a fight against God, a challenge to God. And when it achieves victory it changes man in his own inner behavior, it gives man a kind of stolid solidity, as if the spirit of man had been stuffed with dead substance, and his organic tissues turned into stone."[18]

"Practical" and "absolute" atheism are considered by Maritain to be comprehensive categories (a third—"pseudo-atheism"—is dismissed as unimportant), so the prospective atheist has the choice of classifying himself as a hypocrite or as one constantly engaged in the destruction of values, thereby stuffing oneself with "dead substance." This is hardly an attractive alternative, nor an accurate one, but it does provide Maritain with a vehicle for destroying atheism without worrying about such mundane affairs as fairness, accuracy, intellectual respect and rational arguments.

20

Maritain misrepresents the atheistic position with remarkable ease and audacity and, in doing so, perpetuates many of the nonsensical myths about atheism. To those who believe that only the uneducated and uninformed slander atheism, J. Maritain and his followers provide instructive evidence to the contrary.

VI
What Atheism Is Not

Many of the myths of atheism, such as those put forth by Maritain, depend on assigning characteristics to atheism that do not belong to it. Because of this, it is essential to identify what atheism is *not*.

(a) It is commonly believed that atheism "involves what is called a world outlook, a total view of life."[19] One religionist tells us that atheism "cannot be content with being the simple negation of religious dogmas; it must elaborate its own conception of human life and become a positive reality."[20]

When atheism is represented by theists as a way of life, it is invariably portrayed as evil or undesirable. Conversely, when it is represented by atheists as a way of life, it is portrayed as beneficial rather than harmful. Joseph Lewis, a prominent atheist in the American free-thought tradition, writes that atheism "equips us to face life, with its multitude of trials and tribulations, better than any other code of living that I have yet been able to find." In the opinion of Lewis, "Atheism is a vigorous and courageous philosophy."[21]

To view atheism as a way of life, whether beneficial or harmful, is false and misleading. Just as the failure to believe in magic elves does not entail a code of living or a set of principles, so the failure to believe in a god does not imply any specific philosophical system. *From the mere fact that a person is an atheist, one cannot infer that this person subscribes to any particular positive beliefs.* One's positive convictions are quite distinct from the subject of atheism. While one may begin with

21

a basic philosophical position and infer atheism as a consequence of it, this process cannot be reversed. One cannot move from atheism to a basic philosophical belief, because atheism can be (and has been) incorporated within many different and incompatible philosophical systems.

(b) The label "atheist" announces one's disagreement with theism. It does *not* announce one's agreement with, or approval of, other atheists.

The practice of linking atheism with a set of beliefs, especially moral and political beliefs, allows the theist to lump atheists together under a common banner, with the implication that one atheist agrees with the beliefs of another atheist. And here we have the ever-popular "guilt by association." Since communists are notoriously atheistic, argue some theists, there must be some connection between atheism and communism. The implication here is that communism is somehow a logical outgrowth of atheism, so the atheist is left to defend himself against the charge of latent communism.

This irrational and grossly unfair practice of linking atheism with communism is losing popularity and is rarely encountered any longer except among political conservatives. But the same basic technique is sometimes used by the religious philosopher in his attempt to discredit atheism. Instead of communism, the sophisticated theologian will associate atheism with existentialism—which projects a pessimistic view of existence—and he will then reach the conclusion that atheism leads to a pessimistic view of the universe. It seems that the next best thing to convincing people not to be atheists is to scare them away from it.

While some atheists are communists and some are existentialists, this tells us nothing about atheism or other atheists. It is probable that the Christian, like the atheist, does not believe in the existence of magic elves—but this does not provide a significant area of agreement between the two. And so it is with atheism.

Just as one theist may disagree with another theist on important issues, so one atheist may disagree with another atheist on

22

important issues. An atheist may be a capitalist or a communist, an ethical objectivist or subjectivist, a producer or a parasite, an honest man or a thief, psychologically healthy or neurotic. The only thing incompatible with atheism is theism.

(c) When discussing atheism, many religionists adopt the following procedural rule: if all else fails, psychologize. If you cannot defeat the atheist in the realm of ideas, become his therapist: sympathize with him, inform him of his buried psychological problems that lead to his rejection of god. And, above all, assure him that fulfillment and happiness await him at his neighborhood church.

A philosopher speaks of "the natural desire for God," which, if not fulfilled, "leads to utter frustration."[22] Another philosopher asserts that, if men decide not to believe in a god, "in so far as they are intelligent they are saddened by their decision," because a godless world "would be strikingly short on *joy*."[23] Fulton Sheen tells us that happiness "is an ascension from what is inferior within us to what is its superior, from our egotism to our God."[24] One theologian has gone so far as to state that the phrase "the godless man" involves a contradiction.

> St. John Chrysostom was simply stating the central truth of this tradition in his famous dictim: "To be a man is to fear God". . . . God, who is the Author of nature, is integral to the nature of man. *Therefore, the man who does not fear God somehow does not exist, and his nature is somehow not human. On the other hand, there he is. That is the problem.*[25]

To be an atheist is suddenly to be less than a human being—to be an enigma, a walking paradox, a psychological problem. As one theist puts it, "Unbelief is an interruption in development."[26] Mental health, asserts a psychologist, "demands good interpersonal relations with oneself, with others, and with God"—which, observes Thomas Szasz, "neatly places all atheists in the class of the mentally sick."[27]

These assertions deserve little comment, but it is interesting

23

to note the appalling standard that is used in assessing the relationship between atheism and happiness. If the atheist is unhappy, this is attributed to his lack of belief. By relating happiness to an intimate connection with god, the "happy atheist" is defined out of existence.

The usual pattern for linking god and happiness is as follows: every human being naturally desires the good, the object of happiness. God is the ultimate, self-subsisting good. Therefore, every person naturally desires god as a corollary of his nature as a human being. Happiness divorced from god is a contradiction in terms.

From this dubious line of thought, we have the further conclusion that the atheist is struggling with frustrating internal conflicts. He desires happiness but, by denying god, he denies himself happiness. The atheist is somehow waging a war against himself, against his own nature—and this makes him neurotic, if not schizophrenic.

This theological psychology is Freudianism in reverse. While religionists have become annoyed with the attempts of psychologists to reduce theism to neurotic motivations, these theists do not hesitate to employ the same technique to their advantage against atheists. When the theist announces his belief in a supernatural being, he is usually taken at his word. When the atheist announces his disbelief in a god, however, he is often confronted with: "Oh, not really!" Or: "I'm sorry that you're so unhappy." Or: "I hope that your negative attitude toward life will change."

The atheist also finds his disbelief analyzed with reference to his age. If the atheist is young, his disbelief is attributed to youthful rebellion and immaturity—a "phase" that will hopefully pass. If the atheist is middle-aged, his disbelief is traced to the frustration of daily routine, the bitterness of failure, or the alienation from oneself and one's fellow man. If the atheist is old, the explanation lies in the disillusionment, cynicism and loneliness that sometimes accompany one's later years.

Contrary to what many theists like to believe, atheism is not a form of neurotic rebellion or mental illness. The religionist

24

cannot rid the world of atheists by committing them to an isolated asylum where they can be ignored. To label atheism as a psychological problem is a feeble, almost laughable attempt to evade the fundamental questions of truth and falsity. *Is theism true? What reasons are there for believing in a god?* These are the important issues, and these are the issues to which the theist must address himself if he wishes to confront the challenge of atheism.

Furthermore, there is a gross dishonesty involved in offering happiness as a motivation for believing in a god. Theists who appeal to happiness as a reward for belief display a shocking disregard for intellectuality and the pursuit of truth. Even if theism did lead to happiness (which it does not), this would not demonstrate its correctness. The psychologizing of atheism, therefore, is irrelevant to the subject of theism versus atheism. The theist who attempts to defeat atheism by subordinating truth to emotionalism accomplishes nothing, aside from revealing his contempt for man's ability to think.

VII

The Significance of Atheism

It may be objected that we have reduced atheism to a triviality. It is not a positive belief and does not offer any constructive principles, so of what value is it? If atheism may be compared to not believing in magic elves, why is it important? Why devote an entire book to a trivial subject?

Atheism is important because theism is important. The subject of god is not a remote, abstract topic with little influence in the lives of men. On the contrary, it is the core of Western religion—specifically, the Judaeo-Christian tradition—which includes a system of doctrines dealing with every major branch of philosophy.

If one believes, as I do, that theism is not only false, but is detrimental to man as well, then the choice between theism and atheism assumes a major importance. If considered purely as an abstract idea, theism may be dismissed without extended discussion. But when considered within its proper context—within the framework of its historical, cultural, philosophical and psychological significance—the question of god is among the most crucial subjects of our time.

If, thousands of years ago, a cult of elf-worshipers originated a set of doctrines, a religion, based on their belief in elves—and if these doctrines were responsible for widespread harm—then this book might be entitled *The Case Against Elves.* Historically, however, god has had more appeal than elves, so we are discussing *The Case Against God* instead.

Although atheism is negative in character, it need not be destructive. When used to eradicate superstition and its detrimental effects, atheism is a benevolent, constructive approach. It clears the air, as it were, leaving the door open for positive principles and philosophies based, not on the supernatural, but on man's ability to think and comprehend.

Religion has had the disastrous effect of placing vitally important concepts, such as morality, happiness and love, in a supernatural realm inaccessible to man's mind and knowledge. Morality and religion have become so intertwined that many people cannot conceive of ethics divorced from god, even in principle—which leads to the assumption that the atheist is out to destroy values.

Atheism, however, is not the destruction of morality; it is the destruction of supernatural morality. Likewise, atheism is not the destruction of happiness and love; it is the destruction of the idea that happiness and love can be achieved only in another world. Atheism brings these ideas down to earth, within the reach of man's mind. What he does with them after this point is a matter of choice. If he discards them in favor of pessimism and nihilism, the responsibility lies with him, not with atheism.

By severing any possible appeal to the supernatural—which, in terms of human knowledge, means the unknowable—atheism demands that issues be dealt with through reason and human understanding; they cannot be sloughed-off onto a mysterious god.

If atheism is correct, man is alone. There is no god to think for him, to watch out for him, to guarantee his happiness. These are the sole responsibility of man. If man wants knowledge, he must think for himself. If man wants success, he must work. If man wants happiness, he must strive to achieve it. Some men consider a godless world to be a terrifying prospect; others experience it as a refreshing, exhilarating challenge. How a person will react to atheism depends only on himself—and the extent to which he is willing to assume responsibility for his own choices and actions.

VIII
Theism on the Defense

The task of demythologizing atheism is now sufficiently complete, and the time has come to place the burden of defense where it belongs: squarely on the theist. We will no longer be concerned with rescuing atheism from the fog of misconceptions invented by religionists to obscure fundamental issues. The atheist is not obligated to answer arbitrary assertions, unproven assumptions and sloppy generalizations concerning the nature and consequences of the atheistic position. Atheism is the absence of a belief in a god, nothing more. If the theist wishes to draw monumental implications from this lack of belief, he must argue for his claims.

Without recourse to belittling atheism through mythology and slander, the theist is deprived of his major evasive tool. He is now required to face the issues, to present his beliefs intelligibly, and to argue for the truth of his beliefs. It is the atheist who demands proof from the theist, not vice-versa.

Before proceeding, it is necessary to offer some preliminary remarks concerning the nature of our inquiry. The conflict between theism and atheism centers on the existence or non-existence of a god. This issue involves two major branches of philosophical inquiry: *metaphysics* and *epistemology*.

Metaphysics is the study of reality, of existence as such—in

27

contrast to specialized studies of existence, such as physics (inanimate matter) and biology (living entities). Metaphysics deals with such concepts as matter, consciousness and causality.

Epistemology is "the study or theory of the origin, nature, methods, and limits of knowledge."[28] Epistemology deals with such concepts as truth, falsity, certainty and error.

We will often have occasion to refer to the metaphysical and epistemological implications of theistic belief, so the reader is urged to keep these categories in mind. "What exists?" is a question of metaphysics. "How does one know it?" is a question of epistemology.

Throughout most of this book, we shall be concerned with one question and one question only: *Should theism be accepted as true?* In the final analysis, this is the only important question. After this question is answered, we shall go on to explore the ethical and psychological implications of religious belief, but these areas are secondary to the basic issue of truth.

The theist is now on the defense; he can destroy atheism only by defending his belief in a god. If his defense fails, theism fails—and atheism emerges as the only rational alternative.

2.
The Concept
of God

I

The Meaning of "God"

Knowing what one is talking about is of inestimable value in any dialogue, so the theist, before he sets out to explain why we should believe in god, must first explain what he means by the word "god." What is the theist attempting to establish the existence of? What is the nature of god? How are we to identify him (or it)? At least some of the attributes of this supposed creature must be known before anything can be considered relevant to establishing his existence. As one theist puts it, "With no description or definition to work from, we will literally fail to know what we are talking about."[1] For example, consider the following dialogue:

Mr. Jones: "An unie exists."

Mr. White: "Prove it."

Mr. Jones: "It has rained for three consecutive days—that is my proof."

If this exchange is less than satisfactory, much of the blame rests with Mr. White: his demand for proof is premature. Mr.

29

Jones has not specified what an "unie" is; until and unless he does so, "unie" is nothing but a meaningless sound, and Mr. Jones is uttering nonsense. Without some description of an "unie," the alleged proof for its existence is incoherent.

When confronted with the claim that a god exists, the person who immediately demands proof commits the same error as does Mr. White. His first response should be, "What is it for which you are claiming existence?" The theist must present an intelligible description of god. Until he does so, "god" makes no more sense than "unie"; both are cognitively empty, and any attempt at proof is logically absurd. Nothing can qualify as evidence for the existence of a god unless we have some idea of what we are searching for. Even if it is demanded that the existence of god be accepted on faith, we still must know what it is that we are required to have faith in. As W. T. Blackstone puts it:

> Until the content of a belief is made clear, the appeal to accept the belief on faith is beside the point, for one would not know what one has accepted. The request for the meaning of a religious belief is logically prior to the question of accepting that belief on faith or to the question of whether that belief constitutes knowledge.[2]

The meaning of "god" and other religious terms has been a center of controversy in modern philosophical thought. A. J. Ayer, in his famous *Language, Truth and Logic* (published in 1935), argued that "to say that 'God exists' is to make a metaphysical utterance which cannot be either true or false. And . . . no sentence which purports to describe the nature of a transcendent god can possess any literal significance."[3]

The principle on which Ayer based his rejection of theology is now considered to be defunct, but philosophers continue to debate the pitfalls and merits of religious language. Indeed, much of the recent literature in the area of philosophical theology concerns itself with the meaning and use of religious terms.[4]

Because of this emphasis, most theistic philosophers are painfully aware of the problems of defining and clarifying the concept of god. There remains, however, an insufficient understanding among many theists as to the importance of this task. Defining the concept of god is not an optional chore to be undertaken at the theist's convenience. It is a necessary prerequisite for intelligibility. Assuming that the theist does not believe his theism to be nonsense, he has the responsibility of explaining the content of his belief. Failing this, to state that "god exists" is to communicate nothing at all; it is as if nothing has been said.

What, then, is meant by the word "god"? This is not a simple question. There have been many historical concepts of god, from the anthropomorphic deities of the Greeks to the omnipotent god of Christianity. Some gods are all-powerful, all-knowing and all-good, while others are not. Some gods are objects of reverence, while others are not. Some gods communicate with man, while others do not. Differences such as these make it impossible to give a detailed description of a god that will encompass every religion—and securing widespread agreement on the meaning of "god" is a formidable, if not impossible, task.

Much of the confusion surrounding the idea of god stems from the fact that the word "god" is among the most abused terms in the history of man, ranking with such notorious words as "freedom," "justice" and "love." Atheism is an unpopular stance (especially if one happens to be a clergyman), so some people conveniently attach the word "god" to any belief with a tinge of significance, such as nature, the universe, love or an ultimate goal in one's life. As Antony Flew notes, these idiosyncratic usages of "god" make it "comparatively easy to secure very wide verbal agreement on the existence of God. But much of this is exposed as unreal when we probe the different meanings given to the key word."[5] Today the professed theist

31

and atheist may agree on all major points except an appropriate label for their position—and it is instructive to note that, historically, more blood has been spilled in religious wars between theists of different persuasions than between theists and atheists.

Self-proclaimed theists will have to decide among themselves what, if anything, they have in common when they profess to believe in a god. I shall use the term "god" generally to designate any supernatural or transcendent being, and when I claim not to believe in a god, I mean that I do not believe in anything "above" or "beyond" the natural, knowable universe.

This concept of god carries two obvious implications: first, a god must be something other than part of the natural universe. Second, a god must be a being of some kind which is presumed by the theist to exist.

Although this generic idea of a god is applicable to the traditional varieties of theistic belief, especially within the Judaeo-Christian tradition, some alleged theists object to the portrayal of a god as supernatural or transcendent. These theists point to the "naturalistic" conceptions of god which identify god with some aspect of the natural universe. According to these theories, god is not "out there" above or beyond nature. Instead, he is an integral part of existence and must be regarded as "immanent," or indwelling, rather than transcendent.

Pantheism—the identification of "god" with nature—is a well-known instance of naturalistic theism. But the pantheist (or any alleged theist who wishes to describe his god solely in naturalistic terms) is open to the charge of reducing his god to triviality. If god is taken to be synonymous with nature or some aspect of the natural universe, we may then ask why the term "god" is used at all. It is superfluous and highly misleading. The label of "god" serves no function (except, perhaps, to create confusion), and one must suspect that the naturalistic theist is simply an atheist who would rather avoid this designation.

If one declared a belief in god, while stipulating that the term "god" was used as a synonym for the continent of North America, one's assertion would understandably be ignored or rejected as irrational. To expand this concept of god to include

Europe, Asia, the planet Earth, our solar system—or the entire universe—is equally absurd.

Our second requirement for the term "god"—that it must signify a being which is presumed to exist—has also come under attack by contemporary theologians. Paul Tillich, the most influential Protestant theologian of recent years, has written that "grave difficulties attend the attempt to speak of God as existing."

> ... the question of the existence of God can be neither asked nor answered. If asked, it is a question about that which by its very nature is above existence, and therefore the answer—whether negative or affirmative—implicitly denies the nature of God. It is as atheistic to affirm the existence of God as it is to deny it. God is being-itself, not a being.[6]

For Tillich, to state that "God is being-itself" is the only direct and nonsymbolic statement that can be made about God.[7] God is the name for the "infinite and inexhaustible depth and ground of all being. . . ."[8] Since "God is depth," argues Tillich, "you cannot then call yourself an atheist or unbeliever."

> For you cannot think or say: Life has no depth! Life itself is shallow. Being itself is surface only. If you could say this in complete seriousness, you would be an atheist; but otherwise you are not. He who knows about depth knows about God.[9]

Through a series of linguistic contortions, Tillich manages to erase the distinction between theism and atheism in one fell swoop. In the *Dynamics of Faith*, he comes close to maintaining that atheism is a self-contradictory position.

> The fundamental symbol of our ultimate concern is God. It is always present in any act of faith, even if the act of faith includes the denial of God. Where

there is ultimate concern, God can be denied only in
the name of God ... he who denies God as a matter
of ultimate concern affirms God, because he affirms
ultimacy in his concern.[10]

Walter Kaufmann has aptly termed Tillich's acrobatics as
"conversion by definition." "And," continues Kaufmann, "to
call attention to its occasionally crushing effect on unsuspecting
victims, one may christen it the bear's hug."[11]

Tillich represents an existentialist influence on Christianity,
and—true to the tradition of existentialism—it is difficult to
make sense out of what he says. Tillich denies that he is a
supernaturalist or a naturalist, both of which he considers to be
"insufficient and religiously dangerous solutions." Instead, Tillich's god is "self-transcendent."

God as the ground of being infinitely transcends that
of which he is the ground. He stands *against* the
world, in so far as the world stands against him, and
he stands *for* the world, thereby causing it to stand
for him. . . . Only in this sense can we speak of
"transcendent" with respect to the relation of God
and the world.[12]

At best, Tillich's concept of god is esoteric; at worst, it is
incoherent. By "god," Tillich does not mean simply straightforward material existence. God as "being-itself" or the
"ground of being" is something to which the concepts of
existence and nonexistence cannot apply. Therefore, we shall
do something that spells death for any theologian: we shall take
him at his word. Tillich's god, whatever it is, cannot be said to
exist. The atheist has no quarrel with this assertion. All things
considered, it is a generous concession to the atheistic position.

In his best-selling *Honest to God*, John A. T. Robinson continues the crusade to convert the atheists of the world through
linguistic maneuvers. Following Tillich's lead, Robinson rejects
entirely the notion of a supernatural being who is "out there."

"God is, by definition, ultimate reality. And one cannot argue whether ultimate reality *exists*. One can only ask what ultimate reality is like. . . ."[13]

Contrary to the widespread belief, which has persisted throughout the centuries, that the conflict between theism and atheism concerns the existence or nonexistence of a supernatural being, Robinson assures us that "the line between those who believe in God and those who do not bears little relation to their profession of the existence or nonexistence of such a Being. It is a question, rather, of their openness to the holy, the sacred, in the unfathomable depths of even the most secular relationship."[14]

Aside from its blatant arbitrariness, this contemporary approach has a distinct advantage over the traditional approach to the belief in a god. Whereas the Christian of yesterday had to expend a great deal of time and energy to win converts, the modern theologian has instituted a convenient time-saving device. By juggling a few terms here and there, the atheists of the world (whether they know it or not) are suddenly believers in a god. Through a deft feat of theological legerdemain, Tillich and Robinson have attempted to rid the world of atheism.

The efforts of Tillich, Robinson and other theologians to purge the concept of god of its supernaturalism have come under heavy attack by theists of a more traditional vein. These critics rightly charge that *Honest to God* does not eliminate atheism so much as it extends the term "god" in a confused and arbitrary way to include atheism. E. L. Mascall, an Anglican priest, maintains that Robinson is "so anxious to claim as a Christian anyone who, in spite of his professions of atheism or agnosticism, evidences a serious and generous attitude to life, that he is ready to atheise or agnosticise the Christian faith to almost any extent to bring the professing unbeliever within it."[15] Moreover, Mascall recognizes that "to suggest that 'atheists' are really unconscious crypto-theists is to do them a grave injustice."[16]

To divorce the idea of a supernatural being from the concept of god is to obliterate the basic distinction between theism and atheism. If the so-called "theist" or "Christian" is willing to admit that a supernatural being does not exist, then he has capitulated to traditional atheism, and his continued use of the word "god" carries no metaphysical significance. Robinson's equation of "god" with "ultimate reality" (whatever that means) injects confusion into an already confusing subject. His procedure is no more justified than if an atheist defined atheism as "the serious concern with one's own life"—thereby transforming every person who takes life seriously into an atheist.

Philosophical discussions should be as clear and precise as possible, and to restrict the concept of god to a supernatural being is in the interest of clarity. We have seen that the idea of god is extremely vague, having been used with many different meanings. Since the word "god" is likely to create confusion, we should institute a policy of verbal and conceptual economy in connection with its use. It should not be tacked on as excess baggage to an idea that can be better described in nontheistic terms.

There are important philosophical differences between traditional theism and atheism, differences that focus on the existence or nonexistence of a supernatural being. To adopt the atheistic position in substance, while defining "god" in such a way that one remains a theist or believer in god, is to misrepresent a philosophical position of long historical standing and to evade the major issue dividing theism from atheism. One may have an adverse response to the tag of atheism, and one may prefer to avoid it at all costs—but this is no excuse for adopting misleading and dishonest terminology.

To further illustrate the importance of the supernatural or transcendental element in theism, consider the following hypothetical situation. In another solar system, we discover an alien form of life, a form which is superior to man in all respects. These advanced creatures have an immense life span, superior strength, agility and mobility, and a superior capacity for memory and abstract thought. Does it follow, in virtue of these superior capacities, that these creatures should be designated as gods? No. Because despite the superiority of these creatures in

36

relation to man, they are nevertheless bound by the natural laws of the universe. They are subject to the same physical and logical laws as man. If we did choose to call these beings "gods," this would mean that any creature who is superior to another creature thereby becomes a "god"—which would clearly lead to a chain of absurdities. A dog would be a god with respect to a plant. A man would be a god with respect to lower life forms. A genius would be a god in relation to a man of average intelligence, who would himself be a god when compared to a moron. These uses of "god" may have a place as poetic metaphors, but they are chaotic nonsense if employed philosophically.

In short, the difference between a god and natural existence must be a difference of *kind*, not merely of degree. But this raises the additional problem: What do we mean by a supernatural or transcendent being, as contrasted with a natural being? What is the nature of the difference?

Although "supernatural" and "transcendent" have approximately the same meaning and are often used interchangeably, they may be distinguished for the purpose of analyzing the nature of a god from two perspectives: metaphysics and epistemology.

The term "supernatural" has metaphysical connotations, because it emphasizes the nature of a god in relation to the rest of existence. "Super," in this context, means "above" or "beyond" the natural universe—so a supernatural being is one that exists, in some sense, beyond the realm of the natural universe.

Theists do not wish to imply that a supernatural being resides physically, somewhere in space, beyond the universe. They are the first to agree that this naive concept of a god is easily discarded as nonsense. Rather, theists wish to convey the idea of a being that exists beyond the framework of natural law. A supernatural being is exempt from some or all of the cause-effect relationships that characterize the universe and natural existence. This exemption may be expressed by positing a god as the creator of the universe, the source of natural law, or by investing one's god with special powers that enable it to intervene in the natural course of events (such as through miracles). In any case, a supernatural being is "above" or "beyond" the restrictions imposed by natural law.

This exemption from natural law has profound implications for human knowledge. A god is epistemologically transcendent; *i.e.*, it falls beyond the scope of man's intellectual comprehension. The full nature of god is not merely unknown, it is unknowable. Man's rational capacity does not allow him to understand the nature of god, and any knowledge that man does possess concerning god is necessarily inadequate in some respect. God, by definition, is that which man cannot understand. In the words of Augustine:

> What then, brethren, shall we say of God? For if thou hast been able to understand what thou wouldest say, it is not God. If thou hast been able to comprehend it, thou hast comprehended something else instead of God. If thou hast been able to comprehend Him as thou thinkest, by so thinking thou hast deceived thyself. *This then is not God, if thou hast comprehended it; but if this be God, thou hast not comprehended it.*[17] (Emphasis added.)

To exist beyond the sphere of natural law means to exist beyond the scope of human knowledge; epistemological transcendence is a corollary of supernaturalness. If a god is a natural being, if his actions can be explained in terms of normal causal relationships, then he is a knowable creature. Conversely, if god can be known, he cannot be supernatural. Without mystery, without some element of the incomprehensible, a being cannot be supernatural—and to designate a being as supernatural is to imply that this being transcends human knowledge.

Epistemological transcendence is perhaps the only common denominator among all usages of the term "god," including those of Tillich, Robinson and other modern theologians. While some "theists" reject the notion of a supernatural being in a metaphysical sense, it seems that every self-proclaimed theist—regardless of his particular use of the term "god"—agrees that a god is mysterious, unfathomable or in some way beyond man's comprehension. The idea of the "unknowable" is the universal element linking together the various concepts of god, which suggests that this is the most critical aspect of theistic belief. The belief in an unknowable being is the central tenet of theism, and it constitutes the major point of controversy between theism and critical atheism.

II

Atheism and the Concept of God

Thus far we have discussed the general meaning of the term "god." A god is a supernatural being—which implies, metaphysically, that a god is not subject to the natural laws of the universe; and, epistemologically, that a god transcends human understanding. These are the basic beliefs of theism: the belief in the supernatural and the belief in the inherently unknowable.

The metaphysical and epistemological aspects of the concept of god suggest two critical approaches that may be pursued by the atheist. (a) The atheist may criticize the idea of a supernatural being, or (b) the atheist may criticize the notion of an inherently unknowable being. We shall now discuss these two lines of thought.

(a) The first problem with the designation of supernatural (or any equivalent term) is that it tells us nothing positive about a god. "Supernatural" tells us what a god is not—that it is not part of the natural universe—but it does not tell us what a god is. What identifiable characteristics does a god possess? In other words, how will we recognize a god if we run across one? To state that a god is supernatural does not provide us with an answer.

In addition, the entire notion of a supernatural being is incomprehensible. The theist wishes us to conceive of a being exempt from natural law—a being that does not fall within the domain of scientific explanation—but no theist has ever explained how we can conceive of existence other than "natural" existence. "Natural existence" is a redundancy; we have no familiarity with "unnatural" existence, or even a vague notion of what such existence would be like.

Natural law pertains to the presence of regularity in the universe, and, for this reason, it is sometimes referred to as the "uniformity of nature." Entities behave according to specific causal conditions, and we know that an object will not suddenly disappear or act in an incredible manner without an explanation or causal anticedent. Given the right conditions, an acorn will grow into a tree; it will not mysteriously transform itself into a pumpkin, a snowball, or a theologian. A dog will not sprout wings and breathe fire, a cat will not give birth to an elephant, and a colony of ants will not burst into a chorus of the national anthem.

Natural law is based upon the limited nature of existence. Every entity has a specific nature, specific characteristics, that determine the capacities of that entity. A plant, for example, does not have the capacity to think, and a man does not have the biological capacity for photosynthesis. The capacities, abilities, and potential actions of any existing thing, living or inanimate, are dependent on its characteristics—and since these are always specific and determinate, their resulting capacities are also specific and determinate. The characteristics of an entity determine what an entity can and cannot do; limitations are an integral part of the natural universe, and they constitute the foundation of natural law.

Regularity in nature is the consequence of limitations; entities are limited in terms of their actions. No existing thing can randomly do anything at any time under any conditions. This uniformity in nature permits the systematic study of reality (science) and the formulation of general principles of nature ("laws") which are used in predicting future states of affairs. While the particular scientific laws will change as man's knowledge increases, the principle of natural law itself is a constant; it persists as a corollary of existence.

THE CONCEPT OF GOD

This, in essence, is the meaning of natural existence or natural law. A god, as we have seen, cannot exist within this framework, but according to the theists he must exist nonetheless. This brings us to the considerable problem of how anything can exist as a supernatural being.

If a supernatural being is to be exempt from natural law, it cannot possess specific, determinate characteristics. These attributes would impose limits and these limits would restrict the capacities of this supernatural being. In this case, a supernatural being would be subject to the causal relationships that mark natural existence, which would disqualify it as a god. Therefore, we must somehow conceive of a being without a specific nature, a being that is indeterminate—a being, in other words, that is nothing in particular. But these characteristics (or, more precisely, lack of characteristics) are incompatible with the notion of existence itself.

To be is to be *something* as opposed to nothing, and to be something is to be something specific. If a god is to have any characteristics (which it must to exist), these characteristics must be specific—but to assign definite attributes, to say that a being is this as opposed to that, is to limit the capacities of that being and to subject it to the uniformity imposed by those capacities. A supernatural being, if it is to differ in kind from natural existence, must exist without a limited nature—which amounts to existing *without any nature at all.* *

If we are to talk intelligibly about a god, we must presuppose that this god has characteristics by which it can be identified. But once the idea of supernatural existence is introduced, an existence apart from the limitations of natural law, we exclude the possibility of assigning any definite characteristics to a god—because by so doing we bring our god within the realm of limitations and hence within the realm of natural law.

The theist, even if he agrees with this analysis, is bound to remain singularly unimpressed. To the charge that we cannot

*Some of the ideas discussed in this section, are based on a recorded lecture, "The Concept of God," by Nathaniel Branden in The Basic Principles of Objectivism series (Los Angeles, Academic Associates).

comprehend "supernatural" existence, that it makes no sense to the human mind, the theist is liable to reply, "See, I told you so. God transcends human understanding; he is unknowable."

This is the standard defense against any objection to the metaphysical impossibility of a supernatural being. The theist and the atheist may well agree that a supernatural being cannot be grasped by the human mind; but whereas the atheist wishes to scrap the notion of god for this reason, the theist uses it as evidence that god falls beyond the scope of human understanding. Thus, so long as the discussion remains on this level, an impasse is reached—which indicates that we need to examine a more basic issue. We must move from metaphysics to epistemology. As is often the case, this is where the fundamental disagreement lies; this is where the major battle will take place—and, ultimately, this is where the conflict will be decided.

(b) Leslie D. Weatherhead expresses a central tenet of theism when he writes:

> How can man, an insect on a wayside planet, which is itself of no size or importance, amid a million galaxies that baffle the imagination, put the tiny tape of words around the doings of this august and unimaginable Being who created all that is in the heavens and the heaven of heavens?[18]

The belief that god is basically unknowable is the most important epistemological element of theistic belief. It is shared by all theists to some extent, who disagree only with regard to what degree, if any, god's nature can be known.

We must remember that theism maintains not just that god's nature is unknown to man at the present time, but that god's nature is unknowable *in principle*. Man will never understand god, which is expressed by such terms as ineffable, inexpressible, transcendent and unfathomable.

The most extreme version of this belief is religious agnosticism, which holds that the nature of god is completely unknowable. Thomas McPherson, in an article entitled "Religion as the Inexpressible," defends the agnostic position and carries it to its logical conclusion:

> There are some things that just cannot be said. As long as no one tries to say them, there is no trouble. But if anyone does try to say them he must take the consequences. We ought not to try to express the inexpressible. The things that theologians try to say (or some of them) belong to the class of things that just cannot be said. The way out of the worry is retreat into silence.[19]

McPherson has a point: if one believes that god is inexpressible, then one quite literally has nothing to say and should therefore "retreat into silence." Any attempt to talk about the unknowable will eventually lead to strange and paradoxical assertions, such as that of St. Maximus the Confessor (a Greek theologian of the seventh century), who taught that "that mind is perfect which, through true faith, in supreme ignorance supremely knows the supremely Unknowable. . . ."[20]

If consistently adhered to, theistic agnosticism will result in a dialogue of the following kind:

Theist: "I believe in god."

Atheist: "What is 'god'?"

Theist: "I don't know."

Atheist: "But what is it that you believe in?"

Theist: "I don't know that either."

Atheist: "Then of what possible significance is your original claim to believe in god? How does your 'belief' differ from no belief whatsoever?"

Religious agnosticism suffers from the obvious flaw that one cannot possibly know *that* something exists without some knowledge of *what* it is that exists. In the words of the nineteenth-century-philosopher, Ludwig Feuerbach: "To deny all the qualities of a being is equivalent to denying the being himself. A being without qualities is one which cannot become an object to the mind, and such a being is virtually non-existent."21

If god is completely unknowable, the concept of "god" is totally devoid of content, and the word "god" becomes a meaningless sound. To state that "god exists"—where "god" represents an unknown, a blank—is to say nothing whatsoever. It is on a par with, "Unies exist" or, "A blark exists." The agnostic, by refusing to state the content of his belief, exempts himself from reason and serious consideration. Religious agnosticism is so indefensible that one must regard it as nothing more than the antics of a confused and muddled mind.

Religious agnosticism is predicated on the concept of the "unknowable," and herein lies the root of its irrationality. To posit the existence of something which, by its nature, cannot be known to man is to submerge oneself in hopeless contradictions.

First, we must ask: If god cannot be known, how can god be known to exist? Quoting Nathaniel Branden, "To claim that a thing is unknowable, one must first know that it exists—but then one already has knowledge of it, to that extent."22 To assert the existence of the unknowable is to claim knowledge of the unknowable, in which case it cannot be unknowable.

Second, if god cannot be comprehended, then none of his attributes can be known—including the attribute of incomprehensibility. To state that something is by nature unknowable is to pronounce knowledge of its nature, in which case we are again involved in a contradiction.

When one claims that something is unknowable, can one produce knowledge in support of this claim? If one cannot, one's assertion is arbitrary and utterly without merit. If one can, one has accomplished the impossible: one has knowledge of the unknowable.

Third, to support the existence of the unknowable not only presupposes knowledge—it presupposes *omniscient* knowledge. Again quoting Branden:

> The assertion that a thing is unknowable carries the necessary epistemological implication that the

speaker is omniscient—that he has total knowledge of everything in the universe and, from his unique vantage point, is able to proclaim that certain things are inherently beyond the reach of man's knowledge and understanding.[23]

While some things are presently unknown to man, it is never rational to claim that something is forever unknowable to man. There is no possible evidence that one could adduce in support of this claim. Any evidence would flatly contradict one's initial claim, because it would entail knowledge of the unknowable.

To claim that god is incomprehensible is to say that one's concept of god is unintelligible, which is to confess that one does not know what one is talking about. The theist who is called upon to explain the content of his belief—and who then introduces the "unknowable" as a supposed characteristic of the concept itself—is saying, in effect: "I will explain the concept of god by pointing out that it cannot be explained."

Atheists have long contended that the concept of god is unintelligible, this being a major reason why it cannot be accepted by any rational man. The theist who openly admits this cannot expect to be taken seriously. The idea of the unknowable is an insult to the intellect, and it renders theism wholly implausible.

By criticizing the notion of an unknowable being, we have indirectly destroyed the concept of a supernatural being. We have seen that these ideas are two sides of the same theistic coin. If it is irrational to assert the existence of an unknowable being, it is equally irrational to assert the existence of its metaphysical corollary: a supernatural being. If knowledge of the unknowable is a contradiction, knowledge of the supernatural is a contradiction as well. This has the effect of excluding theism from the sphere of rational consideration, in which case atheism wins by default.

The theist now has two basic alternatives: he can abandon his defense of a supernatural being altogether, or he can continue to proclaim the existence of a supernatural being—while arguing

45

that this being is knowable, at least to some extent, by the human mind.

Since the first choice is a surrender to atheism, the second possibility is usually adopted. The survival of theism requires an escape from agnosticism and a defense of man's intellect to comprehend god in some manner. This brings us to the Christian conception of God, which, especially within the Catholic tradition, has sensed the indefensibility of religious agnosticism and has rejected it accordingly.

3.
The God
of Christianity

I
An Escape from Agnosticism

The Christian God (with a capital "G") is a complex and mysterious creature. Christians debate among themselves concerning God's attributes and the degree to which God's nature can be comprehended by man. There is a strong current in Christian thought which defends the capacity of man to know God through reason, especially within the framework of Thomism (the theology of Thomas Aquinas). There remains, however, a problem regarding the status of this knowledge. Can man have direct knowledge of God's nature? Christians unanimously answer "no." Then what is the nature and validity of our knowledge of God? In what way is it reliable?

If we wish to discover the nature of the Christian God, the *National Catholic Almanac* offers us a generous assortment of attributes from which to choose. According to this source, God is "almighty, eternal, holy, immortal, immense, immutable, incomprehensible, ineffable, infinite, invisible, just, loving, merciful, most high, most wise, omnipotent, omniscient, omnipresent, patient, perfect, provident, supreme, true."[1]

47

This is certainly an impressive list, but one problem immediately becomes apparent: included in this catalogue of characteristics is "incomprehensible." One must wonder how it is possible to declare God's incomprehensibility and simultaneously list twenty-two additional attributes. If God cannot be comprehended, how can the Christian offer us a string of attributes whose function, presumably, is to enable us to understand the nature of God?

The answer lies in the fact that Christianity, like religious agnosticism and all other varieties of theism, maintains that the *true* nature of God—his essence—lies beyond the reach of man's reason. Whatever knowledge of God we may possess is necessarily deficient in some way. According to one Christian:

> .. . there is an important element of truth in the mystical view that God is ineffable. It arises from a vivid awareness of the transcendence of God and provides a salutary warning that finite man can never fully know the essence of God and must never expect to comprehend Him in clear and distinct ideas. But to infer from this that He is wholly ineffable is to overlook the fact that He is immanent as well as transcendent and may be known in a measure through His effects in nature and experience.[2]

Christianity and religious agnosticism thus have a common base: each holds the nature of god to be fundamentally unknowable. In this respect, Christianity is subject to the preceding critique of the unknowable and shares the irrationalism of agnosticism.

But we must take into account that Christianity attempts to provide some means, however inadequate, by which man can know God. The Christian offers some characteristics for his God, so he differs from the agnostic in this respect at least. We must now determine how successful Christianity has been in its escape from the unknowable god of agnosticism.

It is important to note that, although religious agnosticism is blatantly irrational, the agnostic is aware of one vital point: to assign attributes to an entity is to limit the capacities of that entity. An entity can function only within the context of its nature, and to define the nature of god is to *restrict* the capacities of god to that nature.

John Hospers describes the agnostic position as follows:

> What *can* we say truly about God? According to the mystic, nothing at all. Indeed, to say anything about God is to *limit* God. To say that God possesses characteristic A is to say that God lacks the characteristic not-A, and to say this is already to limit God, who transcends all such distinctions.[3]

Since he wishes to retain the idea of an infinite or unrestricted god, the theistic agnostic refuses to assign positive attributes to his god. Rather than run the risk of imposing limits, the agnostic prefers to believe in an unknowable god.

Paul Tillich, by arguing that God cannot be said to exist, exhibits an awareness of this danger. Tillich realizes that existence entails a *finite* nature, and, if God exists, then God must be a finite being. While Tillich does not wish to deny the reality of God, he does sense the pitfall involved in asserting the existence of God. Merely to state that God exists, that God is a being, is to exclude the possibility of an infinite nature—so Tillich resorts to a stance which resembles agnosticism.

Many Christians wish to avoid agnosticism by assigning characteristics to their deity, but these Christians find themselves confronted with a serious dilemma. On the one hand, they favor the notion of a supernatural being, a being without restrictions, a being with an infinite nature. On the other hand, they want a god with characteristics, a god that can be identified. Therefore, they must conceive of a way to give their god a nature while avoiding the consequence of limitations.

The solution of this difficulty has been the introduction of "unlimited attributes"—characteristics of God that do not limit his nature. Hence, we have the traits of omnipotence, omniscience, and other limitless qualities whose function is to give substance to the concept of God without restricting the nature of God. In this way, the Christian hopes to keep his supernatural being without collapsing into the contradiction of agnosticism.

But this enterprise is doomed from the start. An "unlimited attribute" is a contradiction in terms. To specify characteristics is to specify determinate qualities, and these qualities cannot be divorced from limitations. Again quoting Feuerbach: "Dread of limitation is dread of existence. All real existence . . . is qualitative, determinative existence. . . . A God who is injured by determinate qualities has not the courage and the strength to exist."[4]

The phenomenon of the "unlimited attribute" is the central epistemological contradiction of the Christian God. As we shall see, the attributes of the Christian God cannot withstand critical examination; the concept of God is permeated with ambiguities, contradictions and just plain nonsense. Most of these flaws stem from the futile effort of the Christian to endow his God with unrestricted qualities. The result is an insoluble mixture of finite qualities and an infinite being, which transforms the Christian God into a conceptual mess of unequaled dimensions.

When God's attributes are pushed to the limits of absurdity, the Christian invariably falls back on man's inability to comprehend God. If the atheist complains that omnipotence is impossible, or that a benevolent God cannot be reconciled with the existence of evil in the universe, the Christian retreats into the unknowable god of agnosticism. Man, we are told, cannot understand the ways of God.

We have now uncovered an important principle: Scratch the surface of a Christian and you will find an agnostic. The Christian God is simply the agnostic god with window dressing. The characteristics of the Christian God are a first line of defense against agnosticism, but the Christian will eventually seek refuge in the claim that his God, like the agnostic god, is unknowable.

If this is true—if the God of Christianity collapses into agnosticism under scrutiny—then the Christian is no better off than the agnostic, and our previous criticisms of agnosticism will apply to Christianity as well. The Christian will be expressing the inexpressible, thinking about the unthinkable, and presenting knowledge of the unknowable. If this is the case, we must ask the Christian to "retreat into silence" or relinquish his belief. And we shall also have demonstrated why Christian theism must be rejected by any person with even a shred of respect for reason.

II

Knowing the Christian God

The Christian faces this dilemma: if he wishes to retain the notion of a supernatural being, he must insist that God's nature is incomprehensible. On the other hand, if the Christian wishes to escape the plight of agnosticism—which he must to give meaning to the concept of God—he must also argue that man is capable of knowing God in some manner. It seems that this is an impossible task, but various solutions have been proposed.

Traditional Christianity offers us two basic ways in which we may discuss the nature of God: (a) negatively, by stating what God is not, referred to as *negative theology;* (b) positively, by stating what God is, referred to as *affirmative theology.* Some theologians have adopted negative theology exclusively, while others have employed a combination of both. Our concern is with evaluating the success of these approaches in explaining how man can know an unknowable God.

(a) If one examines the list of attributes quoted earlier from the *National Catholic Almanac,* one will find that many of them are negations; *i.e.,* they specify what God is not. These are derived from the *via negativa,* the negative way, which has a history reaching back to the early Platonic influence in Christianity. The negative way was explicitly advocated by Pseudo-Dionysius in the latter part of the fifth century A.D., and it achieved prominence with Thomas Aquinas in the thirteenth century A.D. The negative way is based on the premise that "we cannot know what God is, but rather what He is not."⁵ Negative theology purports to give us an insight to God's nature by specifying which characteristics he cannot possess, thereby differentiating God from finite beings.

Some of God's attributes are obviously negative: "immutable" tells us that God does *not* change; "ineffable" tells us that God *cannot* be described; "infinite" tells us that God is *not* finite; "invisible" tells us that God is *not* visible. Even some terms that appear to be positive are essentially negative. To say that God is "eternal," for instance, is to say that God is "not subject to temporal succession."⁶ Furthermore, attributes such as "omnipotence" and "omniscience" signify capacities *without* limits, so they also stem (at least partially) from the negative way.

The first problem with negative theology is that, if God is described solely in terms of negation, it is impossible to distinguish him from nonexistence—"any Being which had to be characterized entirely in negations would, surely, not be discernible from no Being at all."⁷ God is not matter; neither is nonexistence. God does not have limitations; neither does nonexistence. God is not visible; neither is nonexistence. God does not change; neither does nonexistence. God cannot be described; neither can nonexistence. And so on down the list of negative predicates. If the theist wishes to distinguish his belief in God from the belief in nothing at all, he must give some positive substance to the concept of God.

Moreover, negative theology is incapable of standing by itself. In order to state what God is not, one must have prior knowledge of what God is. Without some positive idea of his nature, it is impossible to determine which characteristics cannot belong to God. If God's nature is a complete blank to man, the Christian cannot list qualities that are supposedly incompatible with that nature. Nothing can be known to be incompatible with the unknowable

How does the Christian know that limits are incompatible with God's nature? Why is it not possible for God to be a

52

material, visible organism? On what basis is it claimed that God cannot be a finite creature? Why does change conflict with the nature of God? These and similar questions cannot be answered without some positive reference to the nature of God.

We see, therefore, that negative theology presupposes the validity of affirmative theology; the negative predicates are possible only if it is possible to know their positive counterparts. If God cannot be known in some positive way, God cannot be known at all—which throws us into blatant agnosticism.

It is important to recognize that the negative way is the vehicle whereby the Christian presents his "unlimited attributes." Characteristics such as infinite, ineffable and immaterial give the appearance of providing God with attributes without imposing restrictions on him. In actuality, however, these characteristics simply push the idea of God beyond man's comprehension; they are thinly veiled agnosticism.

If one were to list the essential traits of man's knowledge of reality and then negate each of these traits, one would arrive at the negative attributes of the Christian God. Defining God with negative terminology may be described as the "non-everything-man-knows" technique. Man, when he perceives reality, is aware of finite, limited existence—but God is infinite and unlimited. Man perceives material organisms with limited capacities—but God is immaterial with unrestricted capacities. Man perceives a world of change—but God is unchanging. Man perceives a knowable, natural universe—but God is an unknowable, supernatural being.

If one set out with single-minded devotion to undercut man's conceptual ability, one could not do better than to posit the Christian God and demand that men believe in him. *God is the negation, the exact reversal, of how man perceives reality.*

To say that God is not this or that appears to provide a partial answer to the question, "What is God?" But when the "this" and "that" refer to the entire context of man's knowledge, negative theology pushes God into agnosticism, and our question remains unanswered.

Infinite, ineffable, immaterial—these and similar characteristics must be negative; if one attempts to express them positively (while retaining their intended context and meaning), one will be enmeshed in a maze of contradictions. What concept could express existence without limitations, when limits are entailed by the concept of existence itself? How can one conceive, in positive terms, of an unknowable being which one knows to exist? How can one conceptualize existence apart from matter, energy and their derivatives (such as consciousness), when these are the only kinds of existence of which we have knowledge?

The answer is simple: we cannot conceive of these things, nor can we conceive of God's other negative qualities—nor will we ever be able to conceive of them. The illusion of qualities without limitations relies on the cloak of negation; when the privilege of dealing solely with negations is denied, there is no possible way to express the concept of an "unlimited attribute." To assign characteristics to a being is to define, limit and restrict the nature of that being. As previously argued, an "unlimited attribute" is a contradiction in terms.

While the negative way logically presupposes positive knowledge of God's nature, most of God's negative qualities, because they entail the inherent contradiction of the "unlimited attribute," cannot be translated into positive terms. The negative attributes of God do not provide us with any real knowledge of God's nature; they are mere pseudo-attributes. Implicit within these characteristics is the premise: "reason will never understand this."

When the contradiction of the "unlimited attribute" is flushed from its hiding place in negative theology, we see that the God of the *via negativa* is just as incomprehensible, if not more so, than the mystical god of agnosticism. The negative way is a cardboard prop of Christianity to conceal its unknowable God. When this prop collapses, theistic agnosticism emerges, complete with its package of contradictions and nonsensical utterances.

(b) Many theologians use negative theology in conjunction with affirmative theology, which allegedly permits the Christian to ascribe positive qualities to his God. If these approaches are combined, it is claimed that we can avoid the dilemma of agnosticism.

Aquinas applied such terms as "knowledge," "life," "will," "love," "justice and mercy," and "power" to the concept of God, and these qualities are clearly positive in nature. But we still have serious problems. Most of the positive qualities commonly attributed to God are of secondary importance because they refer to God's personality rather than his metaphysical nature as an existing being. To say that God is loving or merciful is not equivalent to claiming that he is infinite or ineffable, so we have an imbalance between the positive and negative approaches.

Wisdom, love, knowledge, power—these may be fine qualities, but just what are they qualities of? What is the nature of the being possessing them? Affirmative theology, if it is to rescue God from the oblivion of the unknowable, must accomplish more than list secondary characteristics. If it cannot, affirmative theology is, at best, a useless device.

In addition, the God of affirmative theology is beset by a problem of long historical standing from which he cannot escape. All of the supposedly positive qualities of God arise in a distinctively human context of finite existence, and when wrenched from this context to apply to a supernatural being, they cease to have meaning.

To illustrate this problem, consider the following questions: When the Christian says that God is alive, does he mean that God is alive in the same sense as natural organisms? If so, God must be a material entity who will eventually die. When God is said to be wise or to possess knowledge, is this the conceptual knowledge with which man is familiar? If so, God is capable of error and can acquire his knowledge only through mental effort. When God is said to have a certain power or capacity, is this power similar to the concept as we understand it? If so, God

55

must be limited. When God is said to be loving, is this a love with which we are familiar? If so, God must have emotions with which to feel passion.

If the Christian wishes to use positive characteristics for God while retaining their meaning, he must reduce his God to a manlike or anthropomorphic level. On the other hand, if these predicates do not mean the same when applied to God as they do when applied to natural entities, then they assume some unknown, mysterious meaning and are virtually emptied of their significance. In this event, God is pushed into agnosticism. Frederick Ferré describes the theistic dilemma as follows:

> The theist is caught in a cross fire. Either human language is allowed to retain its meaning, drawn from human experience of the finite, in which case it cannot be about the God of theism, who is not supposed either to be finite or to be properly describable in finite terms; or language, "purified" of its anthropocentric roots, is emptied of meaning for human beings, in which case it can be neither human language nor—for us—"about" God.[8]

The Christian is faced with an either-or situation. Either we can use human language to speak meaningfully of God (in which case God cannot differ in kind from finite existence), or human language cannot be applied to God at all (in which case the word "God" becomes meaningless). By stipulating that God is supernatural and unknowable, the Christian effectively removes God from the domain of language and communication—thereby removing himself from the context of rational consideration.

This objection has a distinguished past. It has been discussed by theologians for centuries, and it still occupies a place of importance in theological debates. The most ambitious effort to rescue God from the anthropomorphic-agnostic dilemma is the doctrine of analogy. This doctrine has been proposed in various forms, some of which are too technical for the present discussion.[9] We shall be concerned with it in its most widely used format, which may be summarized as follows:

When we apply positive qualities to God such as "wise" or "loving" or "good," argues the Christian, we do not use them with the same meaning as when we apply them to finite existence, nor do we use them with completely different and unrelated meanings. Rather, we predicate these qualities *analogically; i.e.,* we base them on a resemblance between God and finite entities.

Since God is incomprehensible, we cannot examine God's characteristics, compare them with man's characteristics, and then conclude that God and man have certain traits in common. Anyway, if this were possible, we would already have direct knowledge of God's nature prior to the comparison, which would eliminate the need for analogy. How, then, can the Christian claim a resemblance between God and man?

We must remember that a supernatural being differs in kind from finite existence, not merely in degree. This unbridgeable gap between God and man prevents the Christian from arguing that God possesses the same qualities as man, but to a greater extent. God is not a superman; the "goodness" of God is not the goodness of man magnified to a tremendous degree, nor is the "intelligence" of God a kind of exaggerated human genius. God and man are diametrically different species, so there can be no intrinsic similarities between the attributes of God and the attributes of man.

We see, therefore, that the analogy between God and man cannot stem from similarities in their natures. No such resemblance is possible. At this point, the doctrine of analogy becomes rather slippery. It seems that analogy "involves the possession of the attribute by both God and man, but each possesses it in a mode proportionate to his nature."[10] D. J. B. Hawkins elaborates as follows:

> . . . while there cannot be a proportion of the finite
> to the infinite, there can be within both the finite and
> the infinite proportions which are similar. Thus the

57

divine goodness is to God as human goodness is to man, and the divine wisdom is to God as human wisdom is to man, and, in general, the divine attributes are to God as the analogous finite qualities are to finite things.[11]

According to this model, the resemblance between God and man is that just as man possesses qualities in a mode appropriate to his finite nature, so God possesses qualities in a mode appropriate to his infinite nature. God's qualities are to God as man's qualities are to man; this is the similarity between God and man.

We have examined this doctrine of analogy (usually referred to as the "analogy of proportionality") because of its historical significance, not because of any intrinsic merit. As an alleged "middle-way" between the extremes of anthropomorphism and agnosticism, the way of analogy is a dismal failure. It has been so thoroughly discredited by philosophers that few theologians outside the mainstream of Thomism care to defend it. We shall discuss only its major flaws, and even these in the briefest terms possible.

To begin with, it is difficult to understand what the doctrine of analogy is supposed to accomplish. We are concerned with the meaning of positive attributes when applied to God, and the way of analogy tells us that God possesses these attributes in a mode proportionate to his nature. But what does this solve? We have not advanced one step closer toward understanding such terms as "wisdom," "knowledge," and "love" when these are predicated of God.

To illustrate the doctrine of analogy, Christians sometimes point to the manner in which we apply common qualities to man and lower life forms. For instance, we may call a dog "loyal," "intelligent," and "loving," and we also apply these terms to man. Now it is obvious that there are certain similarities between dog and man—since both belong to the genus of "mammal"—that permit us to describe them with the same terms; but it is equally obvious that there are vast differences between the two species, so we do not mean these terms in precisely the same sense. Therefore, concludes the Christian, we predicate these qualities to dogs analogically. We say that a dog possesses intelligence within the context of his nature and capacities as a dog, just as man possesses intelligence within the context of his nature and capacities as a man.[12] Extending this model to God, we also say that God possesses his qualities in a manner appropriate to his nature as an infinite being.

This attempt at clarification is doomed to failure. Even if we grant that words such as "intelligence" and "loyalty" can be applied to animals "analogically" (which is itself an unclear claim), we at least know what we are talking about when we use the term "dog." If we say that a dog possesses a quality in proportion to its nature, we at least possess knowledge of its nature. In other words, before we attempt to apply analogical predicates to a dog, we have firsthand, nonanalogical knowledge of what we mean by the word "dog." Unfortunately, we are not similarly privileged when it comes to God.

To say that "the divine goodness is to God as human goodness is to man" is quite meaningless without some direct knowledge of God's nature. We know what man is, and we know what it means to ascribe goodness to man. But we do not know what God is, nor can we know what it means to ascribe goodness to God. As W. T. Blackstone points out, "if one is to know analogically something of God (or any other object), then one must know something of God (or any other object) *literally.*"[13] Analogical knowledge of God's nature presupposes nonanalogical knowledge of God's nature.

If the Christian God is unknowable and completely different in kind from finite existence, we can have no idea of what it means to ascribe a positive quality to his nature—analogically or otherwise—because we have no knowledge of that nature. To say that an "unie" possesses wisdom in proportion to its nature—while stipulating that such wisdom is different in kind from man's wisdom and that the nature of an "unie" is unknowable—contributes nothing to our understanding of "unie" or to the meaning of attributes when applied to an "unie." And so it is with the Christian God. We might just as well claim that God is "yellow" or "slimely," while stipulating, of course, that these qualities do not mean the same when applied to God as when applied to man, and that God possesses them in a mode appropriate to his infinite nature.

As long as the Christian God remains in the realm of the unknowable, as long as he is totally different in kind from anything with which we have experience, we can never meaningfully ascribe positive qualities to God. *To say that God is "good" or "wise" is to say nothing more than some unknowable being possesses some unknown qualities in an unknowable way.* The positive qualities of God only repeat, in a somewhat devious fashion, that God is beyond man's comprehension. As one theologian cryptically admits, "God is so far from being meaningless that its real meaning is more positive than anything we can comprehend."[14]

The doctrine of analogy notwithstanding, affirmative theology is unable to rescue God from the oblivion of agnosticism. Like the negative predicates, the positive attributes of God are simply the means by which the Christian dresses up—and hopefully disguises—his unknowable God.

III

God and Intelligibility

In attempting to provide us with knowledge of an unknowable God, the Christian faces insurmountable obstacles. Negative and positive theology fail to provide us with a method of knowing God, so they cannot give us the needed escape from agnosticism. We shall now examine the major attributes of the Christian God, which will enable us to see in concrete terms how the Christian God collapses into agnosticism—and from there into irrationalism.

Before dealing with the specific qualities, some preliminary groundwork is necessary. We obviously cannot accept the proposed attributes of God uncritically; we must determine if they are intelligible. It does not help us to say that God possesses the attribute "x" unless we understand the meaning of "x." If we are told that an "unie" is "blooey," this does not enable us to understand the nature of an "unie"; instead of one unknown word, we are now facing two.

Our task is to critically evaluate the meaning and use of God's attributes in order to determine the intelligibility of their sum: the concept of God. To achieve this end, we must subject each attribute to one or more of the following questions:

(a) *Is the attribute internally consistent?—i.e.*, does it contain any self-contradictions? Consistency is the backbone of intelligibility. If a proposed quality entails a self-contradiction, it cannot possibly exist, and any being said to possess this quality cannot possibly exist.

(b) *Is the attribute consistent with the other proposed attributes of God?* While it makes sense to say that an "unie" is square or that an "unie" is circular, it is nonsense to suggest that an "unie" is square and circular at the same time and in the same respect. A being with these incompatible qualities cannot possibly exist.

If the concept of God contains contradictory attributes, we may state—with certainty—that God does not exist.

(c) *Is the attribute applied within the proper context?* Concepts do not exist in a vacuum; they are derived within a specific framework and retain their meaning only within that framework. For example, we use the term "red" to describe the color of an object, but suppose that we offered "red" as the shape of an object. Although "red" is a meaningful word, when applied to this improper context, it becomes unintelligible.

We have discussed the problems involved in applying concepts derived from our knowledge of finite existence to a supernatural being who, in the words of one Christian theologian, "has absolutely nothing in common with finite creatures." Due to this radical shift in context, ordinary words, such as "good" and "wise," become meaningless when applied to God.

(d) *Does the attribute give us positive knowledge of God's nature?* We cannot be content with an attribute of God if it merely tells us what God is not. As we have seen, before the Christian can state what God is not, he must have some idea of what God is—and it is with this more fundamental knowledge that we are concerned.

(e) *Is the attribute knowable?* This question is crucial. We are examining the attributes of God on the assumption that they are intended to give us a coherent grasp of God's nature, and this is possible only if the attributes themselves are comprehensible. If they are unknowable, they are useless as qualities. We cannot come to know an unknowable God through unknowable characteristics.

(f) *Is the attribute compatible with known facts?* This question does not affect the intelligibility of the concept of God as such, but it is relevant to establishing the possibility of God's existence. If, for example, we are told that God is the omnibenevolent creator of the universe, we may find this incompatible with the fact of suffering and pain. And if this is the case, we may conclude that God does not exist.

Equipped with these basic, interrelated questions, we shall now turn to the specific characteristics of the Christian God.

IV

God, Being and Existence

The first group of attributes that we shall consider are of particular importance, because they refer to God's nature as a metaphysical being. These are characteristics of God's nature as an (allegedly) existing being, in contrast to his powers and personality quirks. If we are to salvage the Christian God, it is crucial that these characteristics withstand critical evaluation.

(a) The Old Testament tells us that God, cleverly disguised as a burning bush, carried on the following conversation with Moses:

... Moses said to God, "If I come to the people of Israel and say to them, 'The God of your fathers has sent me to you,' and they ask me, 'What is his name?' what shall I say to them?" God said to Moses, "I AM WHO I AM." (Exodus 3. 13-14)

God's cryptic response to Moses sparked a flurry of theological speculation among medieval Christians, but according to their translation, God gave his name as "HE WHO IS." Augustine interpreted this to mean that God never changes, while Aquinas understood it to designate the identity of God's essence with his existence.

The explanation of Aquinas gained wide acceptance, and it remains standard fare today among many theologians. According to Aquinas, "HE WHO IS" expresses "the most proper name of God," and many theologians consider this name to be "the formal constituent of the Divine Nature." Insofar as we can capture the essence of God, "HE WHO IS" is best suited to this task.

"God," explains Aquinas, "is His own being"; his "essence is His being."[15] "HE WHO IS" means that there is no distinction between the *essence* of God and the *existence* of God; they are identical. God's essence *is* existence. As one Thomist writes:

> ... what is characteristic of God, as distinguished from creatures, is, from our point of view, the fact that His essence is not distinct from His Existence, but *is* His Existence.[16]

Aquinas borrowed the metaphysics of Aristotle and altered it somewhat to accommodate Christianity, and one cannot fully understand the distinction between essence and existence without a background in the complex Aristotelian-Thomistic framework. Since a digression of this kind is not desirable, we shall have to simplify as follows: "Essence" (*essentia*) refers to *what* a thing is; "existence" (*esse*) refers to *that* a thing is.[17]

63

Essence, for Aquinas, is the nature or *whatness* of a substance; it is what makes a thing the kind of thing it is. Man is a "rational animal"; this is his essence, this is what makes him a "man."

Existence, for Aquinas, is that which makes an essence real and gives it actual existence. We may define the essence of a unicorn without implying that unicorns actually exist, whereas with a horse, we can specify *that* it exists in addition to what it is. In every finite substance, Aquinas maintains that there is a distinction to be made between the *whatness* and *thatness*—and this is basically the distinction between essence and existence.

The essence-existence dichotomy applies to every being except God. Since God is "altogether simple" and is not composed of parts, there can be no distinction between his essence and existence. Unlike finite creatures, what God is cannot be conceptually divorced from the fact that he exists. His nature is existence as such or, as it is sometimes put, "necessary being." In technical terms, God is *Ipsum esse subsistens*—self-subsisting existence. This is the essence of God and the "fundamental principle of the Divine attributes."

The importance of this attribute cannot be overemphasized. From the identity of God's essence and existence, theologians go on to deduce other qualities of God, such as "infinitude," "perfection" and "immutability." Therefore, we must determine to what extent this attribute gives meaning to the concept of God.

A thorough critique of the above would necessitate a detailed examination and criticism of Thomistic metaphysics. We would have to discuss, not only the distinction between essence and existence, but also the Aristotelian dichotomies of substance-accident, matter-form, and potency-act. And finally, we would require a thorough critique of the Thomistic myth of necessary versus contingent existence. This formidable task clearly falls beyond our present scope, but we can accomplish our goal in a much less complicated fashion.

To say that God's essence is identical with his existence completely fails as an attribute or description of God because it cannot fulfill condition (e) of the preceding section. If we ask the Christian, "Is this characteristic of God knowable to man?— *i.e.*, Can we grasp its meaning?" the answer will be "no." And this cuts the ground from under this attempt to give content to the concept of God.

Without criticizing the metaphysics of Aquinas, let us see what he is trying to establish. First, he tells us that we distinguish between the essence and existence of a substance, that this is a method by which man perceives and gains knowledge of reality. This distinction is how we make sense of things; it is a condition of understanding.

Second, Aquinas tells us that we cannot distinguish between God's essence and existence. What is being asserted here? Simply that God is unlike anything with which we are familiar. Since man comprehends in terms of essence and existence—and since we cannot apply these categories to God—we cannot comprehend God. A basic distinction which we use to understand reality cannot be applied to God, which renders him incomprehensible.

There is no need to argue this point; it is freely admitted by Aquinas: ". . . to know the self-subsistent being . . . is beyond the natural power of any created intellect." Sympathetic interpreters of Aquinas agree. Referring to the identity of essence and existence, F. C. Copleston writes: "We cannot form any clear concept of what this is; for we inevitably distinguish between essence and existence, between what a thing is and the fact that it exists."[18] Etienne Gilson makes the same observation more forcefully:

> . . . since we can in no way conceive of an essence which is only an act-of-being, we can in no way conceive of what God is, even with the help of such attributes. *To make St. Thomas say that we have at least an imperfect knowledge of what God is is to betray his expressly stated thought.* Indeed, he not only says that the vision of the divine essence is not given to us here below, but he states clearly that

"there is something pertaining to God which is *entirely unknown* to man in this life, namely, what God is."[19] (Emphasis added.)

Despite the complicated maneuvers of Christian theologians to escape from agnosticism, despite the abstract dissertations and impressive sounding attributes of God, it always comes down to this: the nature of God is "entirely unknown" to man. The characteristic under consideration—the identity of God's essence and existence—is nothing more than an extremely complicated way of conceding the very point which we are attempting to prove: namely, that *the concept of God is without cognitive content.* The Christian cannot give substance and meaning to the term "God"; it is a blank, an unknowable "something."

The "HE WHO IS" of theologians is strikingly similar to the technique of negative theology. It takes the basic conceptual framework by which man understands reality and then negates the entire framework, while claiming that this captures the essence of God. It says, in effect, "Consider the basic concepts which you need to comprehend reality and understand the world around you. Now contradict each of those concepts—and there you have the nature of God. God is that which you cannot understand."

The identification of God's essence with his existence is not intended to tell us what God is; it is intended to inform us that *we will never know what God is.* "Insofar as God is He Who Is," states one theologian, ". . . He is superintelligible [a euphemism for *un*intelligible.] "[20] "The very uttering of the name which is not and cannot be clear to us," asserts Copleston, "reminds us of the divine mystery and of the divine transcendence beyond all finite things."[21]

The Thomistic interpretation of HE WHO IS, instead of eliminating agnosticism, actually reinforces it. Since we are attempting to bury the Christian God by reducing him to the void of the unknowable, this alleged characteristic of God adds another nail to his coffin. The theologians are killing God in their attempt to save him.

(b) The Christian God is commonly described as "immaterial" or "incorporeal"; he is not composed of matter. Little needs to be said concerning this characteristic, because it is subject to the previous criticisms of negative theology. "Immaterial" tells us what God is not, that he is not composed of matter, but it does not tell us what God is.

Moreover, the notion of an "immaterial being" entails a contradiction and cannot be expressed in positive terms. We cannot imagine an "immaterial being" because the concept of "matter" is essential to our concept of "being." God, claims the Christian, is a "being"—but he does not occupy space, he does not have dimensions, and he cannot be perceived, measured or detected in any way. And these qualifications render the concept of "being" vacuous.

The theologian may object here, pointing out that many words—such as "justice" and "consciousness"—do not signify material objects. The referents of these and many other words are immaterial, so why should the atheist complain when God is also said to be immaterial?

While it is true that "justice" and "consciousness" do not designate material beings, the theist must remember that they do not refer to immaterial *beings* either. "Justice" is a moral abstraction derived from various aspects of man's nature and social interactions. "Consciousness" refers to the state of awareness exhibited by particular living organisms. "Justice" and "consciousness" are not material entities, but they depend on matter for their existence. God, on the other hand, does not depend on matter in any way; he exists in his own right as an independent being. In this context, however, "immaterial" is stripped of meaning.

"Immaterial" does not describe another kind of existence; it negates the concept of existence as we understand it. It is a mistake to suppose that all the theologian means by "immaterial" is that God is not composed of atoms, molecules, energy, and so on (although this is part of what he means). Translated into epistemological terms, "immaterial" stands in contradistinction to the knowable; it designates that which man cannot perceive or comprehend. The basic objection to "immaterial" is that it does nothing more than specify that man cannot understand God. To say that God is "nonmatter" is to say that we can have no sensory experience of God and that we can never conceive of him. This characteristic, therefore, simply throws us into agnosticism.

(c) The third major characteristic of God—"infinitude"—is the catchall, the universal modifier of Christian theology. God is not merely a being; he is infinite being. God is not merely good; he is infinite goodness. God is not merely wise; he is infinite wisdom. And so on down the list. God is exaggeration run amuck.

A detailed examination of "infinite" is unnecessary here, because it carries a simple epistemological message. As a negative term, it signifies "without limits"—and since everything of which man is aware has limits, "infinite" tells us that God is forever beyond our comprehension. This is the chief culprit of the "unlimited attribute" and the "non-everything-man-knows" technique.

Theologians are the first to admit that we cannot understand the infinite, so there is no need to belabor the point. But there is an interesting twist to this characteristic. Many theologians follow Aquinas in arguing that God is not unknowable as such, but, on the contrary, is "supremely knowable." God, Aquinas explains, is "infinitely knowable," and to comprehend God would be to know him to an "infinite degree." But, continues Aquinas, "it is impossible for any created intellect to know God in an infinite degree. Hence it is impossible that it should comprehend God."[22] God is more than we can understand, just as "the sun, which is supremely visible, cannot be seen by the bat by reason of its excess of light."[23]

God is infinite, but man's comprehension is finite, so we have an overflow of the divine nature. God is more than we can pack into the limited mind of man. Thus, instead of characterizing God as unintelligible, theologians prefer to speak of him as "superintelligible."

We are now asked to believe, not that God is unknowable, but that he is "infinitely knowable." He is thus comprehensible

68

to an "infinite intellect" such as himself. But since we cannot understand the infinite, since an "infinite intellect" itself must be unknowable, to say that God is "infinitely knowable" is to say that he is "knowable" in some unknowable fashion—which is to acknowledge that he is incomprehensible, period. There can be no valid distinction between the unknowable to man and the unknowable per se. The attempt of Aquinas and other theologians to draw this distinction, their preference to speak of God as "superintelligible" rather than unintelligible, is theological double-talk in all of its splendor. It does not move us any closer to understanding the concept of God.

After examining the three major characteristics of the Christian God, we see that they are based primarily on the "negative way" and share the basic faults of negative theology. These "attributes" are themselves incomprehensible, and they only serve to plunge us further into agnosticism.

Since the essential characteristics of God cannot be rationally defended, we would be justified in stopping at this point and rejecting the concept of God as irrational. But for further corroboration that the Christian God is simply the agnostic god incognito, we shall turn to the alleged capacities of God, and finally to the notion that God is all-good.

V

The Powers of God

(a) Perhaps the most intriguing capacity of the Christian God is his omnipotence. God is all-powerful; he can do anything. Omnipotence is a hybrid attribute, a combination of negative and positive theology. God has "power" (a positive idea) "without restrictions" (a negative idea). These dual elements make omnipotence susceptible on two fronts, because it shares the flaws of both negative and positive theology.

What does "omnipotence" mean? Does "all-powerful" mean that God can do literally anything? Can he create a square-circle? A married bachelor? To admit these possibilities leads to insuperable difficulties. Since these things are logically impossible, they cannot exist—and any being with the supposed capacity to create the logically impossible must himself be logically impossible. To say that God can do anything, even the logically impossible, is to push one's God into the realm of that which cannot possibly exist.

This problem is an obvious one, and sophisticated theologians have attempted to deal with it. Their solution has been to deny the capacity of God to accomplish the logically impossible, while claiming that this does not detract from his omnipotence.[24]

In short, God's omnipotence is usually interpreted to mean that God can do anything that is conceivable—anything, for instance, that can be drawn or animated in a cartoon. No artist, however skilled, can draw a square-circle; this is a logical impossibility. But an artist can draw the transformation of an acorn into a theologian, or he can illustrate a cat giving birth to elephants—so these are deemed to be "logically possible" and thus within the scope of God's power. If we can imagine it, God can do it.

Despite the fact that many philosophers wish to label the growth of an acorn into a theologian as a "logical possibility," I consider this notion, or any similar to it, to be a travesty of the word "possibility." The fact that we can imagine the mysterious and causeless transformation of an acorn into a theologian does not change the nature of an acorn, a theologian—or any part of reality.

It is important to realize that an entity has a specific nature, specific attributes, that make it the kind of thing it is, and that delimit the *actions* open to that entity. To suggest that an acorn can possess a certain set of characteristics and yet act in a manner which is totally incompatible with those characteristics is, I submit, a contradiction—and it is a contradiction which is as fully impossible as any so-called "logical contradiction."

To accept the idea of an omnipotent God, one must believe that it is in some way "possible" for an entity to act in contradiction to its nature. In a universe containing an omnipotent being, any action would be open to any entity at any time upon the bidding of God. Causality would be a sham, and rational explanation would crumble.

It is into this chaotic world that one must plunge if one wishes to speak of God as omnipotent: a universe without identity, a universe of the unintelligible and the unknowable—a Walt Disney wonderland where pumpkins can turn into coaches, oranges into spaceships, and women into pillars of salt.

Let us explore the implications of omnipotence in more detail. In an examination of theism, John Stuart Mill concludes that there is some evidence of intelligent planning in nature, and in this respect he concurs with most Christians. But Mill recognizes a point which most Christians do not—namely, that "every indication of design in the cosmos is so much evidence against the omnipotence of the designer." Mill rejects omnipotence as an attribute of his god, and his argument deserves to be quoted at length:

> . . . what is meant by design? Contrivance: the adaptation of means to an end. But the necessity for contrivance—the need of employing means—is a consequence of the limitation of power. Who would have recourse to means if to attain his end his mere word was sufficient? The very idea of means implies that the means have an efficacy which the direct action of the being who employs them has not. Otherwise they are not means but an encumbrance. . . . if the employment of contrivance is in itself a sign of limited power, how much more so is the careful and skillful choice of contrivances? Can any wisdom be shown in the selection of means when the means have no efficacy but what is given them by the will of him who employs them, and when his will could have bestowed the same efficacy on any other means? Wisdom and contrivance are shown in overcoming difficulties, and there is no room for them in a being for whom no difficulties exist.[25]

71

Although Mill was wrong in supposing that the universe exhibits intelligent planning, the above passage effectively brings out the problems inherent within the concept of omnipotence. As Mill points out, there can be no obstacles to divine omnipotence—no difficulties that God must overcome—because God's "will" is sufficient to produce *any* effect. The necessity of employing means to accomplish an end is the consequence of limited power; therefore, God cannot be said to employ means in any sense. Extending this argument, we also realize that God cannot be said to *act* in any manner, because actions are required only of a being who must resort to some means in order to accomplish a given end. Nor can God be said to have any kind of purpose, because "purpose" entails *unfulfilled* desires or goals—and these concepts cannot apply to an omnipotent being.

To imagine an omnipotent being, we must imagine a being who has some mysterious "power" to do anything, but who does not employ means, does not act, and does not have any purpose. In other words, the concept of omnipotence attempts to exclude God from *causality*. In some unknowable way, God brings about effects without resorting to causal processes. How would God "cause" an acorn to grow into a theologian? Or how would God "cause" a cat to give birth to miniature elephants? The Christian, unable to answer these questions, resorts to the pseudo-cause of God's will; if God wills something, it happens, mysteriously, inexplicably. The power of God, as most Christians freely admit, is totally unlike any power with which we are familiar. It is different in kind and lies completely beyond the scope of man's comprehension.

We see, then, that omnipotence does not merely entail power, as we understand it, magnified to a tremendous degree; rather, omnipotence is an altogether different kind of power, one that lies beyond our intellectual grasp. To accept omnipotence, we must accept effects without causes and consequences without means. And this is tantamount to magic.

Because the "power" of God is totally beyond the framework that gives meaning to this concept, omnipotence simply tells us that God—an unknowable being—does things in an unknowable way through some unknowable nonprocesses. We cannot understand the meaning of omnipotence, so it seems that we are once again face to face with undiluted agnosticism.

(b) The Christian God is commonly said to be omniscient; he knows everything—past, present and future. Here again we are facing a hybrid characteristic, one that is partially positive and partially negative. Omniscience entails knowledge without limits.

The first problem with omniscience is that it cannot be reconciled with any theory of free will in man. If one believes in an omniscient being, one cannot consistently hold that man has volitional control over his actions. If God knows the future with infallible certainty, the future is predetermined, and man is impotent to change it.

Some theologians (such as Calvin) have enthusiastically embraced predestination, but most theologians, sensing the enormous problems entailed by this doctrine, have attempted to defend some theory of volition. Without volition, morality becomes meaningless: we cannot blame or praise a man for an action over which he has no control. Without volition, the Christian scheme of salvation is a farce; men are predestined for either heaven or hell, and they have no voice in the matter. Why does God create men only to save some arbitrarily, and damn others? Why does the Christian bother to proselytize, since men cannot help what they believe anyway? The problems that arise for theology if it affirms predestination are unsolvable, but they necessarily ensue when omniscience is attributed to God.

Christian theologians have grappled with this problem for centuries. It is even discussed in the Bible by Paul, who writes of those who are "predestined to be conformed to the image of his [God's] Son . . ." (Romans 8.29). According to Paul, God "has mercy upon whomever he wills, and he hardens the heart of whomever he wills" (Romans 9.18). But this raises obvious difficulties.

> You will say to me then, 'Why does he still find fault? For who can resist his will?' (Romans 9.19)

73

These are important questions, but Paul quickly brushes them aside with characteristic indignation.

But, who are you, a man, to answer back to God? Will what is molded say to its molder, 'Why have you made me thus?' Has the potter no right over the clay, to make out of the same lump one vessel for beauty and another for menial use? (Romans 9. 20-21)

Significantly, Paul makes no attempt to defend God from the charge of unfairness; rather, he cites God's absolute authority over man and asserts, in effect, that what God decides to do with man is none of man's business.

Theologians have devised a number of unsuccessful ways to reconcile omniscience and free will. One method is to argue that God's foreknowledge does not "impose" itself on the course of events, and God knows a free action "according to the nature of the event itself—which is free."[26] This, of course, solves nothing, because it evades the central issue. How can an event be "free" in the first place, if God has infallible knowledge of it prior to its happening? Another approach has been to argue that "God does not exist in time at all"[27]—but this serves only to strengthen agnosticism. Other attempts at reconciliation are similarly unimpressive, so it seems that the Christian is forever plagued with the dilemma of preaching a religion of salvation to a world of men who, according to the doctrine of omniscience, are nothing more than automatons.

There is another irritating problem with the idea of omniscience: it contradicts the attribute of omnipotence. If God knows the future with infallible certainty, he cannot change it—in which case he cannot be omnipotent. If God can change the future, however, he cannot have infallible knowledge of it prior to its actual happening—in which case he cannot be omniscient. (This is similar to the issue of in what sense, if any, God can be said to have free will. Does God know his own future decisions? If so, how can those decisions be free? Perhaps God does not make decisions. If so, how can the idea of volition apply to a being with no decisions—and hence no choices—to make?)

The major problem with omniscience is that the "knowledge" of God bears no resemblance to the concept of knowledge as we understand it (which is, by now, a familiar problem). Consider the prerequisites of knowledge. In order to know anything, a being must be conscious, and this presupposes a living organism. If God is said to know everything, therefore, we must presume that God is a conscious, living being.

In what sense can God be said to be alive? God is not even a material being, much less a biological organism with metabolic processes. The concept of life has no meaning when applied to God.

The same is true of consciousness. While some theists refer to God as "pure consciousness," consciousness apart from matter, this amounts to nonsense. Consciousness is the state of awareness present in some living organisms, and it presupposes an entity, a material organism, with this state of awareness.[28]

If consciousness is lifted from its conceptual framework and is presented as something other than a characteristic of life, then it is divorced from its basis in reality and becomes a floating abstraction, a vague idea with no referent in the real world. As with other concepts derived from our experience of natural phenomena, consciousness cannot be extended to a supernatural realm without sacrificing its content.

Now consider what is entailed by knowledge. Man possesses knowledge in the form of concepts; conceptualization is a mental process of abstracting and integrating the concretes of one's experience into mental units, such as "table" or "chair." Abstractions must be abstracted from something; they must be acquired through mental effort. And since man is not infallible, he requires a method to distinguish true beliefs from false beliefs; this is the function of verification.

These two elements—acquisition and verification—are essential to the concept of knowledge as we understand it. Knowledge must come from somewhere, and it must be verified by some means. When the Christian claims that God is omniscient, however, he wishes to exclude acquisition and verification from God's knowledge.

If God acquired his knowledge, this means that at some point in time (*i.e.*, before he had acquired all possible knowledge), God was not omniscient. If God verified his knowledge, this means that his knowledge was uncertain prior to verification. Thus omniscience would cease to be a character trait, an attribute existing eternally with God.

When the theologian posits the omniscience of God, he wishes to convey the idea of nonacquired and nonverified knowledge, knowledge that is immediate and infallible, knowledge inherent in God's nature. But if this is the case, God's knowledge cannot be in conceptual form, which is to say that God's "knowledge" is totally different from man's knowledge. We are once again dealing with a difference in kind rather than degree. The "knowledge" of God is unintelligible and unknowable. To say that God is omniscient is to distort the concept of knowledge beyond recognition. It simply adds another unknowable attribute to an unknowable being.

VI

God and Goodness

The final characteristic of God that we shall consider is omnibenevolence—the quality of being all-good. While God is said to be the epitome of moral perfection, this attribute has been notoriously difficult for Christians to defend, and it functions as a constant thorn in the side of Christian theology.

The first problem with omnibenevolence is reconciling it with the biblical portrayal of God who, in the words of Thomas Jefferson, is "a being of terrific character—cruel, vindictive, capricious and unjust." The Old Testament in particular makes little attempt to absolve God from the responsibility for evil. "Does evil befall a city," asks the prophet Amos, "unless the Lord has done it" (3.6)? The prophet Jeremiah agrees: "Is it not from the mouth of the Most High that good and evil come" (Lamentations 3.38)? And in the book of Isaiah, the biblical Jehovah reports, "I am the Lord, and there is no other. . . . I make weal and create woe, I am the Lord, who do all these things" (45. 6-7).

The Old Testament God garnered an impressive list of atrocities. He demanded and sanctioned human sacrifices (Leviticus 27. 28-29; Judges 11. 29-40; 2 Samuel 21. 1-9). He killed the first-born of every Egyptian family (Exodus 12. 29). He sanctioned slavery (Exodus 21. 2-6; Leviticus 25. 44-46) and the selling of one's daughter (Exodus 21.7). He commanded the killing of witches (Exodus 22.18), death for heresy (Exodus 22.20), death for violating the sabbath (Exodus 31. 14-15), death for cursing one's parents (Leviticus 20.9), death for adultery (Leviticus 20.10), death for blasphemy (Leviticus 24.16), and death by stoning for unchastity at the time of marriage—a penalty imposed only upon women (Deuteronomy 22. 20-21).

The Old Testament credits the Israelites, acting under the auspices of Jehovah, with massacring an incredible number of men, women and children through conquest. Time and again we read accounts where they "utterly destroyed all in the city, both men and women, young and old, oxen, sheep, and asses, with the edge of the sword" (Joshua 6.21). There were exceptions, however. In Chapter 31 of Numbers, we read that Moses, angry with the officers of his army because they had taken captives from a conquered people instead of killing everyone, issued the following orders: "Now therefore, kill every male among the little ones, and kill every woman who has known man by lying with him. But all the young girls who have not known man by lying with him, keep alive for yourselves" (Numbers 31. 17-18).

Jehovah himself was fond of directly exterminating large numbers of people, usually through pestilence or famine, and often for rather unusual offenses. In one instance, he is reported to have killed 70,000 men because David took a census of Israel (2 Samuel 24). In another strange case, he sent two bears to rip apart forty-two children for mocking the prophet Elisha (2 Kings 2. 23-24).

Passages such as the above abound in the Old Testament, and they led Thomas Paine to declare:

> Whenever we read the obscene stories, the voluptuous debaucheries, the cruel and torturous executions, the unrelenting vindictiveness, with which more than half the Bible is filled, it would be more consistent that we called it the word of a demon, than the word of God. It is a history of wickedness, that has served to corrupt and brutalize mankind; and, for my part, I sincerely detest it, as I detest everything that is cruel.[29]

Many theologians are reluctant to identify the Old Testament Jehovah with the New Testament God of Christianity. The Christian God, they assure us, is a being of mercy and love. But this assertion is difficult to defend. While the old god was cruel, he at least restricted his infliction of misery to this life. The Christian God, however, reportedly extends this misery to eternity. According to the New Testament, Jesus repeatedly threatened disbelievers with eternal torment, and we must wonder how the doctrine of hell can be reconciled with the notion of an all-merciful God.

In the *Summa Theologica*, Thomas Aquinas offers this explanation:

> ... punishment is meted according to the dignity of the person sinned against, so that a person who strikes one in authority receives a greater punishment than one who strikes anyone else. Now whoever sins mortally sins against God. ... But God's majesty is infinite. Therefore whoever sins mortally deserves infinite punishment; and consequently it seems just that for a mortal sin a man should be punished forever.[30]

To my knowledge, no one has ever been accused of striking God, so the explanation must be that God, using some peculiar standard of "justice," damns men to endless agony as punishment for insulting his infinite nature. Furthermore, God has complete foreknowledge of each man's fate, so many men are born for no purpose other than to suffer in hell. And why would God create a place of torment in the first place, unless he derived some kind of pleasure or satisfaction from witnessing pain? Whether the Christian deity of fire and brimstone projects love or neurotic sadism on a cosmic scale, will be left to the conscience of the reader to decide.

Many theologians recognize the futility of attempting to reconcile eternal torment with benevolence, so they simply ignore the doctrine of hell or deny it outright. The liberal theologian Leslie D. Weatherhead defends this approach as follows:

> ... when Jesus is reported as consigning to everlasting torture those who displease him or do not "believe" what he says, I *know* in my heart that there is something wrong somewhere. Either he is misreported or misunderstood. ... So I put this alleged saying in my mental drawer awaiting further light, or else I reject it out of hand. By the judgment of a court within my own breast ... I reject such sayings. [31]

Put simply, the New Testament does not say what Weatherhead feels that it should say, so he prefers to ignore the unpleasant (and numerous) New Testament references to hell through the unique epistemological process of "knowing" in one's heart. Or, put even more simply, this theologian will believe what he feels like, contrary evidence notwithstanding.

Even if we bypass the problem of reconciling omnibenevolence with the Bible, the Christian still confronts serious philosophic problems. We shall assume that by omnibenevolence, the Christian means that God never does any evil, that all of his actions are good. Remember that "goodness," in this context, must refer to a standard other than the will of God. Something cannot be defined as good simply because God is responsible for it. If we define the good as anything that God wills, it is ridiculous to talk about the moral worth of God. Morality applies only when there is choice. To say that God has no choice but to be good completely destroys the concept of morality when it is applied to God. If God is incapable of evil, he is neither moral nor immoral; he is simply *amoral*.

To be omnibenevolent, God must be capable of evil but always choose the good. If God deliberately chooses evil, he is immoral. The question now arises: Why is there evil in the creation of an omnibenevolent deity? Why, in a world for which God is ultimately responsible, are there natural disasters that kill millions? Why are there diseases that cause suffering and cripple innocent men, women and children? Indeed, why is there evil and suffering of any kind? Must not God bear responsibility for these things, and do they not demonstrate that God cannot be all-good? This dilemma, known as the "problem of evil," has led some Christians to deny the unlimited power of God and to declare belief in a deity with limited capacities who was unable to create a world without pain and evil. It has led other Christians to write lengthy books on theodicy, which purport to reconcile God's goodness with his other characteristics and the existence of evil.

The problem of evil is frequently considered to be the major objection to the Christian concept of God, and there has been more discussion of omnibenevolence than any other characteristic. But the relative importance attached to this problem is exaggerated. While this is a serious difficulty and one which Christians have failed to solve, it is by no means the most important or basic objection to Christian theism. When considered within the context of other difficulties surrounding the concept of God, this one is minor by comparison. For this reason, we shall not discuss it in as much detail as is customary in a book of this kind.

Briefly, the problem of evil is this: If God does not know there is evil, he is not omniscient. If God knows there is evil but cannot prevent it, he is not omnipotent. If God knows there is evil and can prevent it but desires not to, he is not omnibenevolent. If, as the Christian claims, God is all-knowing and all-powerful, we must conclude that God is not all-good. The existence of evil in the universe excludes this possibility.

There have been various attempts to escape from the problem of evil, and we shall briefly consider the more popular of these. But one point requires emphasis. The Christian, by proclaiming that God is good, commits himself to the position that man is capable of distinguishing good from evil—for, if he is not, how did the Christian arrive at his judgment of "good" as applied to God? Therefore, any attempt to resolve the problem of evil by arguing that man cannot correctly distinguish good from evil, destroys the original premise that it purports to defend and thus collapses from the weight of an internal inconsistency. If the human standards of good and evil are somehow invalid, the Christian's claim that God is good is equally invalid.

One general theological approach to the problem of evil consists of the claim that evil is in some way unreal or purely negative in character. This argument, however, is so implausible that few Christians care to defend it. The first problem with it, as Antony Flew notes, is: "If evil is really nothing then what is all the fuss about sin about: nothing?"

In *Some Dogmas of Religion*, John McTaggart quickly disposes of the claim that evil is in some way unreal:

> Supposing that it could be proved that all that we think evil was in reality good, the fact would still remain that we think it evil. This may be called a delusion or a mistake. But a delusion or mistake is as *real* as anything else. A savage's erroneous belief that the earth is stationary is just as real a fact as an astronomer's correct belief that it moves. The delusion that evil exists, then, is real. But then . . . it

seems certain that a delusion or an error which hid from us the goodness of the universe would itself be evil. And so there would be real evil after all. . . . However many times we pronounce evil unreal, we always leave a reality behind, which in its turn is to be pronounced evil.[32]

As for the argument that evil is purely negative, a privation of the good (as disease may be said to be the absence of health), Wallace Matson provides this illuminating example in *The Existence of God:*

It may console the paralytic to be told that paralysis is mere lack of mobility, nothing positive, and that insofar as he *is,* he is perfect. It is not clear, however, that this kind of comfort is available to the sufferer from malaria. He will reply that his trouble is not that he lacks anything, but rather that he has too much of something, namely, protozoans of the genus *Plasmodium.*[33]

Any attempt to absolve God of the responsibility for evil by claiming that, in the final analysis, there is no such thing as evil is, as Matson puts it, "an unfunny joke." This approach merely ends up by negating our human standards of good and evil, which, as previously indicated, undercuts the argument at its root.

Another common effort to reconcile God and evil is to argue that evil is the consequence of man's freely chosen actions. God, through his gift of free will, gave man the ability to distinguish and choose between good and evil, right and wrong. As a free agent, man has the potential to reach a higher degree of perfection and goodness than if he were a mere robot programmed to behave in a given manner. Thus it is good that man has free will. But this entails the opportunity for man to select evil instead of good, which has been the case in the instances of torture, murder, and cruelty which some men inflict upon others. The responsibility for these actions, however, rests with man, not with God. Therefore, concludes the Christian, evil does not conflict with the infinite goodness of God.

While this approach has some initial plausibility, it falls far short of solving the problem of evil. We are asked to believe that God created man with the power of choice in the hope that man would voluntarily pursue the good, but that man thwarts this desire of God through sin and thus brings evil upon himself. But, to begin with, to speak of frustrating or acting contrary to the wishes of an omnipotent being makes no sense whatsoever. There can be no barriers to divine omnipotence, no obstacles to thwart his desires, so we must assume that the present state of the world is precisely as God desires it to be. If God wished things to be other than they are, nothing could possibly prevent them from being other than they are, man's free will notwithstanding. In addition, we have seen that free will is incompatible with the foreknowledge possessed by an omniscient being, so the appeal to free will fails in this respect as well. In any case, God created man with full knowledge of the widespread suffering that would ensue, and, given his ability to prevent this situation, we must presume that God desired and willed these immoral atrocities to occur.

It is unfair to place the responsibility for immoral actions on man's free will in general. Individual men commit atrocities, not the bloodless abstraction "man." Some men commit blatant injustices, but others do not. Some men murder, rob, and cheat, but others do not. Some men choose a policy of wanton destructiveness, but others do not. And we must remember that crimes are committed by men against other men, innocent victims, who cannot be held responsible. The minimum requirement for a civilized society is a legal system whereby the individual liberties of men are protected from the aggressive activities of other men. We regard the recognition and protection of individual rights as a moral necessity, and we condemn governments that fail to provide a fair system of justice. How, then, are we to evaluate a God who permits widespread instances of injustice when it is easily within his power to prevent them? The Christian believes in a God who displays little, if any, interest in the protection of the innocent, and we must wonder how such a being can be called "good."

The standard reply to this objection is that God rewards the virtuous and punishes the wicked in an afterlife, so there is an overall balance of justice. An extreme variation of this tactic was reported in *The New York Times* of September 11, 1950. Referring to the Korean War, this article states: "Sorrowing parents whose sons have been drafted or recalled for combat duty were told yesterday in St. Patrick's Cathedral [by Monsignor William T. Greene] that death in battle was part of God's plan for populating 'the kingdom of heaven.' "

This approach is so obviously an exercise in theological rationalization that it deserves little comment. If every instance of evil is to be rectified by an appeal to an afterlife, the claim that God is all-good has no relevance whatsoever to our present life. Virtually any immoral action, no matter how hideous or atrocious, can be explained away in this fashion—which severs any attempt to discuss the alleged goodness of a creator from reference to empirical evidence. More importantly, no appeal to an afterlife can actually eradicate the problem of evil. An injustice always remains an injustice, regardless of any subsequent efforts to comfort the victim. If a father, after beating his child unmercifully, later gives him a lollipop as compensation, this does not erase the original act or its evil nature. Nor would we praise the father as just and loving. The same applies to God, but even more so. The Christian may believe that God will punish the perpetrators of evil and compensate the victims of injustice, but this does not explain why a supposedly benevolent and omnipotent being created a world with evildoers and innocent victims in the first place. Again, we must assume that there are innocent victims because God desires innocent victims; from the standpoint of Christian theism, there is simply no other explanation. If an omnipotent God did not want innocent victims, they could not exist—and, by human standards, the Christian God appears an immoral fiend of cosmic dimensions.

Even if we overlook the preceding difficulties, the appeal to free will is still unsuccessful, because it encompasses only so-called *moral* evils (*i.e.*, the actions of men). There remains the considerable problem of *physical* evils, such as natural disasters, over which man has no control. Why are there floods, earthquakes and diseases that kill and maim millions of persons? The responsibility for these occurrences obviously cannot be placed on the shoulders of man. From an atheistic standpoint, such phenomena are inimical to man's life and may be termed evil, but since they are the result of inanimate, natural forces and do not involve conscious intent, they do not fall within the province of moral judgment. But from a Christian perspective, God—the omnipotent creator of the natural universe—must bear ultimate responsibility for these occurrences, and God's deliberate choice of these evil phenomena qualifies him as immoral.

There is an interesting assortment of arguments designed to explain the existence of natural evils. Some theologians argue that evil exists for the sake of a greater good; others maintain that apparent evils disappear into a universal harmony of good. Although something may appear evil to man, we are assured by the Christian that God is able to view the overall perspective, and any apparent evil always turns out for the best. These approaches share the premise that man cannot understand the ways of God, but this simply pushes us into agnosticism. It will not do for the Christian to posit an attribute of God and, when asked to defend that attribute, contend that man cannot understand it.

If we are incorrect in calling natural disasters, diseases and other phenomena evil, then man is incapable of distinguishing good from evil. But if this is the case, by what standard does the Christian claim that God is good? What criterion is the Christian using?

If man cannot pass correct moral judgments, he cannot validly praise *or* condemn anything—including the Christian God. To exclude God from the judgment of evil is to exclude him from the judgment of good as well; but if man can distinguish good from evil, a supernatural being who willfully causes or permits the continuation of evil on his creatures merits unequivocal moral condemnation.

Some Christians resort to incredible measures to absolve their God from the responsibility for evil. Consider this passage from *Evil and the God of Love* in which John Hick attempts to reconcile the existence of an omnibenevolent deity with the senseless disasters that befall man:

> . . . men and women often act in true compassion and massive generosity and self-giving in the face of un-merited suffering, especially when it comes in such dramatic forms as an earthquake or a mining disaster. It seems, then, that in a world that is to be the scene of compassionate love and self-giving for others, suffering must fall upon mankind with something of the haphazardness and inequity that we now ex-perience. It must be apparently unmerited, pointless, and incapable of being morally rationalized. For it is precisely this feature of our common human lot that creates sympathy between man and man and evokes the unselfish kindness and goodwill which are among the highest values of personal life.[34]

Aside from displaying a low regard for man's "highest values" and their origins, Hick illustrates an important point: *There is virtually nothing which the Christian will accept as evidence of God's evil.* If disasters that are admittedly "unmerited, point-less, and incapable of being morally rationalized" are com-patible with the "goodness" of God, what could possibly qualify as contrary evidence? The "goodness" of God, it seems, is compatible with any conceivable state of affairs. While we evaluate a man with reference to his actions, we are not simi-larly permitted to judge God. God is immune from the judg-ment of evil as a matter of principle.

Here we have a concrete illustration of theological "reason-ing." Unlike the philosopher, the theologian adopts a position, a dogma, and then commits himself to a defense of that position come what may. While he may display a willingness to defend this dogma, closer examination reveals this to be a farce. His defense consists of distorting and rationalizing all contrary evidence to meet his desired specifications. In the case of divine benevolence, the theologian will grasp onto any explanation, no matter how implausible, before he will abandon his dogma. And when finally pushed into a corner, he will argue that man cannot understand the true meaning of this dogma.

This brings us to our familiar resting place. The "goodness" of God is different in kind from goodness as we comprehend it. To say that God's "goodness" is compatible with the worst disasters imaginable, is to empty this concept of its meaning. By human standards, the Christian God cannot be good. By divine standards, God may be "good" in some unspecified, unknowable way—but this term no longer makes any sense. And so, for the last time, we fail to comprehend the Christian God.

VII

The Collapse Into Agnosticism

Our journey through the concept of God is complete. After judging religious agnosticism—the belief in an unknowable god—to be indefensible, we examined Christianity's attempt to escape from the irrationalism of agnosticism while retaining the notion of a supernatural being. The escape was a total failure. The attributes of the Christian God are merely a disguise, an elaborate subterfuge designed to obscure the fact that the Christian God is also unknowable. God's characteristics, while supposedly giving us information about God's nature, actually accomplish the reverse: they plunge us further into agnosticism. When stripped of its theological garb, the Christian God emerges as the unknowable god of agnosticism.

The Christian theologian, then, is a kind of dishonest agnostic. While ostensibly explaining the concept of God, he presents attributes that are themselves incomprehensible. Theo-

87

logians frequently acknowledge their use of this technique: ". . . to ask us to accept incomprehensible truths about God," writes the Catholic scholar Etienne Gilson, "is an excellent means of implanting in us a conviction of his incomprehensibility."[35] No atheist has ever put the issue more succinctly.

Where does this leave the Christian? It leaves him believing in the existence of some unknowable being that cannot be coherently described. In other words, the Christian, operating from a conceptual vacuum, is defending the rationally indefensible; he cannot even specify what it is that he believes in. Or, in more blunt terms, the Christian, when he asserts that "God exists," simply does not know what he is talking about. And neither does anyone else.

Having caused the Christian God to collapse into the oblivion of agnosticism, the critical atheist has accomplished his first major task: he has demonstrated the belief in god to be irrational. The general notion of a god (with a small "g") must be rejected because it rests on the muddled notion of the "unknowable." The Christian God, aside from sharing this flaw, also suffers from a terminal case of internal incoherency. God's attributes are unintelligible for the most part, and to the extent that we can make sense of them, they contradict each other.

In essence, the case for atheism is fully established at this point. When undefined, "god" is a meaningless sound. When defined in the traditional manner, "God" slumps back into the muck of unintelligibility. Therefore, a rational man has no choice but to reject theism. Atheism has won by default.

It should be noted that the atheist is now saying *more* than, "I do not believe in god because there is no evidence for its existence." It is logically impossible for god—a concept replete with absurdities and contradictions—to have a referent in reality, just as it is logically impossible for a square circle to exist. Given the attempts to define god, we may now state—with certainty—that *god does not exist.* Thus our atheism has evolved to a more sophisticated level, from the absence of theistic belief to the outright *denial* of its truth.

Let us pause here to consider some of the wider implications of theistic belief. As previously indicated, the conflict between atheism and theism is primarily an epistemological one: it is a conflict between naturalism and supernaturalism, between the knowable and the unknowable. According to atheism, all of existence falls (in principle) within the scope of man's knowledge. According to theism, however, some aspects of existence are forever closed to man's knowledge. This fundamental conflict sets the stage for the inherent antagonism between science and theology.

It is common for modern theologians to argue that there is no conflict between science and religion, that these are concerned with different spheres of human existence. Yet there is a deep-seated friction between these two disciplines with regard to their basic assumptions. Science represents man's attempt to systematize given aspects of reality into a coherent framework of knowledge. Since science is dedicated to understanding reality, it rests on the premise that reality can be understood. Theology, on the other hand, is dedicated to the proposition that an important segment of reality (in fact, its ultimate form) is forever unknowable. There are cross-purposes at work here. Science seeks to make reality coherent; theology seeks to convince us that some aspects of reality are incoherent. To the extent that science succeeds, theology dies of strangulation. (This same principle applies, in a wider sense, between philosophy and theology.)

The conflicts between science and theology, or between philosophy and theology, are offshoots of a more basic conflict, that between reason and theology. Anyone who advocates theism—the belief in the supernatural—simultaneously advocates irrationalism—the belief in the unknowable. This explains why the issue of god is much more crucial than, for example, the issue of flying saucers. While the existence of flying saucers is of immense scientific importance, this controversy has no particular ramifications for epistemology and the efficacy of man's reason. But the same is not true of theism. The existence of a supernatural realm would have profound implications for human reason, and anyone who believes in a supernatural being must also assume certain beliefs concerning the scope and validity of man's knowledge (whether he is aware of these beliefs or not).

If we make a new discovery in the field of science, this simply provides us with one more piece of knowledge. If we were to somehow discover the existence of a god, however, this is a discovery for which we would pay a tremendous price. Theism offers us a bit of "knowledge" which, if true, would destroy the foundation of all present knowledge by obliterating the naturalistic context within which we comprehend reality. Theism represents an attack on man's ability to understand the universe—and the advocacy of theism, theology, attempts to reduce man to a state of perpetual ignorance. The concept of god, as Spinoza put it, is an asylum of ignorance.

This brief discussion sets the context for much of the remaining portion of this book, where we shall discuss the battle between god and reason in more detail. Further discussion is necessary because most theists, especially Christians, will remain unconvinced by an appeal to reason alone. After all, they will argue, we have not touched upon an idea central to Christian belief: the concept of *faith*. For the Christian, reason does not necessarily have the final word. As Richard Taylor expresses it:

A philosophical teacher will often . . . labor long to persuade his audience that the content of Christian faith is unreasonable, which is a shamefully easy task for him, unworthy of his learning. Then suddenly, the underlying assumption comes to light that Christian beliefs ought, therefore, to be abandoned by rational people! A religious hearer of this discourse might well reply that, religion being unreasonable but nonetheless manifestly worthy of belief, we should conclude with Hume that reason, in this realm at least, ought to be rejected. [36]

This moves us deeper within the sphere of epistemology. When discussing religious belief, should reason give way to faith? Is faith capable of ascertaining truths that lie beyond the scope of reason? Can one consistently uphold reason and faith without conflict?

We must now consider the possibility that, although the concept of God cannot be understood through reason, another means of cognition may be available to us through faith. This brings us to the next section which discusses the relation of reason and faith, the nature of reason, and the various theories of faith.

PART TWO:
REASON, FAITH AND
REVELATION

. . . if devotion to truth is the hallmark of morality,
then there is no greater, nobler, more heroic form
of devotion than the act of a man who assumes
the responsibility of thinking.

. . . the alleged short-cut to knowledge, which is
faith, is only a short-circuit destroying the mind.

—Ayn Rand
Atlas Shrugged

4.
Reason
Versus Faith

I

Clarifying the Issue

Confusion is the enemy of purposeful thought. Whether one is engaged in a process of problem solving, or of gaining new knowledge, or of drawing implications from present knowledge, or of directing one's actions, a lack of precision in one's thinking will undermine or completely sabatoge the achievement of one's goal.

The purpose of abstract, philosophical thought is to achieve understanding. A philosophical argument is spurred by an intellectual disagreement, and the purpose of argumentation is to resolve this conflict by reaching a common understanding among the participants. A confused, muddled argument cannot attain this goal because it fails to specify the precise nature of the conflict. Whatever elements a confused argument may contain, it necessarily lacks one ingredient: clarity. Clarity—the precision of thought and communication—is the antidote for confusion; they cannot coexist. Where there is confusion, there is vagueness and the absence of definition.

If confusion is the enemy of purposeful thought, clarity is its closest ally. Specifying the precise nature of the problem to be solved is often a major contributing factor in arriving at a solution. It has been said, with considerable justification, that a question well-asked is half-answered. Applying this principle to the realm of philosophical disputes, we may say that a conflict well-defined is half-resolved.

In order fully to understand the nature of a philosophical conflict, one must grasp the *fundamental* differences that give rise to the conflict. One must investigate the basic issues and apply this knowledge to the disputed issue.

A debated subject is often a symptom, a surface manifestation, of a more basic underlying disagreement. Unless this area is explored—and unless some agreement is reached—the conflict will continue, while becoming repetitious and dull. The result is a kind of "intellectual atrophy," where the argument proceeds without significant progress, where no new material is introduced, and where the participants know beforehand that neither side will convince the other.

This "intellectual atrophy" is typical of the conflict between Christianity and atheism. Volumes are written on the subject of God, pro and con, but fresh material is rarely presented. The Christian presents the standard arguments for the existence of God, and the atheist presents the standard refutations of these arguments. The Christian responds with a flurry of counter-objections, and the atheist retaliates.

Meanwhile, the average bystander becomes confused and impatient. He has observed arguments, but he has not been told why these arguments are important. He has witnessed the disagreements, but he has not been presented with the basic conflicts underlying them. While this person may have absorbed a smattering of divergent theories and ideas, he lacks an overall perspective, a frame of reference from which to integrate and evaluate the particulars that have been thrust upon him. Consequently, he frequently dismisses the philosophical investigation of theism as too abstract, remote and irrelevant to merit his attention. He will leave philosophy to the philosophers; and, while they construct endless debates, he will rely on what he has been taught, or on what his friends believe—or on what his "common sense" and "intuitions" tell him.

Although some philosophers seem to have a vested interest in representing it as such, philosophy is not an esoteric discipline reserved for a select few. As with any specialized field, a detailed knowledge of philosophical issues requires concentrated study, but a basic grasp of the philosophical differences between theism and atheism is available to any person who cares to put forth some effort.

Many Christian laymen are contemptuous of philosophical objections to their belief in God. They may spurn philosophy as irrelevant, while claiming to believe not in "the God of the philosophers," but in "the God of Abraham, Isaac and Jacob." Even if this distinction were valid, it would not change the fact that the Christian implicitly adopts many philosophical beliefs. By his belief in a supernatural being, the Christian commits himself to a metaphysical view concerning the nature of reality. By his belief in the unknowable, he commits himself to an epistemological view concerning the scope of human reason. By his belief in divine moral commandments, he commits himself to an ethical view concerning the foundation of moral principles.

It is the responsibility of the philosopher to identify the underlying assumptions of these commonly held beliefs. A clarification of basic issues is essential to any discussion of theism and atheism. The question of the existence of God is the tip of an iceberg; under the surface, there are crucial problems that must be solved.

Does the theist have reasons for his belief in God? If so, what are they? What is his evidence?—or, more importantly, what is the nature of evidence in general? What does the Christian mean when he claims to know of God's existence?—or, more importantly, what is the nature of knowledge in general? How do we acquire knowledge? How do we distinguish truth from falsity?

These and similar questions fall within the sphere of epistemology, the branch of philosophy which investigates the origin and nature of knowledge. Since the differences between a Christian and an atheist often narrow down to their different responses to the above questions, epistemology is the arena where the deciding battle must be fought.

The conflict between Christian theism and atheism is fundamentally a conflict between *faith* and *reason*. This, in epistemological terms, is the essence of the controversy. Reason and faith are opposites, two mutually exclusive terms: there is no reconciliation or common ground. Faith is belief without, or in spite of, reason.

Explicit atheism is the consequence of a commitment to rationality—the conviction that man's mind is fully competent to know the facts of reality, and that no aspect of the universe is closed to rational scrutiny. Atheism is merely a corollary, a specific application, of one's commitment to reason.

I will not accept the existence of God, or any doctrine, on faith because I reject faith as a valid cognitive procedure. The particular content or object of faith—whether it be gods, unicorns or gremlins—is irrelevant in this context. The statement, "I will not accept the existence of God on faith" is derived from the wider statement, "I will not accept *anything* on faith." Thus, explicit atheism is primarily an epistemological position: if reason is one's only guide to knowledge, faith is necessarily excluded. If theistic doctrines must be accepted on faith, theism is necessarily excluded. A rational man will be without theistic belief, and therefore atheistic.

While some versions of theistic belief may claim to operate only within the sphere of reason, it remains true that all versions of Christianity eventually appeal to the concept of faith. Through faith the Christian claims to transcend reason and gain knowledge inaccessible to man's rational capacity. Even those Christians who attempt to rationally demonstrate the existence of a supernatural being refuse to offer similar demonstrations of the Trinity, the divinity of Jesus, the Resurrection, and other essential Christian beliefs.

Faith is the common thread running throughout the divergent approaches to Christian theism. The Catholic and the

Protestant, the liberal and the fundamentalist, the existentialist and the Thomist—all must rely on the validity of faith as a means of acquiring knowledge. *Faith is the epistemological underpinning of Christianity.* If faith collapses, so does Christianity.

II

The Attack on Reason

Immanuel Kant wrote that he "found it necessary to deny knowledge of God ... in order to find a place for faith." All advocates of faith are Kantians in this respect. In any defense of faith that one cares to examine, one will find an attack on reason.

Some Christians are openly hostile to reason (notably those sympathetic with existentialism). These Christians usually declare that reason is nothing more than an impersonal calculating device, a cold deductive faculty that cannot give meaning and substance to man's life. Faith, on the other hand, is "vital and indescribable"; it "partakes of the mystery of life itself. The opposition between faith and reason is that between the vital and the rational. ..." Christian faith "is not only faith beyond reason but, if need be, *against* reason."[1]

The Church Father Tertullian (A.D. 150-225) stands out as a paradigm of the Christian antagonism to reason. In *De Carne Cristi* he emphasizes the paradoxical nature of Christian belief.

> And the Son of God died; it is by all means to be believed, because it is absurd. And He was buried and rose again; the fact is certain because it is impossible.[2]

Tertullian takes seriously the biblical promise that God "will destroy the wisdom of the wise, and will bring to nothing the understanding of the prudent." "It is philosophy," Tertullian asserts, "that supplies the heresies with their equipment." He wishes "a plague on Aristotle" and poses the now famous question: "What has Jerusalem to do with Athens? . . ."

> After Jesus Christ we have no need of speculation, after the Gospel no need of research. When we come to believe, we have no desire to believe anything else; for we begin by believing that there is nothing else which we have to believe. . . .

> My first principle is this. Christ laid down one definite system of truth which the world must believe without qualification.[3]

Tertullian's explicit advocacy of paradox is extreme even for Christianity, but his open assault on reason is by no means unusual. Many Christians freely admit the conflict between reason and faith and have declared war on reason. Martin Luther, to take a famous illustration, calls reason "the devil's bride," a "beautiful whore" and "God's worst enemy." "There is on earth among all dangers," writes Luther, "no more dangerous thing than a richly endowed and adroit reason, especially if she enters into spiritual matters which concern the soul and God. For it is more possible to teach an ass to read than to blind such a reason and lead it right; for reason must be deluded, blinded, and destroyed." According to Luther, "Faith must trample under foot all reason, sense, and understanding, and whatever it sees it must put out of sight, and wish to know nothing but the word of God."[4]

This gross irrationalism is abhorrent to any person with a semblance of respect for logical thought. The conflict between reason and faith—carried to its extreme in the above examples—is the focal point of critical atheism. For the atheist, to embrace faith is to abandon reason. One atheist defines faith as "the commitment of one's consciousness to beliefs for which one has no sensory evidence or rational proof."[5] Another atheist writes that "Christian faith is not merely believing that there is a god.

It is believing that there is a god no matter what the evidence on the question may be."

"Have faith," in the Christian sense, means "make yourself believe that there is a god without regard to evidence." Christian faith is a habit of flouting reason in forming and maintaining one's answer to the question whether there is a god.6

Many Christians strenuously object to this portrayal of faith as unjustified or irrational belief. On the contrary, they claim that reason and faith are different ways of acquiring knowledge: both can arrive at truth, and neither contradicts the other. To argue that faith rests upon "inadequate evidence," or that faith "is the habit of the irrational or the nonrational" is "entirely unfaithful to the Scriptural and traditional teaching of Judaism and Christianity."7 According to these Christians, the atheist, by representing faith as contrary to reason, is fighting a straw man.

It is true that many Christian apologists have striven to reconcile reason and faith: this was a dominant theme of the later Middle Ages, and it remains an important element of Roman Catholicism. It would be a mistake to attribute to all Christians the overt hostility to reason displayed by Tertullian. However, the historical attempts to reconcile reason and faith are beside the point. The crucial issue is: Have these attempts succeeded? Moreover, can any attempt at rapprochement possibly succeed? To both of these questions, the answer is an emphatic "no."

I am not merely arguing, as a matter of historical fact, that all attempts to reconcile reason and faith have failed. My position is stronger than this. I am asserting that all such efforts must fail, that *it is logically impossible to reconcile reason and faith.* The concept of faith itself carries a "built-in" deprecation of reason; and without this anti-reason element, the concept of faith is rendered meaningless. (Throughout this discussion, the

101

term "faith" refers to a supposedly reliable method of acquiring knowledge. Any other notion of faith is irrelevant with regard to the existence of God and the truth of Christian doctrines.)

In the next two chapters we shall examine the nature of reason and the major theories of faith advocated by Christian apologists. The groundwork for these discussions is presented in the remainder of this chapter, where I defend the position that reason and faith are, and must be, irreconcilable.

III

The Nature of the Conflict

What does it mean to say that reason conflicts with faith? Before we can answer this question, we must have some idea of what it means to accept a belief as true on the basis of reason.

"Reason," to quote Ayn Rand, "is the faculty that identifies and integrates the material provided by man's senses."[8] It is by abstracting the immediately given concretes of his experience into concepts, and integrating these into still wider concepts, that man acquires knowledge and surpasses the ability of lower life forms.

The presence of an idea or belief in one's consciousness does not constitute knowledge; one can have false ideas and false beliefs. If man is to acquire knowledge, he must have a method of distinguishing truth from falsity, beliefs which correspond to reality from beliefs which do not.

To qualify as knowledge (*i.e.*, as a correct identification of reality), a belief must be *justified*; it must warrant acceptance by rational standards. If a belief meets the requirements of these standards, it is a rational belief; if a belief cannot meet the requirements—but is adopted nonetheless—it is an irrational belief.

Specifying criteria for knowledge is a complex and controversial task, and one which we shall discuss in more detail in the following chapter. For the present discussion, we may indicate three minimum requirements that must be fulfilled before any

102

belief can claim the status of knowledge: (a) a belief must be based on evidence; (b) a belief must be internally consistent (*i.e.*, not self-contradictory); (c) a belief cannot contradict previously validated knowledge with which it is to be integrated. If a belief fails to meet any or all of these criteria, it cannot properly be designated as knowledge.

Contrary to widespread opinion, to rationally demonstrate or justify a belief is *not* synonymous with claiming certainty for that belief. Depending on various factors, such as the nature and amount of available evidence, a belief may be categorized as probable to some degree. If this is what the evidence warrants, the belief has been justified. Reason demands that the degree of certitude assigned to a belief must be in accordance with the available evidence. Reason does not demand that every bit of human knowledge must be accepted as certain or closed to further investigation.

To rationally demonstrate a belief is to show that it warrants acceptance according to the epistemological standards of human knowledge. To accept a belief as true on the basis of reason is to accept it because it is capable of rational demonstration.

Now consider the concept of faith. If faith is considered to be a reliable means of gaining knowledge, it is obvious that reason and faith must differ in some way. If they are identical, it is senseless and misleading to use these two words to denote the same intellectual process. "I accept this as true on the basis of reason" cannot be synonymous with, "I accept this as true on the basis of faith." The Christian who attempts to reconcile reason and faith is committed to the position that, while these concepts are not the same, their difference does not render them incompatible.

How does faith differ from reason? This is the question that will ultimately decide the issue of compatibility. Christians have provided many answers to this question (see Chapter 6), but their answers share a common characteristic: all defenses of faith as a means of acquiring knowledge rely upon an (implicit or explicit) deprecation of reason, such as by proclaiming the limits of reason or its undesirability in certain areas. Nor can this be otherwise. The limiting of reason is a necessary ingredient for the concept of faith; it is what makes the concept of faith *possible.*

This point can be illustrated by looking at our original question—How does faith differ from reason?—from a somewhat different perspective. Consider this question: *Why does the Christian employ two concepts, reason and faith, to designate different methods of acquiring knowledge, instead of just using the concept of reason by itself?* In other words, why is it necessary for the Christian to introduce the idea of faith at all? What purpose does it serve that is not served by reason?

The answer is obvious: the Christian wishes to claim as knowledge beliefs that have not been (and often cannot be) rationally demonstrated, so he posits faith as an alternative method of acquiring knowledge. Faith permits the Christian to claim the status of truth for a belief even though it cannot meet the rational test of truth. Thus, the Christian is forced to defend the position that there are two methods by which man can arrive at knowledge: by reason *and* by faith.

Faith is required only if reason is inadequate; if reason is not deficient in some respect, the concept of faith becomes vacuous. The Christian creates the need for faith by denying the efficacy of reason. Without this element of denial, faith is stripped of its function; there are no gaps of knowledge for it to fill.

If reason is comprehensive, if no sphere of reality is exempt from its scrutiny, there are no grounds on which to posit faith as an alternate method of cognition. If reason can tell us anything there is to know, there is no longer a job for faith. *The entire notion of faith rests upon and presupposes the inadequacy of reason.*

This explains why discussions in favor of faith are always accompanied by references to the limits of reason. The Christian must use this procedure in order to prepare the necessary groundwork for faith. Without this preparation, he will be in the position of advocating the use of a concept for which there is no use.

104

The Christian who postures as an advocate of reason is often quite subtle in his attack on reason. Yes, he says, reason provides man with knowledge of reality; yes, reason is vital to man's existence; yes, man's rational capacity is his distinguishing characteristic—*but* some aspects of existence cannot be comprehended by man. Some facts are closed to rational understanding. Reason is fine as far as it goes, but it is limited. And here faith makes its grand entrance. Faith is called upon where reason is said to fail, and faith is represented as a supplement to reason, not an enemy. In the words of Aquinas, faith "perfects" reason.

A Christian may claim that reason cannot fulfill the psychological and emotional needs of man, or that reason is limited in its application, or that reason is defective in some respects—but, regardless of the details, reason must be pushed aside to accommodate faith. Several centuries ago, John Locke noted Christianity's distaste for reason:

> I find every sect, as far as reason will help them, make use of it gladly: and where it fails them, they cry out, It is matter of faith, and above reason.[9]

The thesis that faith is possible only in the absence of reason is substantiated by Thomas Aquinas, who undoubtedly ranks as the most important Catholic theologian in history. In considering the question of whether "it would be superfluous to receive by faith things that can be known by natural reason," Aquinas presents three reasons why reason and faith apply to the same object of knowledge in some instances.

"First, in order that man may arrive more quickly at the knowledge of Divine truth." If a man waits until he has the knowledge required for a philosophical proof of God's existence, "it would not be until late in life that man would arrive at the knowledge of God."

"The second reason is, in order that the knowledge of God may be more general." Those persons who are incapable of grasping or unwilling to grasp the proofs "would be altogether deprived of the knowledge of God, unless Divine things were brought to their knowledge after the manner of faith."

"The third reason," Aquinas writes, "is for the sake of certitude. For human reason is very deficient in things concerning God."[10]

According to Aquinas, a man may first believe something on faith which he later comes to know through reason, or a man may accept as an article of faith something which other men can rationally demonstrate, or a man may use faith to acquire a certainty that reason is impotent to give. In any case, faith serves a function only when reason does not. Aquinas freely admits that reason and faith cannot simultaneously be offered as grounds for belief; they cannot coexist in the same person at the same time with respect to the same object of knowledge.

Etienne Gilson, a prominent Thomist scholar, supports this thesis in a discussion of the Thomistic view of faith:

> Abstractly and absolutely speaking, where reason is able to understand, faith has no further role to play. In other words, we cannot both know and believe [on faith] the same thing at the same time under the same aspect. . . .
>
> . . . since man requires knowledge of the infinite God, who is his end, and since such knowledge exceeds the limits of his reason, he simply must get it by way of faith.[11]

Augustine was actually attracted to Christianity by its insistence that doctrines must be believed without proof. In *The Confessions* he tells how he repented of his "intellectual pride" after many years as a non-Christian and finally turned to the dogmatism of the Catholic Church:

> Being led . . . to prefer the Catholic doctrine, I felt that her proceeding was more unassuming and honest, in that she required to be believed things not demon-

strated (whether it was that they could in themselves be demonstrated but not to certain persons, or could not at all be). . . .[12]

Although Christian doctrines cannot be rationally justified, argues Augustine in *The City of God,* they should not be rejected as false or nonsensical. In support of this, Augustine points out that there are many "marvels" in nature that reason cannot account for, that "the frail comprehension of man cannot master. . . ." If one were demanded to give a rational explanation of these phenomena, one could not do so—except to say that they are "wonders of God's working" that "the frail mind of man cannot explain. . . ."

Among the "wonders" cited by Augustine are the "antiseptic nature" of the peacock that prevents it from rotting like other flesh (a "fact" that Augustine claims to have personally validated); a fountain in Epirus that, "unlike all others, lights quenched torches"; and, perhaps most impressive, mares in Capadocia that "are impregnated by the wind."[13]

As Augustine illustrates, it is by shrinking the range of reason that the Christian attempts to create a sphere for faith. Reason is examined, declared to be ineffective in some area, and faith is assigned to this virgin territory.

If the Christian expands the sphere of reason, he diminishes the boundaries of faith. If reason is declared fully capable of understanding all facts, if no aspect of existence is decreed "off-limits" to man's mind, the need for faith is eliminated. Like air rushing in to fill a vacuum, faith rushes in to fill the void allegedly left by reason. A harness must be placed on reason to manufacture the need for faith. If reason is released from its bondage, faith is its first—and only—victim.

Here we see the critical role of the "unknowable" in perpetuating the Christian scheme of faith. The unknowable is where reason cannot tread; it is the sole province of faith. To relinquish this agnosticism would be to abandon the epistemological function of faith by rendering the concept of faith superfluous and vacuous.

This is why reason and faith are incompatible. Faith depends for its survival on the unknowable, the incomprehensible, that which reason cannot grasp. Faith cannot live in a natural, knowable universe. As Pascal observed, "If we submit everything to reason, our religion will have no mysterious and supernatural element."[14]

A man committed to reason, a man committed to the unswerving use of rational guidelines in all spheres of existence, has no use for the concept of faith. He can adopt faith only at the expense of reason.

IV

Rejoinders and Arguments

Thus far we have seen that faith *must* entail belief in the absence of rational demonstration, because reason and faith cannot coexist in the same person at the same time with respect to the same object of knowledge. The presence of rational demonstration negates the possibility of faith. Since nonrational belief is an integral component of faith, we concluded that reason and faith are irreconcilable.

The Christian may object to this. After all, he may argue, I have shown only that reason and faith are different, not that they are incompatible. Even if we grant that the propositions of faith are believed in the absence of rational demonstration (and therefore may be categorized as nonrational), it does not follow that the propositions of faith are irrational. While faith differs from reason, asserts the Christian, faith is not contrary to reason: it is an auxiliary method of gaining knowledge. The truths of faith are of a different sphere or order than the truths of reason, but both faith and reason can arrive at truth. And since truths never conflict, two methods of arriving at truth—reason and faith—cannot conflict.

This is the general approach usually taken by Christians in their effort to reconcile reason and faith. It rests upon several confusions which we shall now unpack.

108

(a) To begin with, the defender of faith invariably misrepresents "reason" and "rational demonstration" in his attempt at reconciliation. He represents "reason" as a special faculty or compartment of the thinking process, and he represents "rational demonstration" as a special type of demonstration among others. Thus it is argued that there are means of cognition other than reason and kinds of demonstration other than rational. As Richard Robinson points out, the human mind "comes to seem like a toolbox; and these various faculties—reason, intuition, faith, and the rest—are the tools in the box."

> Now the good use of a toolbox involves the good choice of which tool to use for each purpose. There are things that you can do well with a chisel but not with a hammer, and conversely. Hence we come to think that there are things you can do with faith but not with reason, and so on.[15]

This approach allows the Christian to characterize reason and faith as alternative, but not incompatible, ways of acquiring knowledge. Reason has its job, and faith has its job. The critic of faith, according to this view, fails to understand the proper functions of reason and faith. By demanding that a proposition of faith must meet the requirements of reason—or else be denied the status of knowledge—the atheist is demanding that a hammer must meet the requirements of a wrench—or else be denied the status of a tool. Such a position is condemned as narrow-minded. Reason and faith are different, argues the Christian, because they must accomplish different tasks. Reason does what it is capable of, but, as with any instrument, it has its limits. Then we must turn to another instrument—faith—in order to grasp the truths that lie beyond reason. Faith supplements or perfects reason, just as a wrench may supplement a hammer, or complete a task which the hammer begins but is incapable of finishing.

As stated previously, this defense of faith proceeds from a misrepresentation of "reason" and "rational demonstration." Reason is not one aspect of thought, it is the capacity for abstract thought itself. Man's ability to conceptualize—to mentally abstract and integrate concrete particulars—qualifies him as a rational animal. Reason is not one tool of thought among many, it is the entire toolbox. To advocate that reason be discarded in some circumstances is to advocate that thinking be discarded—which leaves one in the position of attempting to do a job after throwing away the required instrument.

"Rational demonstration" is not a special kind of demonstration (such as deductive reasoning); it is the process of demonstrating that a belief fulfills the epistemological requirements of human knowledge. The qualification of "rational" does not imply a contrast with other equally valid forms of nonrational demonstration; it merely emphasizes that demonstration can occur only within the context of principles established by reason. (Technically, when referring to the verification of knowledge, the phrase "rational demonstration" is redundant. A demonstration that is not rational—*i.e.*, that cannot fulfill the basic requirements of knowledge—is not a demonstration in any meaningful sense.)

Reason is the faculty by which man acquires knowledge; rational demonstration is the process by which man verifies his knowledge claims. A belief based on reason is a belief that has been examined for evidence, internal coherence, and consistency with previously established knowledge. There can be no propositions beyond the "limits of reason." To advocate that a belief be accepted without reason is to advocate that a belief be accepted without thought and without verification.

Again quoting Robinson: "On all choices between adopting a proposition and adopting its contradictory, either reason is competent or nothing is. . . . The only alternatives to thinking with reason are thinking unreasonably and not thinking."[16]

Reason does not permit an alternative method of acquiring knowledge. The principles of reason are intended to separate justified from unjustified propositions: if a belief cannot meet the requirements of reason, it is unjustified—without sufficient foundation—and must be condemned as irrational (*i.e.*, contrary to the requirements of reason). Faith, by its very nature as

110

belief in the absence of rational demonstration, must also be condemned as irrational. In this context, "nonrational belief" is irrational.

(b) When arguing for compatibility, most Christians take the position that the propositions of reason do not contradict the propositions of faith—and, therefore, reason and faith do not conflict. With regard to a proposition of faith, claims the apologist, we will not find a proposition of reason that contradicts it.

While it is true that the Christian will never find a contradiction between the propositions of reason and his religious beliefs, this is true only because he will never permit such contradictions to exist. The apologist reduces all contradictions to apparent contradictions, which he claims are ultimately reconcilable.

The Christian typically uses one of two methods to clear up any alleged discrepancies between reason and faith. First, if the battle is not completely lost, he will declare that the apparent conflict results from a defect or limitation in our reasoning capacity. Second, if the evidence of reason is overwhelming, he will be forced to admit the truth of the rational proposition—but he will stipulate that the article of faith was not a "true" article of faith, but rather rested on a misinterpretation of scripture or some other divine source. The Christian will then revise his faith and claim that there was no real conflict all along.

As a brazen example of the first method, a fundamentalist writes:

> . . . no man can possibly presume to make such a statement as: "Science contradicts the Bible," or "The world-view necessitated by modern science disproves the Biblical cosmology." The fact that such statements are made, and in fact quite frequently made, is a sad testimonial to the immodesty and presumption of many scientists, who are merely fallible and sinful human beings like all other men.[17]

111

In case one is puzzled by the connection between being "sinful" and being unable to contradict Christian doctrines, another Christian fills us in as follows:

... when the non-Christian scientist or philosopher begins to reason in the field of philosophy or theology, the very nature of the subject matter, dealing as it does with the ultimate causes of the universe, makes it impossible for him to reason correctly. The distortion brought about by the fall of man into sin completely blocks the intellectual channels of such a non-Christian thinker and prevents him from reasoning correctly.[18]

Even Christians who do not resort to this brand of nonsense will somehow manage to degrade reason in their attempts to salvage religious dogma. As Kaufmann notes, Christianity, from its inception, "has conceived itself as an enemy of reason and worldly wisdom; it has exerted itself to impede the development of reason, belittled the achievements of reason, and gloated over the setbacks of reason."[19]

If there exists a conflict between reason and religious dogma, we are assured that this *apparent* conflict results from our insufficient understanding of divine truths. Whenever consistency, logic or science became uncomfortable for the Christian, he can safely retreat into his incomprehensible God and argue that our problems are a consequence of man's puny understanding.

On occasion, however, even the Christian is forced to acknowledge the supremacy of reason if he is to avoid pushing his beliefs beyond the limits of absurdity. This is where his religion undergoes a rewrite. Previous articles of faith, once disproved, are declared to be unessential, and those beliefs that cannot be discarded without demolishing Christianity are now interpreted "symbolically" instead of literally.

Throughout history Christianity has sought to eliminate scientific principles that conflict with Christian faith, and it has

112

not hesitated to employ intimidation and violence in pursuit of this end. When science finally triumphed, Christianity refused to abandon its appeal to faith. Previous conflicts between religion and science were attributed to misunderstandings. Former articles of faith, after they are conclusively refuted, are now viewed as misinterpretations of the "true" faith; and new theories, such as evolution, are incorporated within Christianity.

It is rather amusing that, after years of violent hostilities between religion and a scientific discovery, a modern Christian will claim that the Christian faith (properly understood, of course) really supported the new theory all along. Evolution ceased to contradict divine creation only after the evidence for evolution became overwhelming. Now every enlightened theologian can deliver an impressive account of how evolutionary theory actually magnifies the greatness of God.

The tragic fate of Galileo is a paradigm case of the conflict between religion and science. The heliocentric theory of the solar system as defended by Galileo was dubbed "atheistic"; and one Church Father, in opposition to it, declared that "geometry is of the devil" and that "mathematicians should be banished as the authors of all hereisies." The Catholic Church with the sanction of Pope Paul V decreed that "the doctrine of the double motion of the earth about its axis and about the sun is false, and entirely contrary to Holy Scripture." Galileo, imprisoned and threatened with torture, was forced to retract his theory and "abjure, curse, and detest the error and the heresy of the movement of the earth." [20] The *Catholic Encyclopedia* candidly states that "the theologians' treatment of Galileo was an unfortunate error; and, however it might be explained, it cannot be defended."[21]

This admission by the *Catholic Encyclopedia* is disturbing. One must wonder why the treatment of Galileo was "an unfortunate error." Was it an error because it is immoral and unjust to coerce any man to change his beliefs, regardless of what those beliefs are? If so, much of the history of the Catholic Church has been a massive "unfortunate error." But this is not the implication of the above passage. One must suspect that the

113

case of Galileo was "an unfortunate error" simply because Galileo was correct and the Catholic Church was incorrect. This apology—like most religious apologies for past mistakes—is one of embarrassment, not of moral disapproval.

Cases of persecution similar to Galileo's (which are also found in Protestantism) are a significant indicator of the extent to which Christians themselves have been aware of the conflict between reason and faith. The issue is not whether Galileo was right or wrong. The issue is: *Why has Christianity found it necessary and desirable to suppress free inquiry with the threat of force?* If reason will only lend support to the dogmas of religion, why have those countries with a strong Church-State alliance displayed such an eagerness to enforce religious dogmas and eliminate dissent through the power of the State? Why has Christianity refused, whenever possible, to allow its beliefs to compete in a free marketplace of ideas? The answer is obvious— and revealing. Christianity is peddling an inferior product, one that cannot withstand critical investigation. Unable to compete favorably with other theories, it has sought to gain a monopoly through a state franchise, which means: through the use of force.

The bloodstained history of Christianity is a dramatic testimony to the conflict between reason and faith, and it illustrates that many Christians, especially those in power, have themselves been aware of the deadly threat that reason poses to faith.

The responsibility of explanation lies with the Christian. If there is no conflict between reason and faith, why has Christianity insisted on rigorous censorship of dissent? If the Catholic Church is an institution committed to rationality and truth, why has it subjected dissenters to torture and death? The man of reason, the man concerned with arriving at truth, supports his ideas with reasons and evidence—not with a torture rack and stake.

Any Christian of today who wishes to parade as an advocate of reason must begin with an unequivocal condemnation of Christianity's brutal past. He cannot be content with criticizing those specific cases where the persecuted party happened to be correct; he must condemn the policy of ideological persecution and censorship *as such*. For the Catholic, this entails that he condemn what has been an official policy of the Catholic Church for centuries—and what remains a policy today, if to a lesser degree, in those countries unfortunate enough to fall under Church domination.

The "unfortunate error" of Galileo was just one among many: the historical conflicts between science and religion are a continual source of embarrassment for contemporary defenders of faith, who must explain why the superior truths of faith have so frequently been displaced by the limited truths of reason. Faith, having fared poorly in direct competition with reason, has since been kicked upstairs. Unlike their ancestors, most modern theologians are unwilling to venture into the realm of science. They prefer to restrict faith to the supernatural and the unknowable—which they believe to be forever beyond the domain of science—thus minimizing the possibility of future (and equally embarrassing) confrontations.

With science left to the scientists and the unknowable left to the theologians, it is unlikely that we will ever again experience such blatant conflicts between science and religion as those in the past. Christian beliefs, especially those of Protestant liberalism, are sufficiently disconnected from the real world that no new knowledge about the real world can affect them.

But confrontations still occur. We have the problem of credibility, or, in many instances, gullibility. Christianity grew up in a time of mysticism and wonder; miracles were commonplace, and men were willing to believe the most fantastic stories. Times have changed. The modern mind, tempered by the progress of science and technology, is less liable to accept at face value stories of virgin births, resurrections and places of eternal torment. We view such incredible doctrines as the products of a primitive and superstitious age—and since Christianity is predicated on these beliefs, it seems that we must reject Christianity for the same reason. But the liberal theologian has come to the rescue.

115

The liberal theologian has dedicated himself to the task of making Christianity palatable to the critical mind. Through "demythologizing" and "biblical exegesis," he seeks to update the traditional doctrines of faith, thereby eliminating any apparent conflicts between reason and the propositions of faith. The liberal purports to give us a glimpse into the "true" meaning of the biblical record—but this meaning usually bears little resemblance to Christianity as it has been known for nineteen centuries.

Liberal Protestants freely concede the historical unreliability of the Bible; in fact, they are largely responsible, through the development of "higher criticism," for its ruthless dissection and demise as a factual source. Rudolph Bultmann, an influential Protestant who popularized "demythologizing," frankly admits that "the whole framework of the history of Jesus must be viewed as an editorial construction, and . . . a whole series of typical scenes . . . must be viewed as creations of the evangelists."[22] While I regard this admission as fatal to Christianity, Bultmann and a host of other modernists do not regard it as destructive in the least. How, then, does the liberal view the Bible?

William Miller explains that the "demythologizer" wishes to "arrive at an accurate picture of the *kerygma,* or real message, of the New Testament." To accomplish this goal, "The Gospels are studied not as historical records but as theological documents from another era that express that era's experience of something that happened then, but also of a kernel of truth that remains valid for today."[23] This raises serious problems. If the Gospels are not considered as "historical records," does this mean that the truth or falsity of the Bible is irrelevant with regard to the truth of Christianity? Or, indeed, can Christianity itself be viewed as true or false?

We must remember that Christianity has a history spanning over nineteen centuries. During this time, with the possible exception of the past few decades, the Christian has defined himself in terms of what he believes to be *true.* The Christian believes in a certain kind of god, and he believes that God has revealed his will to man through the Bible—which includes the doctrines of hell, eternal bliss and the Resurrection of Christ. Many heresies and schisms developed over doctrinal disputes, and heated debates ensued, often culminating in persecution. If the historical record is to count for anything at all, it is quite clear that Christianity has conceived itself as preaching the truth of biblical doctrines and historical incidents. To claim, as does the demythologizer, that the Bible is not to be regarded as historical, is to undercut the historical basis of Christianity—and ultimately to destroy the concept of Christianity as such.

Like many theologians, Bultmann's rejection of traditional doctrines extends to disbelief in the literal Resurrection of Jesus; this too is a myth—a myth with meaning and relevance, but a myth nonetheless. It is at this point that we must wonder how the liberal Christian differs from the non-Christian. Where is the dividing line? In his First Letter to the Corinthians (15.14), Paul warns that "if Christ has not been raised, then our preaching is in vain and your faith is in vain." Paul had a clearer grasp of the issues involved than do modern theologians. If the Resurrection is an "editorial construction," then Christianity is *false.* Period.

The atheist argues that Christian doctrines conflict with reason and should be rejected; the liberal argues that Christian doctrines conflict with reason and should be revised. "Where the heretic would say No, the theologian interprets."[24] But this interpretation, in the hands of the modern liberal, simply distorts Christianity into a grotesque form. It does not reconcile reason and Christian faith.

The reason-faith controversy hinges on the truth of the Christian record, *i.e.,* the Bible. Once the Bible is conceded to be factually incorrect, there is—from the atheistic point of view—nothing further to argue. The theologian may "interpret" to his heart's content, but he will never move one inch closer to refuting atheism.

Another favorite technique of the liberal theologian is to ignore the uncomfortable. Those doctrines beyond the help of interpretation are treated as if they do not exist. This is particularly evident in the case of hell. A conspiracy of silence enshrouds this venerable Christian belief, and one will search in vain among modern theological works for a detailed discussion of it.

Hell is described quite vividly by the New Testament writers, who make no attempt to conceal the hideous fate awaiting nonbelievers. The great Christian theologians also take hell seriously. In his monumental *Summa Theologica*, Thomas Aquinas discusses such pressing issues as whether the damned will be tortured by corporeal fire, whether this fire will be the only method of punishment, and whether the damned will weep with actual tears.[25]

Rarely do we hear the liberal Protestant discuss the fate that awaits nonbelievers. If the liberal denies hell, he must explain why Christianity is important, because there is no longer anything to be "saved" from. If he admits the existence of eternal torment (which is unlikely), he must reconcile vicious cruelty with what is represented as a religion of love and compassion. Typically, the theologian says as little as possible on this subject—which is incredible when one considers the importance of hell as a historical teaching and a religious concept. But to pretend that a doctrine does not exist does not eliminate its conflict with reason.

The liberal theologian is trapped in a dilemma. As a scholar and philosopher, he is ostensibly committed to intellectual honesty and the pursuit of truth—but as a theologian, he is committed to the defense of Christianity. Bultmann expresses this dilemma in a most revealing fashion:

He [Karl Jaspers] is as convinced as I am that a corpse cannot come back to life or rise from the grave, that there are no demons and no magic causality. But how am I, *in my capacity as pastor*, to explain, in my sermons and classes, texts dealing with the Resurrection of Jesus in the flesh, with demons, or with magic causality? And how am I, *in my capacity as theological scholar*, to guide the pastor in his task by my interpretations?[26] (Emphasis added)

Bultmann unwittingly reveals the basic difference between philosophy and theology and their basic source of conflict. Philosophy is committed to the discovery of truth; it is not obliged, as a discipline, to defend any particular set of beliefs at any cost. Such is not the case with theology. *Theology, as a discipline, is concerned with the defense of a particular set of beliefs;* Christian theology is concerned with the defense of the Christian religion. As Kaufmann observes in his brilliant critique of theology, "One must remember that theology, and indeed any systematic discussion of God, was born as a defensive maneuver. It is the product of a distinctive historic situation."[27]

Only if one appreciates the significance of theology as "a defensive maneuver," can one appreciate the function of "demythologizing" and other interpretative techniques. An atheist cannot be a theologian. If a theologian abandons his religious commitment, he ceases to be a theologian. A theologian *qua* theologian is committed to defending his religious commitment, which often leads him to extreme measures to avoid disclaiming Christianity. The theologian risks more than losing an argument; his job is on the line as well.

Interpretation is the life-blood of theology. It is the method by which theology perpetuates its own existence. As Kaufmann puts it, "Theology is . . . a comprehensive, rigorous, and systematic avoidance, by means of exegesis, of letting one's Yes be Yes, and one's No, No."[28]

We thus come full circle to our original problem of reason versus faith. The Christian theologian will never find a contradiction between the propositions of faith and reason, because it is his job to interpret them out of existence. As a theologian, he has decided beforehand that the propositions of faith can be defended, and by defending them he is simply doing theology. Through the prior assumption that his beliefs of faith are true, the Christian necessarily concludes that any "conflict" between reason and faith is a mistake. He does not want contradictions, so he will refuse to accept anything as evidence of a contradiction. There is no apparent contradiction that cannot be explained away—even if it entails the castration of the Christian religion and the sacrifice of reason.

119

(c) There is another important objection to the preceding attempt to reconcile reason and faith: by claiming that the "truths" of faith do not conflict with the truths of reason, the Christian begs the question at issue. Granted, *if* faith can arrive at knowledge, it cannot conflict with reason—but the crucial question is: *Can faith arrive at knowledge in the first place?* Is faith a valid epistemological procedure? Unless the Christian can demonstrate that faith is capable of distinguishing truth from falsity, he cannot uphold the compatibility of reason and faith.

The conflict between reason and faith is not primarily a conflict between the propositions of reason and the propositions of faith: it is a more basic conflict between the epistemological requirements of reason and the nature of faith as a claim to nonrational knowledge. *I am arguing that faith as such, faith as an alleged method of acquiring knowledge, is totally invalid—and as a consequence, all propositions of faith, because they lack rational demonstration, must conflict with reason.*

The incompatibility of reason and faith does not hinge on whether the nonbeliever can provide knowledge which is in direct contradiction to articles of faith. The full weight of responsibility rests with the Christian: he is offering the articles of faith, and he must demonstrate their compatibility with reason. He must show that, although his propositions lack rational demonstration, they should be accepted as true nonetheless. If he fails to do this, his beliefs collapse as unsupported subjective whims.

To illustrate this point, consider the following situation. I claim to be able to arrive at knowledge by the flip of a coin; and, to demonstrate my assertion, I assign "heads" to represent truth and "tails" to represent falsity. While tossing the coin, I utter the proposition, "Phoenix is the capital of Arizona." The coin comes up "heads," indicating that the proposition is true. I repeat the experiment with, "Thomas Jefferson was the first president of the United States." The coin appears "tails," indicating falsity. Since the "truths" of coin flipping are compatible with the truths of reason, must we conclude that coin flipping, as an epistemological method, is compatible with reason?

The answer, of course, is "no, coin flipping is not compatible with reason." But we must understand why it is not. The obvious objection is that, after a few lucky coincidences, the verifications of coin flipping would flatly contradict the propositions of reason. After a fair sampling, approximately 50 percent of the tosses would correspond to rational knowledge, while the other 50 percent would not.

This objection correctly notes that reason must serve as the arbiter of truth, but it misses the crux of the problem. It is not the case, as this objection suggests, that coin flipping can even sometimes arrive at knowledge. While 50 percent of the flips may correspond to rational knowledge, it does not follow that coin flipping is a "semi-reliable" method of gaining knowledge. In fact, it is completely unreliable, because it is not even a method of ascertaining truth in the first place. Since they lack rational support, the propositions of coin flipping—regardless of their specific content—cannot qualify as knowledge claims.

The coin flipping example rests upon an erroneous assumption: it assumes that, since the result of a coin toss may correspond to rational knowledge, coin flipping therefore qualifies as a means of acquiring knowledge. But there are two important issues here that must be distinguished: we must differentiate between *what* one believes (the content) and *why* one believes it (the grounds or justification for belief). *Rational demonstration pertains to justification as well as content.* To earn the status of truth, a proposition must be capable of being justified. When, through sheer coincidence, a coin toss corresponds to actual fact, it has not arrived at a truth; it has not established or justified anything.

Since coin flipping contains no epistemological standards to distinguish truth from falsity, it cannot qualify as a method of gaining knowledge. If I assert a knowledge claim based on a coin toss, it is not the responsibility of the nonbeliever to check my claim against rational knowledge in order to determine whether my method is compatible with reason. It is only necessary for him to point out that I am asserting propositions without offering evidence in their favor—which means that I cannot

121

claim the status of knowledge for any of my propositions. Without cognitive support, I cannot specify why my assertions should be accepted as true—which means that I cannot offer reasons why anyone should take me seriously. Coin flipping as such conflicts with the requirements of reason; therefore, all propositions of coin flipping (*i.e.*, all beliefs based on this procedure) also conflict with reason.

Returning to the concept of faith, we may say the following: if the Christian wishes to argue that the "truths" of faith do not conflict with the truths of reason, he must first demonstrate that faith is capable of distinguishing truth from falsity. He must present the *epistemological credentials* of faith, the method by which faith arrives at truth. How do we distinguish an article of faith from a whim or a coin flip? On what basis does the Christian argue that faith enables one to gain knowledge? What is the justification of faith?

It is thoroughly improper for the Christian to demand that the atheist present propositions of reason that contradict propositions of faith. Although this can be done easily, it is not required to establish the irrationality of faith. As with coin flipping, even if there were cases where propositions of faith coincide with actual fact, this would not prove the rationality of faith. Aside from the content of his beliefs, the Christian must specify why he believes them—and if his justification cannot withstand critical scrutiny, all beliefs accepted on faith collapse as irrational.

We see, then, that one cannot uphold the compatibility of articles of faith with reason until one first establishes the validity of faith as a means of acquiring knowledge. The argument under consideration—that the propositions of faith do not contradict the propositions of reason—is simply question begging, because it presupposes the truth of that which it must demonstrate. The propositions of faith will not conflict with the propositions of reason only if faith can arrive at knowledge, but this is the very issue being disputed. Thus the Christian cannot use this as a link in his argument.

122

V

The Dilemma of Faith

With the preceding groundwork, we now arrive at what may be termed the central dilemma of faith: *Insofar as faith is possible, it is irrational; insofar as faith is rational, it is impossible.* This dilemma is a consequence of the fact that reason and faith cannot simultaneously be offered as grounds for belief. A belief can be based on reason *or* faith, but not both. This makes it impossible for the Christian to maintain the rationality of faith, because as soon as a belief is rationally demonstrated, it ceases to be an article of faith.

Consider the alleged Resurrection of Jesus. Either this belief can fulfill the requirements of knowledge or it cannot. Either it is based on evidence, is internally consistent as a belief, and is capable of integration with one's previous knowledge, or it is not. If the belief in the Resurrection can fulfill these standards, it should be accepted as true—but it has then become a proposition of reason and can no longer be accepted on faith. On the other hand, if the belief in the Resurrection cannot meet the requirements of reason, it may be accepted on faith—but it can no longer claim the status of rational. And so it goes with every article of faith.

By appealing to faith, the Christian wishes to claim the status of knowledge for beliefs that have not fulfilled the minimum requirements of knowledge. Indeed, this is the only context in which the appeal to faith makes sense. But to label as "knowledge" that which has not been rationally demonstrated is a contradiction, because reason demands that nothing be designated as knowledge except that which can fulfill its fundamental requirements.

This is the essence of faith: to consider an idea as true even though it cannot meet the test of truth, to consider an idea as having a referent in reality while rejecting the process by which man knows reality. Regardless of the particular manner in

123

which the Christian characterizes his version of faith, he cannot escape its irrational bias. His only chance of escape, to claim that the articles of faith can also meet the requirements of reason, is a dead end, because it renders the concept of faith inapplicable. Faith is possible only in the case of beliefs that lack rational demonstration.

Since faith must entail belief in the absence of rational demonstration, all propositions of faith—regardless of their specific content—are irrational. To believe on faith is to believe in defiance of rational guidelines, and this is the essence of irrationalism.

Because of this inherent irrationalism, faith can never rescue the concept of God or the truth of Christian dogmas. Faith is required only for those beliefs that cannot be defended. Only if one's beliefs are indefensible—and only if one wishes to retain these beliefs in spite of their indefensibility—is the appeal to faith necessary. If the Christian wishes to argue for the rationality of his convictions, he should stick with presenting evidence and arguments, and he should never appeal to faith in the first place. The Christian who calls upon faith has already admitted the irrationality of his belief; he has already conceded that his beliefs cannot be defended through reason.

If we cannot understand the concept of God, we do not come closer to understanding it through faith. If the doctrines of Christianity are absurd, they do not lose their absurdity through faith. If there are no reasons to believe in Christianity, we do not gain reasons through faith. Faith does not erase contradictions and absurdities; it merely allows one to believe in spite of contradictions and absurdities.

The appeal to faith solves nothing and explains nothing; it merely diverts attention from the crucial issue of truth. In the final analysis, not only is the concept of faith irreconcilably opposed to reason, but it is evasive and quite useless as well.

124

5.
The Skepticism of Faith

I

Spheres of Influence

The conflict between reason and faith may be viewed as a struggle to control *spheres of influence.* Since reason and faith cannot simultaneously reside over any given sphere, the dominance of one requires the exclusion of the other. Once we see that a sphere for faith can be manufactured only at the expense of reason, we can appreciate why the "unknowable" is a central tenet of theism and why Christianity has found it necessary to declare war on reason.

All arguments for faith follow the same basic pattern, which may be divided into three stages: First, we are presented with an alleged need of man, something his nature requires (such as knowledge of ultimate truths). Second, we are told that reason cannot fulfill this need (hence the notion of the "unknowable"). Third, we are introduced to the concept of faith, which we are assured will accomplish the desired task. Faith comes to the rescue, as it were, saving mankind from the strictures of reason.

125

Many critics of faith focus exclusively on the third stage of this progression by objecting to specific theories of faith. Although this is a valuable approach (and one which we shall pursue in the next chapter), it is not the most effective form of refutation. The main source of conflict between reason and faith lies in the second stage of the faith argument. Before the Christian can bring faith to the rescue, he must convince us that something needs to be rescued; he requires a victim to save. This is why he directs most of his energy to creating the epistemological need for faith through denying the efficacy of reason. Defenses of faith primarily consist, not in establishing what faith *can* do, so much as arguing what reason *cannot* do. This suggests that a thorough critique of faith must begin with the alleged inadequacy of reason to fulfill certain needs.

Since an attack on reason, either overtly or through more subtle methods, is a necessary prerequisite for any concept of faith, a defense of reason is the strongest possible argument against faith. Rather than dealing with this or that theory of faith, a defense of reason cuts the ground from under faith as such by denying to it any possible sphere of influence. We shall argue, in effect, that *faith cannot rescue us from the inadequacies of reason simply because reason is not inadequate.*

The methodology of this chapter is based on a principle known as "Occam's razor," after the fourteenth-century theologian, William of Occam. Also called "the principle of parsimony," this dictum states that one should never multiply explanations or increase their complexity beyond necessity. An explanation should be as simple and direct as possible, and any excess baggage should be discarded. Mortimer J. Adler explains the function of this principle as follows:

> . . . Occam's razor is a two-edged instrument—one that works in opposite directions. It eliminates theoretical constructs that cannot be *shown* to be necessary for explanatory purposes; but it also justifies the retention of theoretical constructs the need for which can be *shown*.[1]

126

The Christian's entire defense of faith hinges on whether he can present faith as a "theoretical construct the need for which can be shown." If one believes that reason can be shown deficient in some respect, the door is open for the alternative suggestion that we turn to the sphere of faith.

The adaptation of Occam's razor to the reason-faith controversy consists in demonstrating that faith, as a supposed method of acquiring knowledge, "cannot be shown to be necessary for explanatory purposes." If reason is not inadequate, the door for faith is never opened—and the subject of faith should never arise in the first place.

If faith is to gain a foothold, reason must be attacked, which brings us to the issue of epistemological skepticism. Although skepticism assumes many forms, it is basically the doctrine that reason is unable to know or adequately deal with particular aspects of reality. Although skeptics rarely deny knowledge outright, they may argue that facts cannot be known with certainty, or that man cannot perceive reality directly, or that the foundations of knowledge—such as the laws of logic—are arbitrary constructs of human consciousness and cannot be said to mirror reality.

It is a widespread delusion that Christianity stands as the last threshold against philosophical skepticism. We are repeatedly warned that belief in God provides the only antidote to the skeptical trend in modern philosophy. "In the modern world generally," writes one theologian, "the Catholic Church comes forward as the one and only real champion of reason."[2]

This is a gross distortion of truth, both from a historical and philosophical perspective. Christianity has never been a champion of reason, nor is it so today. Historically, Christianity has demanded unquestioning belief in its dogma, and it has subordinated reason to the "handmaiden of faith." While reason was permitted to explicate and defend religious dogma, it was never allowed to question the truth of dogma as such.

To claim that Christianity somehow provides a bastion of defense against skepticism is worse than false; it is a reversal of the truth. *Christianity thrives on faith, and faith cannot exist*

127

without skepticism. Skepticism is the precursor of faith; it paves the way for faith. Through denying the efficacy of reason, skepticism creates the need for faith. If faith is the epistemological underpinning of Christianity, skepticism is the epistemological underpinning of faith.

The skeptic and the Christian agree that reason is inadequate in some respect, and they disagree only with regard to the conclusion to be drawn from this. Where the skeptic says no, the Christian calls on faith. Where the skeptic wishes to reject some kinds of knowledge as impossible or uncertain, the Christian seeks to preserve knowledge and certainty through faith. The skeptic rejects reason; the Christian rejects reason and then drags in faith. The skeptic and the Christian, united in their belief in the impotence of reason, are philosophical cousins.

In his struggle to create a sphere of influence for faith, the Christian must align with skepticism. While he may later denounce and oppose skepticism, the fact remains that skepticism in one form or another is the method by which the Christian justifies his faith. As noted earlier, defenses of faith are memorable for their careful listing of the many things reason allegedly cannot do. This is the second stage of the faith argument—the denial of spheres of influence to reason—and it constitutes a crucial step in establishing Christianity.

It is interesting to examine some of the ways in which Christians use skepticism to further their goals. Perhaps the most popular method is to declare that reason must be accepted on faith. According to D. E. Trueblood:

> The ordinary view is that knowledge comes first and that faith comes afterward. . . . The truth, however, lies in the precise opposite of all this. *Faith precedes knowledge* and makes knowledge possible. . . . Knowledge is produced when the original *sensa* are interpreted and organized by epistemological faith. Upon such faith rest not only the lofty creeds of ethics and religion, but also the maxims of daily life.[3]

Trueblood also maintains that the existence of a world external to one's consciousness cannot be established through reason and must be believed on faith:

> Of course, we all believe in the existence of the "real world," but it is a wholesome exercise in humility to try to understand *why* we believe in it. We do so by taking a leap, the leap of epistemological faith.[4]

Another common approach is to argue that the basic principles of science—causality, the uniformity of nature, and the reliability of reason—cannot be verified through reason and hence enter the domain of faith. ". . . it is apparent," writes A. F. Smethurst, "that if we look far enough we shall find that modern science rests upon a foundation of religious belief, and is based upon assumptions which can only be justified by *monotheistic* faith. Science rests upon acts of faith."[5] Like many Christians, Smethurst believes that reason must be vindicated through faith:

> What other ground can we find to justify that reliance on the human mind which is essential to science, save faith in God, and in a God of such a character as He Who is revealed by the Christian Revelation?[6]

In *Studies in the Bible and Science,* the fundamentalist H. M. Morris argues that the uniformity of nature must be accepted on faith:

> The scientific method involves . . . the study of *present* natural processes. When men attempt to interpret the events of the prehistoric past or the eschatologic future, they must necessarily leave the domain of true science . . . and enter the realm of faith.[7]

A survey of religious books, especially those written by Protestants, will reveal a deep and thorough strain of skepticism with regard to the efficacy of reason. Reason, we are told, cannot provide its own foundations, or it cannot support the basic principles of logic and science, or it cannot give us factual

129

certainty, or it cannot escape the unreliability of sensory evidence. When the atheist charges that we cannot make sense out of the concept of God, the Christian replies that this should not disturb us, because we cannot make sense out of many things. When the atheist charges that the existence of a supernatural being cannot be demonstrated through reason, the Christian replies that this must be expected, because reason is incapable of demonstrating much of anything. What reason cannot accomplish, however, faith can—and the Christian offers to save us from a skepticism of his own making.

The Christian is committed to a form of transcendental skepticism. What real difference is there between the skeptic who believes that man cannot know reality as it actually is, and the Christian who declares that man cannot know *ultimate* reality (*i.e.,* God) as it actually is? How does the skeptic who bemoans the impotence of reason to comprehend existence differ from the Christian who preaches the impotence of reason to comprehend the *ultimate* form of existence? There are no basic differences here, only differences of degree.

We see, therefore, that Christianity has a vested interest in skepticism—first, to create a sphere for faith and, second, to preserve the notion of an unknowable being who lies forever beyond the scope of reason. For the Christian to oppose skepticism is ideological suicide. The Christian who postures as an enemy of skepticism is biting the hand that feeds him.

Generally considered, a defense of reason is an attack on skepticism. More specifically, our defense of reason shall be an attack on skepticism as employed by the Christian to create a sphere of influence for faith.

II

Universal Skepticism

We shall begin our examination of skepticism with a doctrine known as *universal skepticism.* While few philosophers or theologians explicitly adhere to this position, its basic theme often arises in less sweeping varieties of skepticism. By noting the flaws of universal skepticism, we are able to arrive at the general principles with which to answer other skeptical objections to knowledge.

Universal skepticism is usually stated in one of two ways. In its positive form it consists of the doctrine that man can know nothing. This belief can be easily dismissed, because anyone who defends it finds himself immersed in hopeless absurdities. In asserting that there is no knowledge, the skeptic is asserting a knowledge claim—which according to his own theory is impossible. The universal skeptic wishes to claim truth for a theory that denies man's ability to arrive at truth, and this puts the skeptic in the unenviable position of uttering nonsense. Indeed, he cannot even begin to argue for his position, because the "possibility of knowledge is presupposed in the very possibility of argument, in the very possibility of having recourse to reasons."[8] As Francis Parker explains:

> There is such a thing as knowledge. The assertion of this proposition is necessarily true if there is to be any assertion at all, for its contradictory is self-contradictory. If the assertion "There is no knowledge" is true, then it is false, for that assertion itself purports to be an instance of knowledge. Thus the only alternative to the recognition of the existence of knowledge is, as Aristotle said, a return to the vegetative state where no assertions whatever can be made.[9]

The second form of universal skepticism consists of the doctrine that we must doubt every alleged instance of knowledge. Through this negative formulation, the universal skeptic seeks to avoid the contradiction of asserting a knowledge claim while denying the existence of knowledge. But the doctrine that we should doubt every knowledge claim translates into the positive assertion that man can never attain *certainty*—and this version of skepticism fares no better than the preceding.

We must ask if this "principle of universal doubt" is itself certain, or is it open to doubt as well? If it is known with certainty, at least one thing is beyond doubt, which makes the principle false. If, however, the principle is open to doubt—*i.e.*, if it is not certain—then on what grounds can the skeptic claim greater plausibility for his theory than any other? The logician C. N. Bittle elaborates on this problem:

> Skeptics either have valid reasons for their universal doubting, or they have no valid reasons for it. If they have valid reasons, they surely know something that is valid, and they no longer are real skeptics. If they have no valid reasons, they have no reason to doubt. In the first case their position is inconsistent, and in the second case their position is irrational. Whichever way they turn, their position is untenable.[10]

Why, according to the universal skeptic, should every knowledge claim be doubted? "Because," he will reply, "man is capable of error, and it is possible in any given instance that he has committed an error." We must remember, however, that "error" (or falsehood) is the opposite of "truth"—and the skeptic who appeals to error implicitly admits that a proposition cannot be true and false, correct and incorrect, at the same time and in the same respect. Thus, whether he likes it or not, the skeptic must surrender to the logical principle known as the Law of Contradiction (which states that a proposition cannot be true and false at the same time and in the same respect). As a barest minimum, therefore, the skeptic must concede the validity of the Law of Contradiction and its corollaries: the Law of Identity (A is A, a thing is itself) and the Law of the Excluded Middle (something is either A or not-A).

Here we must note the main source of confusion in the skeptical approach: *the equation of knowledge and certainty with infallibility.* When the skeptic claims that every knowledge claim should be doubted because man is capable of making mistakes, he is simply pointing out the obvious: that man is a fallible being. No one, not even the most resolute antiskeptic, will deny the point that man is fallible. (We must wonder, though, how the skeptic arrived at this knowledge. Is he *certain* that man is fallible?)

The skeptic fails to realize that it is precisely man's fallibility that generates the need for a science of knowledge. If man were infallible—if all knowledge were given to him without the slightest possibility of error—then the need for epistemological guidelines with which to verify ideas, with which to sort the true from the false, would not arise. Man requires a method to minimize the possibility of error, and this is the function of epistemology. A science of knowledge enables us to discriminate between justified and unjustified beliefs; and since the beliefs of an infallible being would not stand in need of verification, he could have no use for epistemological standards. Where infallibility is involved, concepts such as truth, falsity, certainty and uncertainty are stripped of any possible application.

Consider the basic argument of the skeptic. We have seen that fallibility gives rise to epistemological guidelines used to distinguish truth from falsity, certainty from uncertainty, and so forth. The skeptic, however, starts from the same premise—that man is fallible—and uses it to argue that man can *never* achieve truth and certainty. It is because man is capable of error that he *must* distinguish truth from falsehood, certainty from doubt. "But," argues the skeptic, "it is because man is capable of error that he can never attain truth and certainty."

The skeptic thus turns epistemology on its head by using the foundation for a science of knowledge—human fallibility—as a weapon to argue, in effect, that a science of knowledge is impossible to man.

Even if the universal skeptic could consistently adhere to his position (which he cannot), his victory would be an empty one. His claim that man cannot acquire knowledge and certainty reduces to the claim that man is fallible—and this tells us nothing new, except that the skeptic prefers to use epistemological terms while totally ignoring their context.

Since man is not infallible, any concepts of "knowledge" or

"certainty" that require infallibility are, for that very reason, inapplicable to man and totally irrelevant to human epistemology. Even if the skeptical position made sense, it would fail to tell us anything concerning human knowledge and human certainty—which removes it from the realm of serious consideration.

In summary, we have indicted universal skepticism on two counts: first, because it cannot be maintained without contradiction and, second, because it commits what we shall hereafter refer to as the "infallibilist fallacy"—*i.e.*, the equation of epistemological terms, such as "knowledge" and "certainty," with a standard of infallibility, which is completely inappropriate to man and to the science of knowledge in general.

III

The Contextual Nature of Knowledge

The main lesson of the preceding discussion is that man's fallibility does not invalidate his knowledge claims. Man's capacity for error is not sufficient reason to suppose that he has committed an error in any specific instance. The skeptic cannot appeal solely to man's fallibility as the grounds for skepticism; further argumentation is required.

This point has been recognized by a number of philosophers. Thomas Reid, an eighteenth-century Scottish philosopher, wrote a brilliant critique of skepticism in which he maintains that man's fallibility does not preclude certainty. When a skeptic objects to a knowledge claim, argues Reid, "He makes no objection to any part of the demonstration, but pleads my fallibility in judging." But, continues Reid, "I have made the proper allowance for this already, by being open to conviction."[11]

A wise man who has practised reasoning knows that he is fallible, and carries this conviction along with him in every judgment he forms. He knows likewise,

134

THE SKEPTICISM OF FAITH

that he is more liable to err in some cases than in others. He has a scale in his mind, by which he estimates his liableness to err, and by this he regulates the degree of his assent in his first judgment upon any point.[12]

Reid clearly recognizes the absurdity of the skeptic's attempt to turn reason against itself: "To pretend to prove by reasoning that there is no force in reason, does indeed look like a philosophical delirium. It is like a man's pretending to see clearly, that he himself and all other men are blind."[13]

The modern analytic philosopher J. L. Austin argues in a similar vein: the fact that man is *"inherently* fallible," he writes, does not entail that he is *"inveterately* so."

> Machines are inherently liable to break down, but good machines don't (often). It is futile to embark on a "theory of knowledge" which denies this liability: such theories constantly end up by admitting the liability after all, and denying the existence of "knowledge."[14]

According to Austin, if the skeptic wishes to attack a knowledge claim for which evidence has been provided, he must attack the evidence itself; he cannot merely appeal to human fallibility. ". . . being aware that you may be mistaken doesn't mean merely being aware that you are a fallible human being: it means that you have some concrete reason to suppose that you may be mistaken in this case."[15]

D. W. Hamlyn presents a systematic development of this theme in his recent book, *The Theory of Knowledge.* Hamlyn rejects universal skepticism on the grounds that the existence of knowledge "cannot be rationally questioned." Therefore,

> when someone shows skepticism about certain claims to knowledge, what is required is that the ball be put firmly in his court. He is the one who must produce

justification for his position. Skepticism without grounds is empty, and empty suggestions need not be regarded seriously.[16]

The above philosophers have a vital point in common: they adopt what may be termed a *contextual* approach to doubt. Universal doubt is rejected because of its inherent contradiction and presumption of infallibility. Rational doubt arises contextually; that is to say, doubt emerges in specific circumstances when the arguments and evidence offered in support of a proposition are determined to be defective or insufficient. The skeptic cannot bypass the particulars of a knowledge claim and merely assert that, since man is fallible, the knowledge claim deserves to be doubted. To do so is to commit the "infallibilist fallacy."

In order to justify his doubt, the skeptic must take issue with the specific arguments and evidence offered in support of a knowledge claim. If the proposition in question can withstand scrutiny, it qualifies as knowledge; and if the evidence in favor of the proposition is overwhelming, it rationally qualifies as certain knowledge—man's fallibility notwithstanding.

A contextual view of doubt must rest, implicitly or explicitly, on a contextual theory of knowledge and certainty; but none of the preceding philosophers have developed such a theory in detail. Important work in this area has been undertaken by Ayn Rand, the Russian-born novelist and philosopher, whose contextual approach to knowledge provides a solid framework for our critique of skepticism. Rand's basic approach to epistemology (on which much of the previous discussion has been based) is summarized in this excerpt from *Introduction to Objectivist Epistemology*:

Man is neither infallible nor omniscient; if he were, a discipline such as epistemology—the theory of knowledge—would not be necessary nor possible: his knowledge would be automatic, unquestionable and total. But such is not man's nature. Man is a being of

136

volitional consciousness: beyond the level of percepts—a level inadequate to the cognitive requirements of his survival—man has to acquire knowledge by his own effort, which he may exercise or not, and by a process of reason, which he may apply correctly or not. Nature gives him no automatic guarantee of his mental efficacy; he is capable of error, of evasion, of psychological distortion. He needs a *method* of cognition, which he himself has to discover: he must discover how to use his rational faculty, how to validate his conclusions, how to distinguish truth from falsehood, how to set the criteria of *what* he may accept as knowledge.[17]

A thorough presentation of Rand's epistemology is impossible here, but the following brief sketch touches on some basic issues, insofar as they are relevant to our analysis of skepticism.

Man retains his knowledge in the form of concepts. Beginning with the perceptually given concretes of his sensory experience, man forms concepts through a mental process of abstraction and integration. He abstracts, or mentally "lifts out," common characteristics of observed existents, and integrates these characteristics into a single mental unit, a concept, which is used thereafter as an open-ended classification subsuming an unlimited number of concretes of a particular kind. According to Rand, "concept-formation is a method of cognition, man's method, and . . . concepts represent classifications of observed existents according to their relationship to other observed existents."[18]

Conceptualization permits man to store a vast amount of information which can be called to conscious awareness when needed. From basic, low-level concepts, man expands his range of knowledge, step by step, in a hierarchical fashion. To validate his concepts, man "has to discover the rules of thought, *the laws of logic*, to direct his thinking."[19] Concepts are symbolized by words, and words are arranged in grammatical sentences to express propositions. A true proposition identifies a

REASON, FAITH, AND REVELATION

fact of reality; a false proposition purports to identify a fact, but fails to do so.

With one exception, which we shall discuss shortly, Rand regards all concepts—and hence all knowledge—as contextual. This means that concepts are formed and validated within the context of previous concepts, and new knowledge is acquired and validated within the context of previous knowledge. We thus have what may be described as an inverted pyramid of knowledge, a complex system of interrelated ideas, each concept depending for its validity on previous concepts from which it is genetically derived. But it is logically impossible to have an infinite regress of concepts; there must be a fundamental underpinning, a foundation to set the context. This foundation, for Rand, consists of axiomatic concepts. These are the basis of man's knowledge:

> An axiomatic concept is the identification of a primary fact of reality, which cannot be analyzed, i.e., reduced to other facts or broken into component parts. It is implicit in all facts and in all knowledge. It is the fundamentally given and directly perceived or experienced, which requires no proof or explanation, but on which all proofs and explanations rest.
>
> The first and primary axiomatic concepts are "existence," "identity" (which is a corollary of "existence") and "consciousness." One can study what exists and how consciousness functions; but one cannot analyze (or "prove") existence as such, or consciousness as such. These are irreducible primaries. (An attempt to "prove" them is self-contradictory: it is an attempt to "prove" existence by means of non-existence, and consciousness by means of unconsciousness.)[20]

The contextual nature of knowledge and the role of axiomatic concepts are the basis for an important principle concerning skepticism. Since these three concepts—existence, identity, and consciousness—are implicit in and presupposed by all propositions, any attempt to deny them results in a kind of self-contradiction known as the Fallacy of the Stolen Concept. This fallacy, writes Nathaniel Branden, "consists of *the act of using a concept while ignoring, contradicting or denying the validity of the concepts on which it logically and genetically depends.*"[21] Branden elaborates as follows:

> All of man's knowledge and all his concepts have a hierarchical structure. The foundation or ultimate base of this structure is man's sensory perceptions; these are the starting-point of his thinking. From these, man forms his first concepts and (ostensive) definitions—then goes on building the edifice of his knowledge by identifying and integrating new concepts on a wider and wider scale. It is a process of building one identification upon another—of deriving wider abstractions from previously known abstractions, or of breaking down wider abstractions into narrower classifications. Man's concepts are derived from and depend on earlier, more basic concepts which serve as their genetic roots. For example, the concept "parent" is presupposed by the concept "orphan"; if one had not grasped the former, one could not arrive at the latter, nor could the latter be meaningful.
>
> The hierarchical nature of man's knowledge implies an important principle that must guide man's reasoning: When one uses concepts, one must recognize their genetic roots, one must recognize that which they logically depend on and presuppose.[22]

The principle that knowledge is contextual, and the consequence of ignoring this fact—the Fallacy of the Stolen Concept—are essential for understanding the basic flaw in the majority of skeptical arguments. In order to present his arguments, the skeptic must employ words and concepts; and if these words and concepts are to have meaning, they must be employed within the conceptual framework that makes them possible. Skeptics typically argue as if concepts exist in a vacuum—as if any kind of question or demand is legitimate—and they proceed to mistake the ensuing chaos for profundity.

To say that the skeptic commits the Fallacy of the Stolen Concept is to say that the skeptic "steals" concepts to which he has no epistemological right. The skeptic presents an argument which, if valid, would undercut the logical foundations that the skeptic himself must use in presenting the argument. Most skeptical arguments cannot be maintained without *presupposing* the truth of that which they are attempting to invalidate, which forces the skeptic into the mire of self-contradiction. The introductory text *Philosophical Problems and Arguments* expresses this principle as follows:

> . . . a fundamentally important goal of thought and language is to make sense of things. What makes sense is certified by our epistemic standards; consequently, those standards reflect our conception of reality. The skeptic is implicitly and clandestinely rejecting those very standards and conceptions. By so doing he is also rejecting the very language he speaks. But now the epistemic treachery is exposed; and once seen for what it is, we may readily conclude . . . that skepticism is a sham and a delusion.[23]

IV

Skepticism and the Primacy of Faith

Among Christian theorists, overt skepticism is most often employed by Protestant theologians who wish to establish some variant of the "primacy of faith" doctrine. These theologians argue that due to the inadequacies of reason, we must have faith in reason, faith in logic, faith in the existence of the external world, and faith in the basic tenets of science. If the atheist objects to the irrationality of Christian faith, the Christian replies that the atheist faces the same problem—except that the atheist places his faith in reason and science instead of in God and the immaterial world.

This ploy to vindicate faith through skepticism is a failure twice over: it is useless and fallacious. Let us suppose, for the sake of argument, that the atheist is required to have "faith" of some kind, such as faith in the laws of logic. As a barest minimum, the atheist can give an intelligible meaning to his "faith" by specifying what he has faith in, the object of his faith.

Such is not the case with Christian faith in the existence of God. As demonstrated in Chapter 3, theologians are unable to provide a coherent and consistent description of God; so faith in God, aside from being unjustified, is also unintelligible. The Christian may just as well claim to have faith in the existence of square circles. Because the concept of God is incoherent, the primacy of faith, even if true, is stripped of its major impact. The Christian can never reduce the beliefs of an atheist to the same depths of irrationality as the concept of God.

This temporary concession to the primacy of faith doctrine is far too generous. Every attempt of the Christian skeptic to give faith priority over reason is doomed to failure. We shall briefly examine four versions of the skeptical approach—(a) faith in the efficacy of reason, (b) faith in the laws of logic, (c) faith in the existence of the external world, (d) faith in the principles of science—and we shall see how each commits some form of common skeptical fallacies.

(a) What does the Christian mean when he says that we must have faith in reason? According to A. F. Smethurst, "we must have some degree of faith in our capacity to distinguish truth from error and to make theoretical constructions which bear some measure of relationship to reality."[24] In other words, faith in reason means that we must have faith in the existence

141

of knowledge. Can we "prove" that our alleged knowledge of reality is accurate? No, answers the skeptic, so we must accept on faith the capacity of the human mind to acquire knowledge of reality.

This skeptical argument has been substantially answered in our previous discussion. We accept the existence of knowledge, not because of some mysterious faith, but simply because we have no other choice. The only alternative is universal skepticism, which we have already discarded as indefensible.

While it is legitimate to ask, "What does man know?" or, "How does man acquire knowledge?" it is not legitimate to ask, "*Can* man acquire knowledge?" The mere asking of this question already presupposes knowledge on the part of the questioner, including knowledge of language, man, and a consciousness with the capacity to understand the question, as well as to distinguish a satisfactory from an unsatisfactory answer. Without knowledge, no questions can be asked, and no questions can be answered. Any argument against knowledge is thus self-refuting. As D. W. Hamlyn puts it:

> If knowledge is not possible, how can discussion about its possibility have any hope of reaching a conclusion? How can it even take place? The parties involved might mouth words, but this would not be *discussion.* Thus the skeptic who doubts the possibility of knowledge in general is in the position of Aristotle's skeptic who doubts the principle of contradiction; he only has to be made to say something, and he is convicted out of his own mouth. He cannot both doubt the principle and enter upon discussion to support his case.[25]

Our acceptance of knowledge is not arbitrary or capricious; on the contrary, it is absolutely mandatory. The only alternative—the denial of knowledge—is chaotic nonsense. In no way whatever does our confidence in reason rest on an act of faith. Reason is quite capable of vindicating itself.

(b) The three laws of logic may be stated in different ways, depending on whether they refer to things, classes or propositions. Here is the formulation from a standard text on logic:

1. The Law of Identity: For things, the law asserts that "A is A," or "anything is itself." For propositions: "If a proposition is true, then it is true."

2. The Law of Excluded Middle: For things: "Anything is either A or not-A." For propositions: "A proposition, such as P, is either true or false."

3. The Law of Contradiction: For things: "Nothing can be both A and not-A." For propositions: "A proposition, P, cannot be both true and false."[26]

These principles are simple enough, and few people would be foolish enough to deny them outright. But some Christian theorists deny them indirectly; that is to say, they argue that the laws of logic are without rational foundation and must be taken on faith. On what grounds is this assertion made? Usually on the grounds that the laws of logic, strictly speaking, cannot be proven true. Therefore, concludes the theologian, in the absence of proof, we must accept them on faith.

What does it mean to say that the laws of logic cannot be proved? Formal proof involves an inference from a set of given premises, and in the case of logical laws, there are no available premises from which they can be derived. Any attempt to prove the Law of Identity, for example, would result in question begging, because any attempted proof would presuppose the Law of Identity. The laws of logic are incapable of proof. (There are excellent discussions of the principles of logic in other sources, such as John Hospers' *An Introduction to Philosophical Analysis* and Brand Blanshard's *Reason and Analysis*, so I will restrict this discussion to a few brief comments.)

First, the laws of logic are fundamental to all concepts, thought and communication. We cannot prove them because they are presupposed by the very concept of "proof," and to demand proof for them is to commit the Fallacy of the Stolen Concept. Even the denial of these principles entails their acceptance. Therefore, we accept the laws of logic because we must accept them; they are self-evident and necessarily true. Faith plays no part here.

Second, the laws of logic are not, as is sometimes supposed, only one set of basic principles among many possible sets. These laws are not selected arbitrarily or by convention. Quoting Hospers:

> If the principles of logic weren't already true *before* you established any verbal conventions, you couldn't even establish any conventions. If a convention could also be a non-convention, what would it mean to say that it was a convention after all? Don't you see how the truth of the principle is presupposed in the very attempt *to say anything at all*—whether about conventions or about anything else? Reality lays down these First Principles . . . If we don't follow them, we talk nonsense. [27]

In *The Nature of Thought*, Blanshard dismisses the notion of so-called "alternative logics":

> Remove the law of contradiction from your system and replace it with a substitute, and what do you get? Some bizarre alternative system? No. You get no system at all, and no assertion at all, for you have removed the condition of intelligible statement in any system whatever. It is odd to call such a law a 'linguistic convention'. A convention can be exchanged for something else. But when you changed the law of contradiction, what would you change *to*? Such laws cannot be abandoned, nor are they in fact abandoned by any of the so-called alternative logics. . . . [28]

The laws of logic are prerequisites for consistency and intelligibility. We accept them because they are necessarily true, not because we have "faith."

(c) To doubt the existence of an external world seems absurd to most people—as, indeed, it is—so it is curious that many philosophers regard the existence of an external world as a serious topic of philosophical debate. And rising from the dust of the skeptic's claim that we cannot demonstrate the existence of an external world, is the theologian, ready to offer faith as the basis for belief.

Why, according to some Christians, must the existence of the external world be accepted on faith? Because, they will argue, reason is incapable of providing evidence or proof that the universe exists independently of consciousness. I am trapped, so to speak, within my private world of consciousness, and I can never get "out there" to demonstrate conclusively that a universe exists apart from myself.

The doctrine that only I exist, and that the universe is nothing more than a product of my consciousness, is known as solipsism. Solipsism is rarely defended outright, because when it is, we have the ludicrous picture of a man informing other men that they do not exist. Bertrand Russell once related an amusing incident of this kind:

> As against solipsism it is to be said, in the first place, that it is psychologically impossible to believe, and is rejected in fact even by those who mean to accept it. I once received a letter from an eminent logician, Mrs. Christine Ladd Franklin, saying that she was a solipsist, and was surprised that there were no others. Coming from a logician, this surprise surprised me.[29]

Many philosophers have pointed out that man's use of language, his ability to communicate, presupposes the existence of an external world that functions as a common frame of reference. If words are to have meaning, they must have referents; and if men are to communicate with words, their words must have common referents. If one is trapped within one's private world of consciousness, if one is unable to perceive an independent universe, then one has no way to compare one's own use of language with the usages of other men. Therefore, since the skeptic must employ language in order to communicate his argument, he implicitly concedes the existence of an external world.

This flaw in the skeptic's position is only one among many: to deny the existence of the external world involves a great many stolen concepts. To deny objective existence is to obliterate the distinction between truth and falsehood. A true proposition identifies a fact of reality, and if there is no reality to be identified, there can be no truth. Similarly, external reality provides the objective framework for the presentation of evidence, and to deny independent existence is to destroy the standard that makes evidence possible. And, again, the concept of objective proof has application only in an objective world. The skeptic who questions the existence of an external universe thus forfeits his epistemological right to language, and such concepts as truth, evidence and proof.

These objections are very brief, but the basic point should be clear. As with other skeptical positions, to argue against the existence of an external world is effectively to remove oneself from the sphere of rational discourse. We accept the premise of an external world in the name of necessity, intelligibility and consistency, not in the name of faith.

(d) The claim that we must have faith in science centers around two main points: first, we supposedly cannot demonstrate the uniformity of nature and, therefore, must accept it as an article of faith; second, the laws of science are constantly undergoing revision, so, according to the skeptic, we can never claim to know any specific law with certainty. The first of these issues is discussed elsewhere in this book and I will not repeat it here.[30] The second issue has also been substantially answered in the previous discussion of the "infallibilist fallacy," but I will summarize its application to this problem.

146

As scientific knowledge increases, man will continually revise and update many of his scientific principles, but this does not preclude the possibility that many scientific laws can be known with certainty. Certainty does not mean "static." It simply means that, *within the context of one's knowledge,* the evidence for a given proposition is overwhelming. If one's method is correct, future knowledge will expand and refine our present knowledge, but it will not contradict it. Thus, where we have substantial evidence for the truth of a proposition, it is extremely unlikely that this proposition will be contradicted by future evidence, although it may require revision in some cases.

Depending on the nature and degree of available evidence, a scientific law may be possible, probable or certain. These are different stages of an evidential continuum. As the amount of evidence increases, so will the degree of certainty.[31] Certainty does not require infallibility or omniscience, and to claim certainty is not to claim the theoretical impossibility of error (although this is the case in some instances, such as with mathematical truths).

We must remember that scientific inquiry does not differ radically from other fields of inquiry. To exclude certainty from science is to exclude it from other fields as well. We no more accept science on faith than we accept other branches of knowledge on faith, so the argument that science cannot attain certainty eventually leads to the conclusion that certainty is impossible. And for reasons already presented, this variety of universal skepticism is untenable.

V

Skepticism and Sense Perception

Perhaps the most concerted attack of skepticism is directed at the validity of sense perception. Sense perception constitutes the starting point, in effect, of knowledge, and to undercut the reliability of sensory evidence is to undercut the basis of man's knowledge. It comes as no surprise, therefore, that one will often find a Christian theologian (usually a Protestant) employing skeptical arguments against the senses to his advantage. If the atheist demands sensory evidence of God's existence, the Christian quickly points to the supposed unreliability of sense experience, while suggesting that God transcends such crass and ineffective methods of revealing himself. Instead, God chooses a purer way to reveal himself; the Christian experiences God directly, without the aid of intervening sense perception, and the Christian insists that the knowledge of God gained in this manner far surpasses the flimsy capacity of man's physical sense organs.

The following dialogue between a skeptic and an antiskeptic covers the primary arguments against the senses. Although the specific issues are different from our previous discussions, it is instructive to note that the skeptical fallacies remain basically the same. The informal, conversational format of this dialogue will hopefully make for interesting and entertaining reading.[32]

Skeptic: "You claim that man gains knowledge of reality through his senses, but I submit that our sense are deceptive. Since we cannot rationally defend the reliability of sensory evidence, we must place trust in them as a matter of *faith*."

Antiskeptic: "Why do you say that?"

Skeptic: "Because our senses give us contradictory testimony, and even you stress that contradictions cannot exist. Look, I'll prove it to you by taking this pencil and placing it in . . ."

Antiskeptic: "Excuse me for a moment. If I understand correctly, you are going to demonstrate that our senses do not give us accurate knowledge of reality. Is this correct?"

Skeptic: "Yes."

Antiskeptic: "Then you cannot start from the prior assumption that our senses *do* give us accurate knowledge of reality,

148

because this would entail accepting the truth of the very proposition which you wish to disprove. Do you agree?"

Skeptic: "Of course."

Antiskeptic: "Then you won't mind if, from this point on, I don't grant you this assumption."

Skeptic: "Naturally. Now may I proceed with my demonstration?"

Antiskeptic: (staring in opposite direction—no answer).

Skeptic: "I said, may I proceed?"

Antiskeptic: (startled). "Did I hear something?"

Skeptic: (irritated). "I'm talking to you."

Antiskeptic: "I beg your pardon."

Skeptic: "Are you going to be serious or not? Here I am trying to carry on an intelligent philosophical conversation, and you're acting silly."

Antiskeptic: (squinting his eyes). "It looks and sounds like you are talking to me, but then I can't be certain, since I never trust what I see and hear. In fact, I can't be sure that you are actually sitting there."

Skeptic: "I insist that you behave reasonably!"

Antiskeptic: "If I could only trust what I see and hear, I might be able to reply—assuming of course that I could trust you, if you're really there, to hear what I actually say. But, then, I couldn't be sure that what I hear myself saying is what I've said, because . . ."

Skeptic: "All right, you've made your point. Have it your way. Assume, for the sake of argument, that we are communicating accurately. I admit that it cannot be proven, but assume it for now."

Antiskeptic: "Why?"

Skeptic: "So I can make my point."

Antiskeptic: "I must assume, in other words, that my senses are *not* deceptive—at least as they pertain to this conversation—so that you can get your argument off the ground to 'prove' that this entire assumption is unfounded. If your argument is correct, you don't have the means with which to make your point. Through your attempt at communication and argument, you are admitting the validity of sense perception—and, therefore, by arguing that sense perception is deceptive, you cut the ground from under your own feet and become mired in a hopeless absurdity."

Skeptic: "I'll restate my argument somewhat. I don't deny that, for practical purposes, we act on the assumption that our senses enable us to perceive without deception. Language, as you have pointed out, depends on this assumption. What I wish to argue is that our naive trust in our senses is without logical foundations. Although we may have faith in our senses from day to day, they are not as reliable as the average person thinks—and I can demonstrate this by showing you an example where our senses are unreliable, because they give us contradictory information. If this is true, then we have no way of ascertaining when we are being deceived and when we are not."

Antiskeptic: "Your argument hasn't changed any; you have merely elaborated it. Like all skeptics, you seem to think that you can assume as true the very thing you are trying to disprove, and you attempt to skirt this problem by stipulating that you are doing so for practical purposes because we make these assumptions in everyday life. You claim that, as a philosopher, you have discovered reasons to doubt the validity of sense perception. My point is this: regardless of whether you call your use of language 'practical' or whatever, by attempting to communicate you commit yourself to a certain philosophic context—namely, the context that makes communication possible. Once you are working within this context, it is completely irrational to turn around and declare that the foundations of that context are rationally unfounded. If the premise that our senses give us accurate knowledge of reality has no basis in reason, then any argument that occurs within that context has no basis in reason either—which includes your argument."

Skeptic: "I see your point, but I think I can convince you if you will only watch my demonstration."

Antiskeptic: "Any attempted proof will itself depend on the *prior* validity of sensory evidence, so you are again attempting the absurd."

Skeptic: "But there are such obvious cases of deceptive sensory appearance, it seems absurd to me to deny their existence. As I was about to demonstrate before, if I take this straight pencil and place it in . . ."

Antiskeptic: "Straight pencil? How did you ascertain that it is straight and that it is a pencil?"

Skeptic: "It's quite obvious."

Antiskeptic: "I agree, but you must presuppose the ability of your senses to give you accurate knowledge of reality."

Skeptic: "I'll rephrase my argument. Here we have what *appears* to be a straight pencil, although I'll admit that I cannot prove it. Mind you, I'm not saying that it really is a straight pencil, but only that it appears to be so. Now when I place what appears to be a straight pencil in this glass of water . . ."

Antiskeptic: "You mean, when you place what appears to be a straight pencil in what appears to be a glass of water. . . ."

Skeptic: "Have it your way. Anyway, as you can now witness, the pencil appears to be bent."

Antiskeptic: "Does it?"

Skeptic: "Well, you're not at a very good angle. Get down more level with the water line."

Antiskeptic: "Do you mean to say that your monumental disproof of the senses requires a certain angle?"

Skeptic: "Don't be smart, just look. You must admit that it now looks bent."

Antiskeptic: "Yes, although a better description would be 'disjointed.'" *(Long pause.)*

Skeptic: "Well?"

Antiskeptic: "Well what?"

Skeptic: "What do you think now?"

Antiskeptic: "I told you what I think—the pencil does look 'bent' in water."

Skeptic: "Yes, go on."

Antiskeptic: "With what?"

Skeptic: "With the conclusion, of course."

Antiskeptic: "But I already gave you my conclusion: the pencil does appear to be bent under water."

Skeptic: "But what about the contradiction?"

Antiskeptic: "A contradiction?"

Skeptic: "Yes. The pencil appeared to be straight, and now it appears to be bent. If I remove it from the water, it once again appears straight."

Antiskeptic: "I agree with you on that point."

Skeptic: "But that's a contradiction!"

Antiskeptic: "It is?"

Skeptic: "Of course! How can the same pencil be straight and bent?"

Antiskeptic: "We didn't say that it *is* straight and bent; we merely said that it *looks* straight out of water and *looks* bent in water. Where is the contradiction?"

152

Skeptic: "But that must be a contradiction."

Antiskeptic: "The Law of Contradiction—which is one of the basic laws of logic—states that an object cannot be A and non-A *at the same time and in the same respect.* You're showing me a pencil that looks straight at one time and in one respect (out of water), but that looks bent at another time and in another respect (in water). You must remember the context. We are perceiving the pencil through two different mediums, air and water. Since light travels more slowly through water than through air, it takes longer for the light waves to reach our eyes from the submerged portion. What we are perceiving is not a contradiction, but simply a straight pencil that appears bent in a specific context, *i.e.,* in water. No defender of sensory experience would claim that an object must appear the same in every situation, but this has no effect whatsoever on the validity of the senses. For example, if I placed the pencil in a glass of tar, would you then express surprise because part of the pencil had 'disappeared'? Would this show that we cannot trust our senses? On the contrary, it is through our senses that we understand that the pencil is submerged in tar, and it is through our senses that we discover that light will not penetrate tar. In other words, it is through our senses that we gather the information with which to explain why the same object appears differently under different conditions. We solve the alleged instances of 'sensory deception' through a further appeal to sensory evidence—just as you must presuppose the validity of the senses in the very attempt to disprove the validity of the senses."

Skeptic: "Since you claim that I have not presented you with a legitimate instance of a contradiction, I will appeal to another version of this argument which will fulfill your requirements. If we feel the pencil while it is in water, it will feel straight. The pencil *looks* bent but *feels* straight at the same time and in the same respect, *i.e.,* while it is in water. That should cinch my argument."

Antiskeptic: "No, because we are dealing with two different sense modalities, which again changes the context. Also, this demonstration, like all others, presupposes the validity of sense perception—which renders your conclusion invalid. For example, in order for your alleged contradiction to be a contradiction, it must be true that we are seeing and feeling the same object. After all, if we were seeing and feeling different objects, you would not even raise the possibility of a contradiction. Now I must ask you how you know that you are seeing and feeling the same object?"

Skeptic: "It's very simple to see that we are dealing with the same pencil."

Antiskeptic: "Of course, but *you* must establish that you are seeing and feeling the same object without recourse to the senses. And this, I submit, is impossible. Furthermore, in order for you to maintain that we are receiving contradictory evidence, you must assume that two different sense modalities—sight and touch—can furnish us with information concerning the same aspect of the same object. This raises the question: On what basis do you claim that there is a contradiction between '*feeling* straight' and '*looking* bent'?"

Skeptic: "I must say again that it seems quite obvious."

Antiskeptic: "If it seems obvious, it is only because our past experience has permitted us to make the correlation between what we see and how an object feels. Without this previous sensory evidence, no such correlation would be possible. Thus, your argument is unintelligible without presupposing the validity of sensory evidence."

Skeptic: "I don't understand what you're saying here. Are you claiming that there is no problem whatsoever in the example I have presented?"

Antiskeptic: "It depends on what you mean by a 'problem.' There is a kind of problem here, but it is scientific, not philosophical. Because there is a change in perception when the pencil is submerged in water, it calls for an explanation—but this explanation, as I have pointed out, consists of appealing to *more* sensory evidence in order to establish why the pencil appears bent in water. A primitive man with no knowledge of light refraction may be genuinely puzzled by our phenomenon, but if he wishes to arrive at a solution, he can do so only through more research. For him to blame his senses, aside from being unjustified, would not solve or explain his dilemma.

"I would like to emphasize a major source of confusion in your argument against sense perception. To speak of our senses 'deceiving' us is, at best, a sloppy metaphor. Philosophically, it is nonsense. Our senses are simply physical organs with no will of their own. To say that they 'deceive' us makes no more sense than to claim that our hearts or our lungs 'deceive' us. Sense organs respond to physical stimuli from the external world; they have no capacity to deceive or misrepresent. They simply transmit sensations according to their physiological characteristics, which our brains then automatically integrate into percepts. We may *misinterpret* the basic data given to us, but there can be no question about the validity of the data *per se*. For example, a man may see what he believes to be a lake in the middle of a desert, whereas what he actually sees is only a reflection of light waves off the sand, or, in other words, a mirage. The man is mistaken in his identification of the sensory evidence—he has not properly interpreted the data given to him—but his senses have not somehow 'deceived' him. The light waves that reach his eyes actually do exist, but the man's interpretation as to the causal origin of these waves is mistaken."

Skeptic: "It seems that you have opened the door for an entirely new set of objections against the senses. Even if our senses, properly speaking, do not 'deceive' us, how can we be sure that our interpretation of sensory evidence is correct? To use your example, how could the man in a desert decide if what he perceives is a real lake or merely a mirage?"

Antiskeptic: "By appealing to more sensory evidence. In this case, he may not be able to decide with certainty until he approaches the area where the lake is supposed to be and sees that there isn't one."

155

Skeptic: "But isn't it possible for me to doubt my interpretation of sensory evidence in every instance? How can I ever be certain that what I identify as the object of my perception is in fact the actual object and not merely a mirage, illusion, or hallucination? Is it not possible to doubt that you are *really* sitting there, even though I am presented with the perception of a man? After all, you may be a mirage as well."

Antiskeptic: "This throws us into the problem of universal skepticism, which was refuted in the preceding section. Can you doubt every instance of sense perception? On a practical level, this is impossible—but even if you were an exceptional person with the psychological capacity to doubt everything, your universal doubt would be blatantly irrational and self-contradictory. To doubt every interpretation of sensory evidence is logically absurd.

"You must realize that to talk of deception, whether in the form of a mirage, illusion or hallucination, makes sense only in contrast to a wider context of nondeception. In order to say that one's interpretation of sensory evidence is incorrect, one must be able to distinguish incorrect from correct interpretations. Otherwise, what would it mean to speak of mistaken identification? Mistaken as opposed to what? What would it mean, for example, to speak of counterfeit coins, unless in contradistinction to genuine coins?

Skeptic: "I understand your objection and I think I can respond to it. I won't deny that in order for us to identify incorrect interpretations of sensory evidence, we must be able to recognize, in principle, a case of genuine interpretation. But my point is this: how, in any *specific* instance, can we be sure that we are correct? The man in the desert, after all, may have felt absolutely certain that he was perceiving a lake, but he was wrong anyway. I may feel absolutely certain that I am perceiving you right now, but isn't it possible that I too am mistaken? It is perfectly conceivable that you are a figment of my imagination. Can you demonstrate to me that you are real and not merely a hallucination, or must I accept my interpretations on faith?"

156

Antiskeptic: "Your demand that I somehow prove to you that I am not an hallucination is totally inappropriate and unjustified. First of all, since you admit that you must be able to identify correct interpretations in order to distinguish incorrect interpretations, simply apply your criteria to this specific instance. Here I am sitting next to you in plain view. You can see me, hear me, and even touch me if you wish. If these conditions do not qualify this as a case of genuine perception, I fail to see what conditions could possibly satisfy you.

"Doubt is not justified merely on the grounds that you can somehow 'imagine' that you are mistaken. In the face of such overwhelming evidence you wish to doubt the correctness of your judgment, then you must provide the grounds of your doubt. If your skepticism is to be more than empty talking, you must justify your doubt. This must consist of specifying why, in our particular circumstances, there is reason to suppose that our perceptual judgment is in error. Doubt cannot be applied indiscriminately; it arises *contextually* in specific circumstances when there is reason to suppose that we may be mistaken.

"To illustrate the contextual nature of doubt, consider the case of the mirage. If we are in the middle of a desert on a very hot day, and if we see what appears to be a lake in the distance, I may say, 'There is a lake,' and you may reply, 'Perhaps not; you may be mistaken. It may be a mirage.' If I ask why you doubt that it is a lake, you may reply: 'Because light waves often reflect off of the desert sand and give the appearance of water. We are in a situation where this occurs quite frequently, so I have reason to doubt.' Or perhaps you are very familiar with the area and know for a fact that there is no lake, in which case you would not simply doubt my assertion, but would claim that I am positively mistaken. In either case, there is something about our specific situation that causes you to doubt the veracity of my perceptual identification.

"Now suppose that we are in the middle of a forest and we stumble across a lake. We decide to take a swim and after an hour of splashing around, you suddenly declare, 'I doubt if this is a real lake.' Your doubt in this context would be utter nonsense. If I ask you why you doubt, and you reply, 'It's conceivable that I am having a hallucination,' I will press you further by asking, 'But what reasons do you have for supposing that you are hallucinating at this particular moment?' If you fail to offer reasons and merely assert that a hallucination is conceivable, I will reply (without going into a detailed criticism of your use of 'conceivable' here) that you are uttering an unsupported, arbitrary proposition—and you do not deserve serious consideration until such time as you are prepared to offer arguments in support of your claim.

"You see, then, that doubt is appropriate in some circumstances and inappropriate in others. It should be quite clear that your doubt of my existence is unfounded, and it must therefore be discarded as irrational. Our context is such that there is no reason to doubt our interpretations of sensory material. If you wish to cling to your doubt, you must offer reasons—reasons that pertain to *this specific context*—as to why doubt is necessary. If you fail to do so, then there is no reason why anyone should listen to you."

Skeptic: "You've covered this ground thoroughly, so I want to move to another (and in my opinion) more serious objection. You mentioned earlier that our senses operate according to a physiological process. Is this correct?"

Antiskeptic: "Yes, perception involves a causal chain of physiological events."

Skeptic: "Precisely. But all that we are immediately aware of is the end link of that causal chain. We are aware of percepts, but only as they present themselves to our consciousness, *i.e.*, only as they interact with our sense organs. There is, for example, no such thing as sound existing independently of consciousness; it is simply the product of waves interacting with our ears. All of external reality is filtered through our senses before it reaches us, and this prevents us from ever perceiving reality accurately."

Antiskeptic: "There are two major flaws in your argument. First, it involves the original stolen concept of depending on communication which would be impossible if not for the

158

assumption that we do perceive reality correctly. Second, I would like to ask you how we came to know of the causal chain involved in perception. After all, it is not self-evident."

Skeptic: "It was a scientific discovery."

Antiskeptic: "You mean to say, then, that it is an accurate, true discovery that describes the actual nature of sense perception?"

Skeptic: "Yes, of course."

Antiskeptic: "Then your use of the causal chain in perception commits you to the position that we perceive reality accurately, since you are claiming that this causal chain is objective fact and not merely an idea in your mind."

Skeptic: "But don't you agree that all we ever have direct awareness of is immediate sense data?"

Antiskeptic: "No. What we have direct awareness of is reality, and we are given this awareness through perception. Perception is our means of awareness, not the object of awareness. Every perception is perception of *something*.

"You want to argue that we are aware only of ideas or perceptions in the mind rather than external reality. You then claim that we need to infer the existence of the external world using these perceptions as a starting point. I am arguing that no such inference is necessary. We have direct and immediate contact with reality through sense perception.

"All that the causal nature of perception tells us is that perception necessarily entails a *means* of perception; certain causal conditions must be present before perception is possible, and once these conditions are satisfied, we have perception. Perception of what? There is only one possible answer: of reality. There is no other alternative. If your perceptions are not of reality, just what are they perceptions of?"

Skeptic: "They are perceptions of the interaction between the external world and my senses."

Antiskeptic: "No. The interaction causes the perception; the interaction is not the object of perception, but simply that which makes perception possible. Again, I must ask you, what is it that you are perceiving, if not reality?"

Skeptic: "I don't think I understand this argument."

Antiskeptic: "I'll rephrase it somewhat. You claim that our senses, because of the physiological process involved in perception, distort reality in some way. Correct?"

Skeptic: "Yes."

Antiskeptic: "Now is this distortion caused by our particular sense organs—I mean, is there something peculiar about the sensory apparatus of man?—or will there be distortion whenever there is perception, regardless of the nature of the organism involved?"

Skeptic: "Since all perception would involve a causal chain, there would doubtless be distortion regardless of the nature of the sense organs involved."

Antiskeptic: "So what you are actually telling me is this: While there may be a reality out there, unfortunately we can never see it because we have eyes, or we can never hear it because we have ears, or we can never smell it because we have noses. In other words, you consider sense organs to be an *obstacle* to perception, rather than the *means* of perception.

"You must remember that man is a physical organism who perceives through physical sense organs. These sense organs operate according to specific physiological processes determined by their nature—and this must be true of any sensory apparatus, regardless of the organism involved. Where you have perception, there must be a means of perception. This is what makes perception possible. What you wish to claim, however, is that our means of perception is what invalidates perception—that any act of perceiving, by its very nature, is not really perception but distortion. Aside from the many stolen concepts in this line of thought, it strikes me as a blatantly absurd argument."

Skeptic: "Even if you are correct, there are other arguments against the senses."

160

Antiskeptic: "Yes, but they differ only in details, not in essentials. No man can escape the fact that his knowledge is gained through sensory experience; all of his concepts, words and arguments depend on and presuppose this fact. Whenever a man opens his mouth to speak—assuming that he intends to communicate intelligibly—he is admitting the validity of sensory experience. All of the so-called arguments against the senses would not be possible without the prior assumption that our senses are reliable. The skeptic cannot avoid self-contradiction."

Skeptic: "Even if I accept what you say, there is yet another problem—and this one is raised quite frequently by Christians. I'll agree, as will many Christians, that we gain knowledge of reality through our senses, and that this knowledge is accurate. This does not prove, however, that our senses are our *only* method of perception. You want to limit knowledge to that which is gained through sensory experience, but this seems unjustifiably dogmatic. After all, the Christian claims that he gains knowledge of God, not through his senses, but through direct experience with the divine nature. As an atheist, you will not grant credence to his claim. But why? How do you know that we are limited to perception through our senses?"

Antiskeptic: "If the Christian has discovered a new means of perception, I am perfectly willing to listen to his claim, provided that he is willing to argue for his assertion. Perhaps man possesses perceptual powers of which he is presently unaware. I don't see any evidence for this, but I'll grant the possibility for the sake of argument. My argument with the Christian is that he claims to have experienced God, but he refuses to explain the process by which he, a physical organism, experienced this supernatural being. I won't limit him arbitrarily to the traditional five senses, but I will demand that he present evidence for his new perceptual powers. Has he discovered a new sense? Fine, then let him tell us about it so we can test it.

"No Christian has ever succeeded in explaining just how he perceives his mysterious God. He claims to have knowledge of a mysterious, unknowable being, having gained this

161

knowledge in some mysterious, unknowable manner. This is totally unacceptable.

"If the Christian wishes to be taken seriously, he must explain, not only what he claims to know, but how he claims to know it. If he did not acquire his knowledge through the senses, by what means did he acquire it? The burden of explanation lies with him. If he upholds his belief in the absence of rational grounds, then he is the dogmatist, not the atheist. The atheist simply wants to know what the theist believes in and how he acquired his knowledge. If explanations are not forthcoming, the atheist will remain an atheist."

6.
The Varieties
of Faith

I
The Bible, Faith and Misology

Although the idea of faith is central to Christianity, the Bible gives us little information concerning the nature of faith. We are told that men must have faith, and we are informed in rather gruesome detail as to what awaits those who lack faith—but nowhere are we told precisely what faith is. The biblical statement most resembling a definition is found in Hebrews 11. 1: "Now faith is the assurance of things hoped for, the conviction of things not seen." While this is not very illuminating, it does suggest why critics of Christianity have likened faith to wishful thinking and emotionalism.

John Hick has observed that "the validity of faith in divine existence . . . is simply taken for granted and acted upon. The biblical writers are not conscious of their belief in the reality of God as being itself an exercise of faith, but only of their confidence in his promises and providence."[1]

While the biblical authors are vague with regard to the nature of faith, they are extremely clear on other related issues, such as the role of reason and the necessity for blind obedience. By examining these topics, we are able to arrive at a better perspective as to the meaning of biblical faith.

The biblical antagonism to reason is one of its most striking features. The Bible is a paradigm of *misology*—the hatred of reason. This attitude permeates the Bible, beginning with the book of Genesis. Adam and Eve, we are told, were evicted from their blissful state of ignorance as a result of eating from the tree of knowledge. When the serpent was tempting Eve, he told her that "God knows that when you eat of it your eyes will be opened, and you will be like God, knowing good from evil." The serpent was correct: man did acquire knowledge, and Christianity views this defiant act as the source of man's inherent evil.

According to the New Testament, Jesus openly admitted the absurdity of his teaching:

> I thank thee, Father, Lord of heaven and earth, that thou hast hidden these things from the wise and understanding and revealed them to babes. (Matthew 11.25)

Jesus was fond of delivering his messages in the form of parables, and at one point he admitted that he *intended* for these parables to be confusing:

> To you has been given the secret of the kingdom of God, but for those outside everything is in parables; so that they may indeed see but not perceive, and may indeed hear but not understand.... (Mark 4. 11-12)

The apostle Paul, who in many respects had more influence on Christianity than did Jesus, was quite candid in his hostility to reason. "See to it," he warned, "that no one makes a prey of you by philosophy and empty deceit, according to human tradition, according to the elemental spirits of the universe, and not according to Christ" (Colossians 2.8).

Paul announced that "We are fools for Christ's sake," but he saw nothing wrong with being a fool.

> ... the word of the cross is folly to those who are perishing, but to us who are being saved it is the power of God. For it is written, "I will destroy the wisdom of the wise, and the cleverness of the clever I will thwart." ... Has not God made foolish the wisdom of the world? For since, in the wisdom of God, the world did not know God through wisdom, it pleased God through the folly of what we preach to save those who believe. ... God chose what is foolish in the world to shame the wise. ... (I Corinthians 1. 18-27)

And again:

> Let no one deceive himself. If any one among you thinks that he is wise in this age, let him become a fool that he may become wise. For the wisdom of this world is folly with God. (I Corinthians 3. 18-19)

Like his predecessors, Paul argues that the truths of Christianity transcend reason:

> The unspiritual man does not receive the gifts of the Spirit of God, for they are folly to him, and he is not able to understand them because they are spiritually discerned. (I Corinthians 2. 14)

Paul's contempt for reason is further illustrated by his willingness to deceive if it will hasten the spread of Christianity:

> ... if through my falsehood God's truthfulness abounds to his glory, why am I still being condemned as a sinner? And why not do evil that good may come?—as some people slanderously charge us with saying. Their condemnation is just. (Romans 3. 7-8)

To the Jews I became as a Jew, in order to win
Jews; to those under the law I became as one
under the law—though not being myself under the
law—that I might win those under the law. To
those outside the law I became as one outside the
law ... that I might win those outside the law. To
the weak I became weak, that I might win the
weak. I have become all things to all men, that I
might by all means save some. I do it all for the
sake of the gospel.... (I Corinthians 9. 20-23)

Considering the biblical assaults on "wisdom" and "understanding," Tertullian and Luther displayed a clear grasp of
Christian essentials when they attacked reason and philosophy.
The misology of the Bible is its most repugnant trait; there is a
constant demand that one must believe without evidence or
thought, and that one must regard absurdity as a desirable
aspect of Christianity. To accept faith in the biblical sense
means to believe in defiance of rational guidelines; it is blatantly
anti-reason, and the biblical writers make no effort to conceal
this fact.

Another significant element of biblical faith is its intimate
association with virtue. Jesus does not demand that people
believe in him in the name of *truth*; he demands that they
believe in him in the name of *morality*. Acceptance by faith is a
virtuous act. "Blessed are those who have not seen and yet
believe," and as Paul warns, "whatever does not proceed from
faith is sin."

This tie between faith and virtue is responsible for the
Christian equation of doubt and disbelief with immorality. One
is not morally free to investigate the truth of the Christian
doctrine by means of reason; instead, one must believe uncritically or be condemned as immoral. A man is thus forced to
choose between morality and truth, virtue and reason. The
paragon of virtue, according to this view, is the man who refuses
critically to evaluate his ideas—and one can scarcely imagine a
more vicious form of irrationalism.

166

Closely related to the preceding is the Christian appeal to reward as a motivation for faith. Virtues should be rewarded, and if faith is a virtue, faith should be rewarded. Jesus sweetens the prize by the promise that the man of faith will be endowed with miraculous powers. "All things are possible to him who believes."

> . . . he who believes in me will also do the works that I do; and greater works than these will he do, because I go to the Father. Whatever you ask in my name, I will do it . . . if you ask anything in my name, I will do it. (John 14. 12-14)

> . . . if you have faith as a grain of mustard seed, you will say to this mountain, 'Move hence to yonder place,' and it will move; and nothing will be impossible to you. (Matthew 17. 20)

Unlike many of his other teachings, these statements by Jesus are quite clear. *Anything* asked in the name of Jesus will be granted, including the miraculous transportation of a mountain. It would take very few examples of mountain moving to convert the atheists of the world, but the modern Christian is reluctant to defend these grandiose claims of faith, much less attempt an actual demonstration.

Despite the awkward failure of the omnipotent faith doctrine, Christians still appeal to a reward for faith, but this prize cannot be collected until after the expiration of our present life. Faith, we are told, is necessary for salvation:

> For God so loved the world that he gave his only Son, that whoever believes in him should not perish but have eternal life. (John 3. 16)

Where we have bribery we usually have blackmail. If the prospect of eternal life does not provide sufficient motivation

167

for belief, we are also informed that the man who lacks faith—
the skeptic, atheist or disbeliever—faces the wrath of an omnipotent God:

> He who believes in the Son has eternal life; he who
> does not obey the Son shall not see life, but the
> wrath of God rests upon him. (John 3. 36)

Jesus warns us to "fear him who can destroy both soul and
body in hell," and he predicts an ominous fate for sinners:

> ... if your hand causes you to sin, cut it off; it is
> better for you to enter life maimed than with two
> hands to go to hell, to the unquenchable fire. And if
> your foot causes you to sin, cut it off; it is better for
> you to enter life lame than with two feet to be
> thrown into hell. And if your eye causes you to sin,
> pluck it out; it is better for you to enter the kingdom
> of God with one eye than with two eyes to be thrown
> into hell, where their worm does not die, and the fire
> is not quenched. (Mark 9. 43-48)

If the implications of this passage fail to sink in, it is
probably because few Christians of today take its message
literally. Such was not the case, however, with earlier and less
sophisticated Christians who were moved to self-castration as a
means of eliminating temptation.

Paul, who is reported to have struck a man blind for opposing
Christianity (Acts 13. 8-11), writes that "he who has doubts is
condemned " (Romans 14. 23).

> A man who has violated the law of Moses dies with-
> out mercy at the testimony of two or three witnesses.
> How much worse punishment do you think will be
> deserved by the man who has spurned the Son of
> God ... and outraged the Spirit of Grace? ... It is a

fearful thing to fall into the hands of the living God. (Hebrews 10. 28-31)

Like Jesus, Paul makes no attempt to veil his threats. His ultimatum between faith and torment is specific and graphically stated. Jesus, warns Paul, shall be

revealed from heaven with his mighty angels in flaming fire, inflicting vengeance upon those who do not know . . . the gospel of our Lord Jesus. They shall suffer the punishment of eternal destruction. . . . (II Thessalonians 1. 7-10)

The threat of punishment for disbelief is the crowning touch of Christian misology. Believe in Jesus—regardless of evidence or justification—or be subjected to agonizing torture. With this theme reverberating throughout the New Testament, we have intellectual intimidation, transcendental blackmail, in its purest form. Threats replace argumentation, and irrationality gains the edge over reason through an appeal to brute force. Man's ability to think and question becomes his most dangerous liability, and the intellectually frightened, docile, unquestioning believer is presented as the exemplification of moral perfection.

The biblical portrait of Christian faith is far removed from the approach of modern liberals who represent Christianity as a reasonable, benevolent philosophy of life interested in the pursuit of truth. There is nothing reasonable about intellectual blackmail, nor is there anything benevolent about threats of violence. As for Christianity's alleged concern with truth, Christian faith is to free inquiry what the Mafia is to free enterprise. Christianity may be represented as a competitor in the realm of ideas to be considered on the basis of its merits, but this is mere disguise. Like the Mafia, if Christianity fails to defeat its competition by legitimate means (which is a foregone conclusion), it resorts to strong-arm tactics. Have faith or be damned—this biblical doctrine alone is enough to exclude Christianity from the domain of reason.

II

Faith as Authoritative Trust

The most concentrated efforts to reconcile reason and faith have been made by Catholics and other Christians who follow the approach outlined by Thomas Aquinas. According to Aquinas, faith is not subjective whim or believing simply because one feels like it, nor does faith consist of belief in the absence of evidence. Rather, faith is a method of acquiring knowledge which, while differing from reason, is not incompatible with reason.

For the Thomists, faith is basically *trust in authority*, or "assent to or acceptance of the word of another that something is true."[2] Faith "is believing something on the authority of another."[3]

Like reason, faith is considered to be a form of intellectual assent to the truth of a proposition. In the case of reason, however, the object of knowledge is "seen," whereas the object of faith is "unseen." This means that we accept something as true on the basis of reason when we personally verify it for ourselves, and we accept something as true on the basis of faith on the testimony of an authority, in the absence of personal verification.

This authoritative concept of faith is often defended on the grounds that everyone must have faith of some sort, even if one does not believe in God. While the atheist may not have faith in the supernatural, he must at least have faith in human authority. Because we cannot personally verify each of our beliefs, we must rely on various authorities. Children believe their parents—on faith. Students believe their teachers and textbooks—on faith. We believe the statements of scientists—on faith. We accept the advice of our doctors and lawyers—on faith.

The man who says that he will believe only what he can prove is fooling himself. Even in a human way the

170

THE VARIETIES OF FAITH

knowledge that we derive from our own experience is pitiably small in comparison to what we accept on the authority of others. We must have faith then.[4]

Considering the obvious need for faith, asks the Christian, why should faith in God be condemned as irrational? In essence it is identical with the faith employed by millions of persons every day, except that the Christian places his trust in a divine authority rather than man. As one Christian puts it, "it is natural to have faith. . . . It is only that the kind of faith and the prevailing objects of faith may differ from age to age."[5]

Faith, therefore, is inescapable. Without it our sphere of knowledge would be drastically reduced to the fraction of our present knowledge that is directly verifiable by each individual. Whenever we consult an authority, maintains the Christian, we leave the realm of reason and enter the domain of faith. Even the hardened atheist is a man of faith.

In discussing this notion of faith as an appeal to authority, we must distinguish between two applications of this concept. (a) The Christian may claim to have faith *in* God, meaning that he places trust in the authority of God and accepts divine revelation as true on this basis. (b) The Christian may claim to have faith *that* God exists, where the trust is placed in a person, a "religious authority," who supposedly has knowledge of God's existence. The first of these approaches is typical of Catholicism, the second of Protestantism.

(a) If one believes in the existence of God, and if one believes that this God has revealed propositions to man through the Bible, then one will accept the Bible as true on "faith"—even if the Bible is undemonstrated—because of one's trust in the authority of God. By having faith in God, a confidence in his authority, the Catholic justifies his belief in revelation.

This concept of faith, however, is totally irrelevant to the choice between theism and atheism. Before one can trust an authority, one must believe in the existence of that authority. Before one can accept God as an authority, one must believe in

171

the existence of God. Before one can have faith *in* God, one must believe *that* God exists. Therefore, this concept of faith *presupposes* the existence of God.

Catholic theologians are well aware of this, and they generally maintain that the existence of God must be demonstrated through reason before their notion of faith becomes applicable. These "proofs" from natural theology (examined in Part III) are the "preambles of faith" or the "motives of credibility." Furthermore, once the existence of God has been established, it is necessary that a given proposition can be shown to be an actual revelation from God. "To assent to a truth on faith," writes one Catholic, "one must be certain that God has revealed *this* truth." This requires a "rule of faith," a means to distinguish genuine revelation, and this is the function of the Catholic Church: "... the Church determines and defines what is contained in the deposit of faith and in tradition."[6]

Because this idea of faith presupposes the existence of God and revelation, it cannot be used to establish the truth of theism, and there is no need to comment on it at length. We should note, however, the misleading use of "faith" in this context, as supposedly contrasted with "reason."

If one believes in the existence of an omniscient, infallible being, then it hardly requires an act of "faith" to accept the testimony of this being. If God is incapable of error, the only possibility of his statement being false is that he chose to lie. If deceit is incompatible with one's idea of God (as it is in Christianity), no possibility of falsehood remains.

Working from the premise that an omniscient, infallible being exists and that this being has revealed a proposition to man, it is a short, logical—and uncontroversial—step to conclude that this proposition is worthy of belief. What stronger evidence could one ask for? If the proposition comes from an infallible, non-deceitful God, it cannot be false; therefore, it must be true. This is the logical elimination of possible alternatives. It is clearly an act of reason, and to call it "faith" is highly misleading.

Thus, even if we were to grant the existence of God and revelation, the appeal to faith would be unnecessary. Reason must be the final court of appeal in any and all circumstances.

172

(b) Since the world is dismally short of burning bushes that talk and tablets personally inscribed by a divine being, the Christian has considerable difficulty producing his chief witness—God—to testify in his own behalf. God does not even present himself, much less his credentials of authority. This brings us to the second version of "faith" as authoritative trust: trust placed in *human* religious authorities as a basis for accepting the *existence* of God.

The appeal to religious authority is usually presented in a manner similar to the following: There are many fields of specialized knowledge, argues the Christian, which are not open to personal verification by each and every individual. Much of our knowledge depends on our faith in authorities, *i.e.*, our trust in the testimony of men who have devoted considerable time and effort to a particular field and who have thus acquired specialized knowledge. The subject of theism is essentially no different than these other spheres of inquiry. Those men, such as the ancient prophets, who have devoted their entire lives to the quest for religious truth possess the superior wisdom and insight one acquires as a result of diligent and disciplined study. While these religious authorities sometimes disagree over points of detail, they agree unanimously on one issue: that there exists some kind of transcendant being, a being beyond the realm of the natural universe. Therefore, concludes the Christian, it seems blatantly unreasonable to rely on authority in so many areas of human inquiry and yet deny the overwhelming testimony of religious authorities concerning the existence of God. If we are to have faith in human authorities, which we obviously must, we cannot arbitrarily refuse to have faith in the testimony of religious authorities as well.

This appeal to authority as a source of religious knowledge is beset by serious problems. To begin with, we must recognize that authority is never a primary source of knowledge. A proposition is not worthy of belief merely because a supposed authority testifies in its behalf. The authority himself must be able to rationally defend his position through proof and argumentation; indeed, it is his ability to do so that qualifies him as an authority in the first place.

173

REASON, FAITH, AND REVELATION

Suppose that one were to maintain that authority is the final court of appeal (in some instances at least). What would be the consequences? In *The Nature of Thought*, Brand Blanshard writes:

> . . . if one person is justified in appealing to authority without reasons, then others are similarly justified. They would even be justified in accepting authorities that said precisely the opposite of what is said by one's own authority. But it is obvious that in this event one or other authority is wrong, and therefore that whatever justified appealing to it must similarly be wrong. In the light of its consequences, the unreasoning appeal to authority is thus self-destructive.[7]

The appeal to authority is not a special method of acquiring knowledge; it is just one of the many ways which reason employs to gather evidence in the search for truth. We accept the testimony of authorities in some cases, but never uncritically. The appeal to authority is simply an epistemological short cut that must always occur within rational guidelines.

What are these guidelines? First, the authority must be willing to present evidence in support of his beliefs. Second, the proposition of the authority must be verifiable in principle by any person who cares to take the time and effort required. Third, the propositions of the authority can never contradict the laws of logic. A contradiction can never be true, regardless of the academic qualifications of the person advocating it.

Once we see that the appeal to authority, rather than being an alternative to reason, must always be subsumed under the principles of reason, we can readily judge the religious appeal to authority to be an evasion.

Suppose that the theist calls upon his authority to testify for the existence of god. This person claims to be an expert in theological issues, having devoted his entire life to such studies, and he personally assures us of the existence of a god. We then ask this "expert" the same questions that we asked the novice

174

before him—namely, "What do you mean by the term 'god'?" and, "What evidence do you have for the existence of such a being?" Either this religious authority can answer these questions satisfactorily or he cannot. If he can, the issue is decided in his favor solely within the sphere of rational argumentation, and his alleged expertise is irrelevant to the validity of his arguments. If he cannot, he should not be believed under any circumstances, his alleged expertise notwithstanding. Thus, to argue that we must have faith in a religious authority is to evade the central issue: *i.e.*, Can the theist produce rational grounds in support of his belief? An appeal to authority does not answer this question.

There is a further problem with the notion of a "religious authority." This designation is ambiguous. As an illustration, consider what it would mean to speak of an astrology expert. To say that Mr. Jones is an authority on astrology would mean that Mr. Jones has a thorough knowledge of the *doctrines* of astrology, but this does not necessarily imply that Mr. Jones personally believes in the truth of astrology. In fact, we shall assume that Mr. Jones considers astrology to be false.

Now we encounter another astrology expert, Mr. White, who in addition to possessing comprehensive knowledge of astrology, also believes these doctrines to be true. Here we have two legitimate authorities, Mr. Jones and Mr. White, who disagree concerning the truth of astrological doctrines, but both qualify as experts nonetheless. Clearly, therefore, the truth or falsity of astrology cannot be determined by an appeal to either of these authorities (since they contradict each other), so we must listen to the *arguments* of each authority and then judge on the basis of available evidence.

Suppose, however, that I persist in defending the truth of astrology through an appeal to authority. "After all," I argue, "Mr. White has studied astrology intensively for many years, and he believes in the truth of its doctrines. What right have we as mere laymen to question the soundness of his judgment?"

Now suppose that someone points out to me that Mr. Jones, whose knowledge of astrology is comparable to that of Mr.

White, does not personally believe in astrological doctrines. On the contrary, he considers them to be false. In response to this I reply that Mr. White is the only qualified authority, and only his testimony should be seriously considered. It is obvious that I am using the notion of "authority" in a peculiar way here. The only substantial difference between Mr. White and Mr. Jones is that the former believes in astrology while the latter does not. If I disqualify Mr. Jones as an authority on this basis, I would justly be accused of circular reasoning. I wish to appeal to an authority in support of my belief, yet I am unwilling to accept anyone as an authority unless he agrees with me in the first place. Is it any wonder, then, that all astrological "authorities" will somehow defend my position?

Now transpose these authorities to the realm of religion. Mr. Jones and Mr. White have similar educational backgrounds; each is thoroughly schooled in the doctrines of various religions. Mr. Jones is an atheist, while Mr. White believes in god, but both qualify as religious authorities due to their comprehensive knowledge of religious doctrines. If we apply the concept of "authority" with its usual meaning, there is no necessary connection between being a "religious expert" and believing in a god.

If the theist may appeal to his religious authority (Mr. White), the atheist may appeal to his own religious authority (Mr. Jones). If the theist may argue that his authority must be accepted on faith, the atheist may argue that his authority must also be accepted on faith. We then have an inevitable clash of authorities, which makes us realize that the original appeal to authority was an epistemological dead end.

Why is it that many theists do not recognize the inevitable conflict to which their appeal to authority will lead? Simply because they refuse to accept anyone as a "religious authority" unless he first believes in god. The theist will call on Mr. White for testimony, but he will ignore Mr. Jones. Mr. White will qualify as a "religious authority," but Mr. Jones will not—and the only difference separating them is the belief in the truth of theism.

Why is it that all religious authorities unanimously agree on

176

the existence of a supernatural being? Simply because the Christian considers the belief in a god to be a *defining characteristic* of a "religious authority." The Christian surveys ancient and contemporary history for religious scholars who believed in theism, and these comprise his cadre of religious authorities. The Christian thus manufactures his experts to meet desired specifications, and atheists will never be able to make the grade. The religious authorities will always testify in support of theism because they were selected as experts with this condition in mind. The Christian falls into the same pattern of circular reasoning as the previous defender of astrology.

The Christian faces the following dilemma: If he wishes to appeal to religious authorities in support of theism—and if the notion of "authority" is used in its customary way to designate anyone with specialized knowledge of religious doctrines—then the appeal to authority will automatically fail due to the contradictory testimony of various authorities, some of whom will be atheists and disbelievers. In this case, the Christian will have to resort to rational arguments independent of authority, which is what he should have done in the first place. On the other hand, if the Christian appeals to religious authorities while stipulating that the belief in theism is a necessary condition of authority, he will be guilty of arbitrarily defining his authorities into existence, which renders his appeal to authority useless. Once again, he will be forced to relinquish the appeal to authority and return to rational arguments.

We have seen that the Christian cannot escape the onus of proof through an appeal to authority, but what of the claim that our everyday trust in authority is based on an act of "faith"? Is this true?

It is obvious that the term "faith" is used in a variety of ways. Many persons (including atheists) speak of "faith" in their friends, doctors, and so on. But this tells us nothing, except that a word may have a number of different applications. We are concerned strictly with the concept of "faith" in a philosophical sense, *i.e.*, as an alleged *alternative* to reason. Can the idea of faith as authoritative trust qualify in this respect?

Recall the context in which the idea of faith was introduced

177

in Chapter 4. After concluding that the concept of God cannot withstand rational examination, we set out to consider the possibility of a sphere of knowledge that is inaccessible to reason, a sphere open only to faith. We then reached, in Chapter 4, the central dilemma of faith: "Insofar as faith is possible, it is irrational; insofar as faith is rational, it is impossible."

By representing faith as trust in authority, the Christian seeks to escape this dilemma. Trust in authority, he tells us, is an act of faith, but it is not irrational. What does this entail? First, the Christian must maintain that trust in authority is *not* an act of reason, because if it is, why bring in the notion of faith at all? We are thus presented with the following dichotomy: propositions of reason are those that are personally verified, and propositions of faith are those that are accepted on the authority of another.

This dichotomy between reason and faith rests on the "tool-box" theory of reason, which was refuted previously (Chapter 3, Part IV, Sec. a). Reason and faith are represented as different "tools" to be applied in different circumstances. Where reason is inadequate, faith comes to the rescue. Reason, argues the Christian, pertains to beliefs that are personally verified ("seen" to be true) by the individual concerned, such as firsthand observation of a scientific experiment. Faith is applicable when we must accept the word of another person, such as when we believe the testimony of a scientist without having personally witnessed his experiments.

This conception of "reason" is severely restricted and distorted. It is true that propositions of reason should be "personally verified," but this simply means that each individual should consider all available evidence for himself before reaching a decision. A person should critically evaluate his beliefs; this is personal verification.

This is not what the advocate of faith means by "personal verification." The Christian wishes to use this phrase to differentiate knowledge that is directly acquired through perceptual observation from knowledge that is gained inferentially through the testimony of other people. But to isolate knowledge that is

178

acquired through others as the sphere of "faith" is totally unjustified. We acquire knowledge in a variety of different ways, but all knowledge must eventually meet the requirements of reason. All appeals to authority must be subsumed within the guidelines of reason. The appeal to authority is not a different means of acquiring knowledge; it is one aspect of rational inquiry, not an ultimate ground of truth.

A rational appeal to authority is fundamentally nonauthoritarian. For example, if we accept the testimony of physicists concerning the truth of scientific theories, we do so not because of their authority (*i.e.*, not because they say so), but because we believe that they are able to provide strong evidence in support of their positions. Again quoting Blanshard:

> If we ask why they [the physicists] do accept certain results, the answer is very simple; given the conditions, they have seen these results to be necessary; and they are ready to supply the data and the reasoning to anyone who can follow. In short, they do not take these things to be true because they are authorities; they are authorities because they can see these things to be true. . . . The court to which in the end we shall take our appeal is not authority, but those reasons through seeing which an authority becomes an authority, namely, those that condition or determine the truth itself. . . . If this higher warrant is there, authority is superseded; if it is not there, authority fails. In neither case is authority itself the final court of appeal.[8]

The subservience of authority to reason is evident when we consider the many conflicting authorities from which we must choose. Even as laymen, we must judge between doctors and quacks, competent and incompetent lawyers, scientists who are consistent and scientists who contradict themselves. As Richard Robinson puts it:

179

Complete submission to an authority, far from being commendable, is a grave irresponsibility. We are responsible for all our opinions, however ignorant we may be in the field, because we are responsible for our choice of any authorities on whom we rely. All submission to an authority should be based on, and revocable by, our own judgement whether he is an authority; and this judgement should be revised from time to time in the light of the best considerations then available.[9]

The Christian is left with two alternatives. He can cling to the artificial dichotomy between reason and authority, while claiming that the latter is the province of faith. While this carves a sphere of influence for faith, it divorces authority from reason, which invites everyone to play it deuces wild through indiscriminate and conflicting appeals to authority. On the other hand, the Christian can concede that authority must always bow to reason, but this entails that faith (or trust in authority) must also be subservient to reason. In this event, faith is reduced to a subcategory of reason, in which case it cannot claim a separate sphere of its own. This renders the concept of faith epistemologically useless, since the Christian can no longer appeal to knowledge which is supposedly beyond the limits of reason.

We thus confront the dilemma of faith. In order to claim the sphere of authority for faith, the Christian must deny it to reason—but then the appeal to authority becomes irrational. In order to retain the rationality of authority, the Christian must place it within the bounds of reason—but then it becomes impossible to claim that faith provides us with a special kind of knowledge. The first alternative gives us irrational faith; the second alternative gives us "rational faith" with no purpose. We must reject the first because it is unreasonable. We must reject the second because the term "faith" is superfluous. There are rational and irrational appeals to authority, and this is the only

THE VARIETIES OF FAITH

distinction that needs to be made. The consideration given to an authoritative statement depends, not on *who* says it, but on *why* he says it.

III

Voluntarist Theories of Faith

Voluntarist theories of faith are those that regard faith as an act of will. Traces of this approach are found in medieval writers such as Irenaeus, Augustine, and Aquinas. Faith, according to Aquinas, "is an act of the intellect assenting to the Divine truth at the command of the will moved by the grace of God. . . ."[10] Retaining this element of voluntary consent permitted Aquinas to argue that acceptance on faith is a "meritorious act."

Later Christian writers have placed a much heavier emphasis on the voluntaristic aspect of faith:

> The distinctive feature of faith, in contrast with mere belief, is the element in it of will and action. . . . Faith is not merely the assent that something is true, it is our readiness to act on what we believe true.[11]

Many Christians now view faith as a subjective, emotional commitment to the truth of Christianity. Insofar as any voluntarist theory of faith concedes its own irrationality, it is not worthy of discussion. Commitments, even highly emotional ones, should not be arbitrary or irrational. On the contrary, it is precisely in crucial times of decision that we must rely on reason the most. Granted, we must sometimes act without complete certainty, and we may sometimes make the wrong decisions, but this does not alter the vital life-and-death distinction between rational and irrational commitment. Commitment, far from being irrational or "subjective," should always be based on the best available knowledge. Blind, unthinking commitment is unadulterated fanaticism, and the fanatics of this world have left millions of dead in their wake.

Some voluntarist theories do not explicitly advocate irrationality. They maintain that reason can only go so far, at which time we must make a commitment on faith, a decision that falls beyond the scope of reason. As one theologian puts it, a man "must pursue the way of argument as far as it can take him, and then make a leap of faith in the direction of the evidence, acting *as though* it were sound."[12]

Two thinkers are representative of this second voluntarist approach: Blaise Pascal, the French philosopher, mathematician, and scientist of the seventeenth century; and William James, the celebrated psychologist and philosopher. We shall briefly examine each of their views.

Pascal, in his famous "wager," argued as follows:

> ... "God is, or He is not." But to which side shall we incline? Reason can decide nothing here.... According to reason, you can do neither the one thing nor the other; according to reason, you can defend neither of the propositions.
>
> ... but you must wager. It is not optional. You are embarked. Which will you choose then? Let us see. Since you must choose, let us see which interests you least. You have two things to lose, the true and the good; and two things to stake, your reason and your will, your knowledge and your happiness; and your nature has two things to shun, error and misery. Your reason is no more shocked in choosing one rather than the other, since you must of necessity choose. This is one point settled. But your happiness? Let us weigh the gain and the loss in wagering that God is. Let us estimate these two chances. If you gain, you gain all; if you lose, you lose nothing. Wager, then, without hesitation that He is.[13]

There are many things that can be said about Pascal's wager, all of them bad, but we shall confine ourselves to a few brief remarks.

First, Pascal's claim that reason can defend neither theism or atheism is plainly false. The onus of proof, as we have seen, is solely on the theist. If he fails to make his case, reason resides with atheism. Pascal was correct in his assertion that the existence of God cannot be rationally demonstrated, but he was mistaken in his belief that the existence of God is therefore an open question. In fact, Pascal was himself a rigorous agnostic theist who held that God is "infinitely incomprehensible." "We are then incapable," Pascal asserts, "of knowing either what He is or if He is." This confession is an overt surrender to the rationality of atheism.

Second, Pascal's wager is not an argument in any intellectual sense; rather, it is an attempt at psychological intimidation. He is arguing, in effect, that we ought to believe in God because we may be rewarded for it—which implies, of course, that if we fail to believe in God, we will suffer the consequences. The threat of eternal torment for disbelievers is not specifically stated in Pascal's argument, but it is clearly implied.

Third, Pascal constructs a fallacious—and hideous— dichotomy between knowledge and happiness. We must wager one or the other, he argues, so which will we choose? Such a choice may exist in the mind of the Christian, but reality decrees no such thing. Quite the contrary, it is only through the *integration* of knowledge and decision that happiness can be achieved.

Fourth, Pascal's comment to the effect that one has nothing to lose through a commitment to theism, even if it remains undemonstrated, is absolutely incredible. But Pascal demands even more, for he is not just speaking of theistic belief in general; he is referring to the doctrines of Catholicism. One should become a Catholic, he states, on the possibility that Catholicism is correct, in which case one will have gained eternal happiness and avoided eternal torment. In reply to the objection that it is difficult to make oneself believe in the absence of sufficient reasons, Pascal recommends that one begin in the same way that most people come to accept Christianity: through blind obedience and ritual:

> Follow the way by which they began; by acting as if they believed, taking the holy water, having masses said, etc. Even this will naturally make you believe, and deaden your acuteness. . . . What have you got to lose?[14]

What have we got to lose? Intellectual integrity, self-esteem, and a passionate, rewarding life for starters. In short, everything that makes life worth living. Far from being a safe bet, Pascal's wager requires the wager of one's life and happiness.

Finally, Pascal is guilty of inconsistency. He positively states that reason cannot prove the truth of Christian theism, and he mistakenly regards Catholicism and total disbelief as the only two alternatives. Such is not the case. What of other non-Christian religions that prescribe punishment for Christians? If reason cannot decide, how are we to choose between alternative religions? Indeed, it is possible to have an unlimited number of religious doctrines, each of which prescribes eternal torment for all other beliefs. We would then have a complex crossfire of damnation threats, with no means of choosing among them. Once Pascal disallows an appeal to reason, he commits himself to a hopeless situation, for he denies himself the possibility of condemning *any* religious commitment as false or unreasonable, even if that belief is virulently anti-Christian.

Antony Flew has appropriately tagged Pascal's infamous wager as an appeal "to prudence in the rat-race for salvation." [15] It is also a terrible argument, if it can be called an "argument" at all. Few Christians use it today except as a last resort, where it tends to be embarrassing. The voluntarist theory of faith underlying Pascal's wager (or any similar approach) must be discarded as irrational.

In his famous essay, "The Will to Believe," William James presents a voluntaristic theory of faith that is modeled after Pascal's wager in some respects, although it is more thoroughly argued. Also, unlike Pascal, James appeals to happiness in this life rather than in an afterlife as the primary motive of belief.

"The Will to Believe," states the author, is "an essay in justification *of* faith, a defence of our right to adopt a believing attitude in religious matters, in spite of the fact that our merely logical intellect may not have been coerced."[16] In other words, James contends that some propositions are worthy of belief even though the evidence in their favor is insufficient to compel our rational assent. These propositions must be accepted through "voluntarily adopted faith."

"Faith," writes James in another essay, "is synonymous with working hypothesis," where the believer's "intimate persuasion is that the odds in its favour are strong enough to warrant him in acting all along on the assumption of its truth."[17] When should we employ faith? When we are confronted with a "genuine option" that cannot be decided through reason.

In order for an option (*i.e.*, a choice between two propositions) to be "genuine," it must fulfill three criteria. First, the option must be "living"; *i.e.*, it must present two real possibilities to the individual concerned. Second, the option must be "forced"; *i.e.*, there cannot be a middle ground of indecision between the two propositions. Finally, the option must be "momentous"; *i.e.*, it must represent an important decision.

James goes on to argue that many genuine options cannot be resolved through rational deliberation, but we must make a decision nonetheless. In these instances, *"Our passional nature not only lawfully may, but must, decide an option between propositions... for to say, under such circumstances, 'Do not decide, but leave the question open,' is itself a passional decision—just like deciding yes or no—and is attended with the same risk of losing the truth."*[18] According to James, the "religious hypothesis" is one such option.

The choice between religion and disbelief, argues James,

185

fulfills the preceding three criteria: it is "living," "forced," and "momentous." This option presents two important alternatives from which we *must* select a course of action. To remain indecisive is equivalent to rejecting the religious hypothesis, because "although we do avoid error in that way *if religion be untrue*, we lose the good, *if it be true*, just as certainly as if we positively chose to disbelieve."[19]

James is arguing that reason cannot settle the issue of religious truth, but we are forced to act either in accord *or* against religion whether we like it or not. Therefore, a person is justified in following his emotions and accepting religion on faith, because "we have the right to believe at our own risk any hypothesis that is live enough to tempt our will."[20] James agrees with Pascal that religion offers great personal rewards. If it turns out to be true, our gain is tremendous; if it turns out to be false, our loss is trivial. Given these odds, how can we stubbornly refuse the voluntary assent of faith?

James's argument for faith suffers from the same basic flaws as Pascal's wager. Like Pascal, James contends that reason is unable to reach a conclusion in the sphere of religion—which opens the door for faith. James calls on skepticism to pave the way for faith, and much of his essay is devoted to an attack on the efficacy of reason. "Objective evidence and certitude are doubtless very fine ideals to play with," he writes, "but where on this moonlit and dream-visited planet are they found?"[21] Most of our important beliefs depend on faith. "Our belief in truth itself, for instance, that there is a truth, and that our minds and it are made for each other—what is it but a passionate affirmation of desire, in which our social system backs us up?" We believe that we possess truth, but if a skeptic asks us *how* we know this, can logic find a reply? "No! certainly [?] it cannot. It is just one volition against another—we willing to go in for life upon a trust or assumption which he, for his part, does not care to make."[22]

James concludes, in effect, that every person pretty well believes what he wants to believe anyway, so there is no reason to condemn beliefs based on subjective emotions. Knowledge ultimately narrows down to arbitrary, subjective commitment; James's voluntarist approach is made possible by this underlying skepticism. Without it, faith is denied a sphere of influence, and "The Will to Believe" collapses into dust.

Moreover, "faith" as conceived by James is devoid of cognitive worth. It does not enable us to determine the truth or falsity of propositions and thus cannot qualify as a means of acquiring knowledge. As John Hick observes, it merely "authorizes us to believe ('by faith') any proposition, not demonstrably false, which it might be advantageous to us, in this world or another, to have accepted."[23] "The Will to Believe" is nothing but a license for wishful thinking.

James attempts a counter-argument against this objection. *"There are ... cases,"* he maintains, *"where faith creates its own verification."* Faith is "essential and indispensable" to this class of truths. "The truths cannot become true till our faith has made them so."[24]

What are these truths? Basically, they are cases where one's subjective commitment is a determining factor in bringing about the truth that one desires. Consider a man who is about to jump over a wide chasm. If he refuses to believe that he can leap the chasm because he does not have sufficient evidence for this belief, this lack of confidence may very well contribute to his failure. If, on the other hand, his desire to leap the chasm motivates him to believe that he can actually leap it, this confidence may very well contribute to his success. This man's faith in the absence of evidence, argues James, brings about the desired truth. Faith has created fact.

This argument is easily demolished. James blurs the distinction between believing something to be true and acting with conviction. A man's desire to accomplish a goal will frequently contribute to his success, but desire is *not* the same as knowledge. Furthermore, the above illustration has no relevance whatsoever to the issue of religious belief. A strong emotional commitment may help achieve a desired goal in the future, but it cannot alter present facts. A god will not spring into existence if only one believes strongly enough. A desire for an afterlife, however intense, cannot create a heavenly paradise. Facts are facts, independently of one's desires, fears and hopes. "The Will to Believe" notwithstanding, wishing will not make it so.

Implicit throughout the voluntarist approach to faith is the assumption that because we must sometimes act without complete certainty, we must therefore appeal to our emotions and act on faith. But the choice between certainty and emotionalism is a false alternative. Certainty does not entail infallibility, and we cannot expect absolute guarantees of success in our endeavors. We often act on partial knowledge, and we sometimes take considerable risks. It is precisely this chance of failure that necessitates our alliance with reason. Reason tells us when we may fail, when we have a reasonable chance for success, and when we will most certainly succeed (within one's context of knowledge). To abandon reason in favor of emotion is to surrender responsible decision making to whim. *If anything will guarantee failure and unhappiness, it is the delusion that one's feelings can abrogate the function of reason.* In the words of George Santayana:

> To be boosted by an illusion is not to live better than to live in harmony with the truth; it is not nearly so safe, not nearly so sweet, and not nearly so fruitful. These refusals to part with a decayed illusion are really an infection to the mind. Believe, certainly; we cannot help believing; but believe rationally, holding what seems certain for certain, what seems probable for probable, what seems desirable for desirable, and what seems false for false.[25]

James derides the efficacy of reason and then exhorts us to accept desire as a guide to knowledge. We are once again asked to abandon reason as a means to happiness. Anyone who advocates such a dichotomy does face a serious problem, but the problem lies within himself—and the problem is psychological, not philosophical.

In summary, James assumes that the concept of god is a reasonable hypothesis to begin with, that reason cannot decide the issue of religious belief, that one's emotions can justify belief in the absence of evidence, and that theistic belief provides a greater degree of happiness than disbelief. All of these assumptions are false. "The Will to Believe," as Walter Kaufmann aptly puts it, "is an unwitting compendium of common fallacies and a manual of self-deception."26

IV

The End of Faith

The preceding theories of faith were selected with specific features in mind. The Bible is the core of Christianity, and its overwhelming irrationalism is significant as a pace-setter. The Bible, especially the New Testament, vividly illustrates the theme of the previous chapter: that reason must be attacked to create a sphere of influence for faith. Although the New Testament is technically unpolished, its philosophical message is crystal clear: reason and criticism must succumb to faith, blind obedience and threats of violence. In its own modest way, the Bible is a remarkable compilation of vulgar skepticism. Can we understand its enormous appeal within the context of men living hundreds of years ago? Perhaps. Can we understand why contemporary, intelligent scholars persist in treating the Bible as something more than a mildly interesting collection of documents written over a span of centuries? Or can we understand why enlightened theologians parade as devout Christians and yet ignore the blatant intellectual oppressiveness and viciousness of the Bible? I, for one, cannot.

Our second variety of faith—faith as authoritative trust—has a distinguished historical background and may be termed the classical view of faith. We discussed two variations of this approach: faith *in* God, and faith *that* God exists. The first conception, aside from being superfluous, is totally irrelevant to

189

the choice between theism and atheism. The latter approach rests on the mistaken notion that authority somehow constitutes an independent court of appeal apart from reason. The skepticism here is subtle. It consists of arbitrarily limiting "reason" within a narrow framework and then awarding the remaining large sphere of knowledge to "faith." This permits the Christian to posture as a friend of reason, while maintaining that reason and faith are different, though reconcilable, methods of attaining knowledge. In a sense, this kind of skepticism is more reprehensible than an overt hostility to reason, because it is dishonest. The Christian cripples reason and then presents himself as a friend of this mutation that he has created.

Finally, we discussed two voluntarist approaches to faith. These theories are important because they represent a critical transition from a *cognitive* view of faith to an *emotive* view. There is no attempt to represent faith as a method of cognition; faith is frankly conceded to be an emotional commitment, an act of will, without rational justification. More than any other approach, the voluntarist theory of faith strives to give philosophical respectability to the practice of believing something simply because one "feels like it." Here the skepticism is overt. We are constantly reminded that reason is impotent in the crucial areas of man's life, and that we must frequently act on our feelings in the absence of rational demonstration. A sphere of influence is created for voluntarist faith through an open declaration of war on reason. The voluntarist wishes faith to rule, not through negotiation, but through brutal conquest.

Although there are other important and sophisticated theories of faith, to examine them would degenerate into a tiresome routine. The general objections to faith established in the previous two chapters, combined with the specific applications in this chapter, should provide the reader with sufficient information to project the criticisms that would be made against other theories.

Where does this leave the term "faith"? Must every rational man banish it from his vocabulary? No, not necessarily. We mentioned previously that "faith" has a number of different, if

190

somewhat vague, applications. There is nothing objectionable to speaking of "faith" in one's friends, and so on. What *is* objectionable, however, is to elevate this nebulous concept to an *epistemological status*. In a strictly philosophical context, there is no room for faith; reason, a previous tenant, has hung out the "no vacancy" sign.

Thus, after a journey spanning three chapters, we must abandon faith and return to the realm of reason. We must exclude any diversion to faith as an alleged substitute for reason and consider Christian theism solely on its rational merits. This is not arbitrary or subjective; it is simply a matter of necessity. If we wish to acquire knowledge, we must respect the method by which man acquires knowledge. If we are to know anything, we must establish cognitive guidelines. The Christian may experience this strict adherence to reason as restrictive, but it is not the atheist who decrees these restrictions—it is reality.

7.
Revelation

Revelation is a disclosure, a direct communication, from a god to a man. Since Christian theology relies heavily on revelation, and since most theologians claim that revelation must be accepted on faith, it is appropriate to discuss this subject in conjunction with faith.

We must keep in mind that revelation, since it entails a communication from God to man, presupposes the existence of God—so one must first accept the existence of the Christian God before one can believe in Christian revelation. Our problem is complicated by the failure of Christian theology to provide us with a coherent meaning for the term "God." We know roughly that the Christian God is supposed to be a kind of supernatural being—since this is entailed by the definition of "god"—but we do not have an intelligible, noncontradictory description of this mysterious being.

Therefore, because we cannot understand the meaning of "God," the alleged source of Christian revelation, we cannot make sense out of the Christian's claim to have received a communication from this being. He might just as well claim to have received a revelation from an "unie."

We thus see at the outset that no appeal to revelation can rescue the Christian God. But various kinds of revelation occupy an important place in Christianity, so, if only for the purpose of comprehensiveness, we shall discuss two of the most popular varieties: the Bible and miracles.

The purpose of this chapter is twofold: first, to present some relevant (and hopefully interesting) background material concerning the validity of Christian revelation; and, second, to demonstrate that no appeal to revelation can establish the truth of supernaturalism in any form.

I

The Bible

The primary source of Christian revelation is the Bible, a compilation of material claimed by its defenders to have been inspired by God. Through selected authors, God chose to reveal himself to man—and the result, the Bible, constitutes the foundation of the Christian religion.

Christians disagree radically among themselves concerning the veracity of the biblical record. On one extreme we have fundamentalists who uphold the Bible as literally infallible, and on the other extreme we have liberals who—to put it more bluntly than they would care to—take the alleged factual accuracy of the Bible with a grain of salt. The fundamentalist position is described by Professor W. F. Tillett as follows:

Those who hold the view commonly designated as plenary and verbal inspiration claim that the biblical writers were divinely secured against any and all mistakes by virtue of their divine inspiration, and affirm, further, that that which constitutes the Bible a divine book is the fact that the Holy Spirit so dominated

194

and guided the minds and pens of those who wrote as to make their writings free from mistakes of any and all kinds, whether it be mistakes of history or chronology or botany or biology or astronomy, or mistakes as to moral and spiritual truth pertaining to God and man, in time or eternity. According to this view of biblical inspiration, whatever the Bible says must be true because it is God's own Word; what it says is what God says.[1]

This traditional view of the Bible has posed more of a problem for Protestants than for Catholics. It has been said that when Protestantism abandoned the authority of the Church and left the Bible to individual interpretation, it effectively surrendered the inerrancy of the Bible. Considering the many sectarian disputes within the ranks of Protestantism, this statement is well founded. The Catholic Church, on the other hand, recognizing the possibility of contradictory interpretations of the Bible, maintains that "the Roman Pontiff, when he speaks *ex cathedra* . . . is possessed of that infallibility with which the divine Redeemer willed that His Church should be endowed for defining doctrine regarding faith or morals."[2] Using the Church as a final arbiter in the case of doctrinal disputes has enabled Catholicism to escape many of the theological battles so common among Protestant theologians.

Every Christian believes that the Bible is "inspired" in some way, but there is widespread and bitter disagreement over what it means to be inspired. Fundamentalists, as we have seen, argue that the Bible is factually correct in every respect. To admit error in any instance, they maintain, is to surrender the principle of divine inspiration. If the Bible is conceded to be mistaken or based on superstition in some instances, what is to prevent us from rejecting all of the supernatural accounts in the Bible—including the life and Resurrection of Jesus—as myths?

Liberals disagree. They point out that the Bible, a collection of books written over a span of approximately one thousand years, was written by fallible men who were not exempt from the prejudices and superstitions of their day. God revealed himself to man, not through written propositions, but through historical incidents such as the life of Christ. The Bible derives its inspiration, not from the men who recorded these events, but from the divine nature of the events themselves. The Bible does not reveal propositions about God; it reveals God himself through his actions. Thus, concludes the liberal, it is not necessary to believe that the Bible is accurate in every detail; it is only necessary to believe that the biblical writers were witnessing acts of God within their historic framework. And although they may have misinterpreted or exaggerated these events at times, we are able, through interpretation guided by faith, to reach the true meaning of these inspired events. Rather than accept the Bible uncritically as the fundamentalist would have us do, we must subject the Bible to textual and historic criticism in order to gain a true perspective of the biblical message.[3]

The meaning of inspiration is a controversy which we can safely leave for Christians to decide. The attitude of the atheist towards the alleged inspiration of the Bible was summed up nicely by Robert G. Ingersoll, the famous nineteenth-century "infidel":

> Now they say that this book is inspired. I do not care whether it is or not; the question is, Is it true? If it is true, it doesn't need to be inspired. Nothing needs inspiration except a falsehood or a mistake.[4]

Whatever else may be said about the fundamentalist, he at least comes to grips with the problem of atheism, for from an atheistic viewpoint, the accuracy of the Bible is the only relevant consideration. If the Bible is true, so is Christianity. If the Bible cannot withstand critical examination, neither can Christianity.

In judging the veracity of the Bible, we immediately confront the fact that it abounds with incredible stories and primitive superstitions. These elements alone disqualify it as worthy of belief. While the Bible may have *some* historic and literary

196

value, it simply cannot be accepted at face value. In public libraries, one will appropriately find it shelved next to the mythology section.

While disclaimers of the Bible are common fare today, they would have led to execution in some countries a few centuries ago—so it is understandable why detailed critiques of the Bible are a fairly recent phenomenon. But the roots of biblical criticism extend centuries into the past. As early as the sixteenth century, scholars noted discrepancies among various translations of biblical manuscripts which, along with some textual irregularities, raised doubts concerning the validity of traditionally assigned dates and authors.[5]

The seventeenth-century philosopher Thomas Hobbes is usually given credit for launching a rationalistic approach to the Bible. In his *Leviathan*, he denied the traditional belief that Moses wrote the first five books of the Old Testament (the Pentateuch), using as evidence passages that could not have been written until after the death of Moses. Hobbes also suggested that we must follow the dictates of reason in determining what qualifies as genuine revelation:

When God speaketh to man, it must be either immediately; or by meditation of another man, to whom he had formerly spoken by himself immediately. How God speaketh to a man immediately, may be understood by those well enough, to whom he hath so spoken; but how the same should be understood by another, is hard, if not impossible to know. For if a man pretend to me, that God hath spoken to him supernaturally and immediately, and I make doubt of it, I cannot easily perceive what argument he can produce, to oblige me to believe it. . . . For to say that God hath spoken to him in the Holy Scripture, is not to say that God hath spoken to him immediately, but by mediation of the prophets, or of the apostles, or of the church. . . . To say he hath spoken to him in a dream, is no more than to say he dreamed that God

197

spake to him; which is not of force to win belief from any man. . . . So that though God Almighty can speak to a man by dreams, visions, voice, and inspiration; yet he obliges no man to believe he hath so done to him that pretends it; who, being a man, may err, and, which is more, may lie.[6]

Hobbes was as close to an infidel as one could be in his time and remain alive. Though he professed theism, notes J. M. Robertson, "nothing is more certain than that he was no orthodox Christian; and even his professed theism resolves itself somewhat easily into virtual agnosticism on logical pressure."[7] While Hobbes did not reject Christianity outright, his treatment of religion stirred controversy. His terse distinction between religion and superstition reflects the attitude, not of a devoted believer, but of philosopher cynical of religious claims: "*Fear* of power invisible, feigned by the mind, or imagined from tales publicly allowed, RELIGION; not allowed, SUPERSTITION."[8]

Through his rejection of traditional Christian doctrines, such as the efficacy of prayer and the existence of hell, Hobbes gained the reputation of a religious skeptic. The English Parliament condemned the *Leviathan* in 1666, and Hobbes was ordered to cease writing further books on controversial topics.

The next milestone in biblical criticism was Baruch Spinoza's *Theologico-Political Treatise,* published anonymously in 1670. Spinoza outlined the purpose of this treatise:

> As I pondered over the facts that the light of reason is not only despised, but by many even execrated as a source of impiety, that human commentaries are accepted as divine records, and that credulity is extolled as faith . . . I determined to examine the Bible afresh in a careful, impartial, and unfettered spirit, making no assumptions concerning it, and attributing to it no doctrines, which I do not find clearly therein set down. With these precautions I constructed a method of Scriptural interpretation. . . .[9]

Spinoza was proposing a radical procedure for his time: that the Bible, like any other book, be examined objectively for evidences of dates, authorships, and reliability. Though he concluded that he "found nothing taught expressly by Scripture, which does not agree with our understanding, or which is repugnant thereto," Spinoza's interpretation of the Bible scarcely won him friends in the Christian community. Subjecting the Bible to a much closer scrutiny than Hobbes had done, Spinoza reached a number of unacceptable conclusions:

> Of the authors . . . of many of the books, we are either in complete ignorance, or at any rate in doubt. . . . Further, we do not know either the occasions or the epochs when these books of unknown authorship were written; we cannot say into what hands they fell, nor how the numerous varying versions originated; nor, lastly, whether there were not other versions, now lost. [10]

Spinoza also pointed to various mistakes, contradictions and impossibilities in the Bible—in short, he rejected its infallibility. Concerning the miracles recorded in the Bible, Spinoza wrote:

> We may, then, be absolutely certain that every event which is truly described in Scripture necessarily happened, like everything else, according to natural laws; and if anything is there set down which can be proved in set terms to contravene the order of nature, or not to be deducible therefrom, we must believe it to have been foisted into the sacred writings by irreligious hands; for whatsoever is contrary to nature is also contrary to reason, and whatsoever is contrary to reason is absurd, and, *ipso facto*, to be rejected. [11]

The *Treatise* was the most effective attack on Christian supernaturalism yet published. It was promptly condemned by a Dutch clerical synod and placed on the forbidden Index of the

Catholic Church. Wishing to avoid as much controversy as possible, Spinoza wrote the *Treatise* in Latin, so that it would be accessible to scholars but not to laymen. He vetoed a plan to have it translated into the vernacular Dutch, where it would enjoy wide readership. In the preface, Spinoza explains that his work was intended for philosophers. "To the rest of mankind," he writes, "I care not to commend my treatise, for I cannot expect that it contains anything to please them: I know how deeply rooted are the prejudices embraced under the name of religion. . . . Therefore the multitude . . . I ask not to read my book; nay, I would rather that they should utterly neglect it, than that they should misinterpret it after their wont."[12]

Biblical research continued after Spinoza, but the constant threat of persecution in many countries guaranteed that this information would not be used as a weapon against Christianity. America was one of the first countries where freedom of speech was relatively secure, and Thomas Paine, the inspirational spark behind the American Revolution, published an overt attack on Christianity in the late eighteenth century. Now considered a classic of free-thought literature, the *Age of Reason* still stands as one of the most trenchant critiques of the Bible and Christianity ever published.

Like many of his colleagues, Paine believed in the impersonal god of deism, a god who created the universe and then left it to its own devices. Paine was suspicious of organized religion in any form: "All national institutions of churches, whether Jewish, Christian or Turkish, appear to me no other than human inventions, set up to terrify and enslave mankind, and monopolize power and profit."[13]

Paine was extremely hostile to revealed religion, especially that of Christianity:

> The most destestable wickedness, the most horrid cruelties, and the greatest miseries that have afflicted the human race have had their origin in this thing called revelation, or revealed religion. It has been the

most dishonorable belief against the character of the Divinity, the most destructive to morality and the peace and happiness of man, that ever was propagated since man began to exist. It is better, far better, that we admitted, if it were possible, a thousand devils to roam at large, and to preach publicly the doctrine of devils, if there were any such, than that we permitted one such impostor and monster as Moses, Joshua, Samuel, and the Bible prophets, to come with the pretended word of God in his mouth, and have credit among us. . . .[14]

Of all the systems of religion that ever were invented, there is none more derogatory to the Almighty, more unedifying to man, more repugnant to reason, and more contradictory in itself, than this thing called Christianity.[15]

Because Paine believed in a benevolent deity, he appealed to what he termed "moral evidence against the Bible" to show "that the Bible is not entitled to credit as being the word of God." Referring to the many atrocities recorded in the Bible, Paine states:

To charge the commission of acts upon the Almighty, which, in their own nature, and by every rule of moral justice, are crimes, as all assassination is, and more especially the assassination of infants, is matter of serious concern. The Bible tells us, that those assassinations were done by the *express command of God*. To believe, therefore, the Bible to be true, we must *unbelieve* all our belief in the moral justice of God; for wherein could crying or smiling infants offend? And to read the Bible without horror, we must undo everything that is tender, sympathizing, and benevolent in the heart of man. Speaking for myself, if I had no other evidence that the Bible is fabulous than the sacrifice I must make to believe it to be true, that alone would be sufficient to determine my choice.[16]

Paine was a master of polemical style, and passages in the *Age of Reason* range from bitter to humorous. His comment on Matthew 27.51-53 is a good example of the latter. These passages report an incident during the crucifixion of Jesus.

And, behold, the veil of the temple was rent in twain from the top to the bottom, and the earth did quake, and the rocks rent; and the graves were opened; and many bodies of the saints which slept arose, and came out of the graves after his resurrection, and went into the holy city, and appeared unto many. (King James Version.)

After noting that none of the other three Gospels mention this remarkable occurrence, Paine argues that this event, had it actually occurred, would have been far too significant for the other New Testament writers to ignore. He then subjects this report to the full force of his wit:

It is an easy thing to tell a lie, but it is difficult to support the lie after it is told. The writer of the book of Matthew should have told us who the saints were that came to life again, and went into the city, and what became of them afterward, and who it was that saw them—for he is not hardy enough to say he saw them himself; whether they came out naked, and all in natural buff, he-saints and she-saints; or whether they came full dressed, and where they got their dresses, whether they went to their former habitations, and reclaimed their wives, their husbands, and their property, and how they were received; whether they entered ejectments for the recovery of their possessions, or brought actions of *crim. con.* against the rival interlopers; whether they remained on earth, and followed their former occupation of preaching or working; or whether they died again, or went back to their graves alive, and buried themselves.[17]

Much of the *Age of Reason* concerns the authenticity and veracity of the Old and New Testaments. Like Spinoza before him, Paine appealed to internal evidence to prove that the Old Testament books could not have been written by their traditionally ascribed authors. And since many of these books testify to miraculous events, "if it should be found that the books ascribed to Moses, Joshua and Samuel, were not written by Moses, Joshua, and Samuel, every part of the authority and authenticity of those books is gone at once; for there can be no such thing as forged or invented testimony, more especially as to things naturally incredible, such as that of talking with God face to face, or that of the sun and moon standing still at the command of a man."[18]

"The New Testament," writes Paine, "compared with the Old, is like a farce of one act, in which there is not room for the very numerous violations of the unities. There are, however, some glaring contradictions, which . . . are sufficient to show the story of Jesus Christ to be false."[19] Furthermore, charges Paine, the four Gospels "have been manufactured, as the books of the Old Testament have been, by other persons than those whose names they bear."[20]

Most modern theologians would agree with Paine that the New Testament contains a mass of contradictions and that the Gospels (or at least three of the four) are of unknown authorship, written anywhere from 40 to 150 years after the death of Jesus. This brings out a curious parallel between many non-Christians and liberal Christian theologians regarding their view of the Bible. Yet most theologians couch their rejection of the Bible in theological terms, which gives them the appearance of strengthening Christianity while ripping the reliability of its source book to shreds. Few theologians would care to pursue their research to its logical conclusion and finally assert, as did

Paine, that the biblical account of Jesus "has every mark of fraud and imposition stamped upon the face of it." Despite these impolite terms, however, this conclusion reached by an arch-infidel of two centuries ago is not dissimilar from the conclusion reached through modern biblical scholarship.

Many of Paine's biblical criticisms were not original with him, nor did he have the background necessary for a thorough analysis of the Bible. Some of his comments on the Bible seem naive and simplistic by today's standards, but this is irrelevant when we remember that Paine was concerned only with destroying the doctrine that the Bible is the infallible word of God, or indeed the product of any supernatural being. And viewed in this context, the *Age of Reason* was—and is—a resounding success.

Critical examinations of the Bible are so commonplace today that they have lost most of their sting. While there are disagreements over points of detail, there is a general consensus among moderate and liberal theologians that the inerrancy doctrine of the Bible is blatantly indefensible. A few theologians, the more honest among them, are remarkably frank in their disclaimers. For example, Alfred Loisy, one of the leaders in the movement known as "Catholic Modernism," published two works whose tone is sometimes reminiscent of Thomas Paine. Loisy, a widely acknowledged biblical scholar, was a professor at the Institut Catholique in France from 1889 until his excommunication from the Church in 1908. Loisy firmly denied any supernatural influence in the Bible. Concerning the New Testament, he wrote:

A long, slow process brought the Gospels to their present form without any sign of divine initiative at the beginning or the end or at any point between the two; at a given time they were selected, from among many, by the Church authorities and the text of their content finally determined. . . . The apostolic Epistles, authentic or not, are personal works called forth by particular occasions. Moreover a consid-

erable part of them are forgeries, for which it would
be unseemly enough to make God directly responsible. . . . In short, the idea of God as author of books
is a myth, if ever there was one, and a myth redolent
of magic. . . . The books reputed all divine are simply
not filled with truth from beginning to end—far from
it! They contain as many errors as books of their
kind, written when they were, could be made to
hold.[21]

After citing numerous contradictions between the various
stories of the Resurrection, Loisy concludes:

From all this the conclusion follows that what we
have here is not a historical tradition of a factual
resurrection . . . but an assertion of faith. The stories
of imagined apparitions are, for the most part, apologetic constructions for buttressing belief by clothing
it in material form. Whence it follows in this crucial
case, as in that of miracles in general, that the only
history we can glean from stories of supernatural
magic is the history of belief.[22]

Loisy found it incredible that learned scholars, especially his
Catholic colleagues, continued to defend the infallibility doctrine. Since the evidence against this belief is so overwhelming,
he bluntly accused other theologians of intellectual dishonesty:

In the supernatural so understood we have here no
part or lot, for the plain reason that it is untrue, that
it crumbles to pieces, save so far as it is held together
by the ignorance of the believing masses, and by the
wilful blindness of the theologians who refuse to see
what is before them; nor can the suspicion be avoided
that these theologians sometimes play a part which
ranges them with opportunists, apologetic politicians,
exegetical strategists, rather than with those who

205

really and personally believe in this false super-naturalism, which they seem determined to impose as a perpetual burden on the religious mind. We beg to tell them, and to say it once for all, that their pretensions are preposterous and their assumption of infallibility an unpermitted revolt against exact knowledge. [23]

Returning to the subject of atheism, we must determine what, if anything, can be said in defense of the Bible. Is it possible to demonstrate that the Bible contains a supernatural element?

In considering this question, we must remember that the Christian assumes the full burden of proof. It is not necessary for the atheist to prove that the Bible contains contradictions or that many biblical books are forgeries in order to debunk the alleged supernaturalism of the Bible. Even if the Bible were consistent, or even if all its books were written by their purported authors, this would not begin to establish any supernatural influence. For this reason, we shall not pursue these problems in this chapter. For further information, the reader may consult any of a vast number of books dealing with biblical research. [24]

Many Christians openly concede that the Bible must be accepted as an article faith, but this has no relevance to our present goal. Our task is to determine the philosophical possibility of using the Bible as a means of establishing Christianity. Can we somehow start from the Bible itself and, with the aid of some self-authenticating procedure, use it as an argument for supernaturalism? Does the Bible contain anything that cannot be explained except with reference to a supernatural being?

Some fundamentalists think so. They argue that the Bible contains accurate prophecies which provide overwhelming evidence of a supernatural influence. Since the biblical writers were able to predict future events with accuracy, such as events in the life of Jesus, we must conclude that they were inspired by God.

It is true that prophecy was very popular among many biblical writers, but whether they were successful or not is another matter entirely. We must first keep in mind that many of these attempts at prophecy are of such an obscure nature that any of a variety of events could be interpreted as fulfillment. Also, the Bible as we have it today is the result of much editing and interpolation, and many of the books that have traditionally been ascribed to one author are now known to be the work of different anonymous men. So there is considerable reason to suppose that many alleged prophecies (especially those which are predicted and fulfilled in the same Old Testament book) were manufactured after the fact in question.

But let us consider an area where there is an indisputable chronological gap between the prediction and its alleged fulfillment: the Old Testament prophecies of a Jewish messiah which, according to Christianity, were fulfilled by Jesus. The New Testament abounds with references to Old Testament predictions of a future savior, and the biblical authors went to great lengths to pound Jesus into the mold of Jewish messianic expectation. In their enthusiasm, however, they resorted to blatant distortions.

While the Jews were anticipating the coming of a savior, they visualized him as a military conqueror who would liberate them from centuries of oppression. Because Jesus did not fit this image, he was not widely accepted by the Jewish community; but the Gospel writers, eager to verify the messiahship of Jesus, referred to the Old Testament on many occasions. As an example of the distortion and context-dropping that resulted, consider the first reference to prophecy in the New Testament. Referring to the supposed virgin birth of Jesus, the author of Matthew writes:

All this took place to fulfil what the Lord had spoken by the prophet: "Behold, a virgin shall conceive and bear a son, and his name shall be called Emmanuel" (which means, God with us). (Matthew 1. 22, 23)

207

This is a reference to the Old Testament passage, Isaiah 7.14:

> Therefore the Lord himself will give you a sign. Behold, a young woman shall conceive and bear a son, and shall call his name Immanuel.

To begin with, this appeal to prophecy is based on a mistranslation. The Hebrew word *almah*, which means "young woman" or "maiden," is made to read "virgin" (for which the Hebrew is *bethulah*) by the author of Matthew—thus conveniently switching the Old Testament passage to meet his particular requirements. According to *The Interpreter's Bible*, "if Isaiah had wished to make clear that he had in mind a miraculous virgin birth, he would have had to use the specific term *bethulah*."[25] The King James Translation retains the mistranslation of Isaiah 7.14 as "virgin," but the more honest Revised Standard Version correctly renders it "young woman."

In addition to this, the entire intent of the Old Testament passage has been mutilated by the author of Matthew. This is evident to anyone who cares to examine the entire context of Isaiah 7.14. Taken in its full context (beginning with 7.1), this child is meant to be a sign to Ahaz (King of Judah) that he will not be defeated in battle by Pekah (King of Israel) and Resin (King of Syria). The birth of this child is reported in Chapter 8 of Isaiah; in no way can it be construed as a reference to the future birth of a messiah, much less the birth of Jesus 750 years later. The author of Matthew was very free in ignoring context. (For an interesting sidelight, see II Chronicles 28, where Ahaz was conquered in battle despite God's promise to the contrary.)

For another astounding prophecy, turn to Matthew 2.15, which refers to Jesus' alleged flight into Egypt to escape Herod's mass slaughter of children (a slaughter, incidentally, for which there is no corroborating historical evidence, even among the writings of the Jewish historian Josephus who reported the atrocities of Herod in meticulous detail).

> [Joseph and Jesus] remained there until the death of Herod. This was to fulfil what the Lord had spoken by the prophet, "Out of Egypt have I called my son."

208

Observe the context of this "prophecy," which was taken from Hosea 11.1:

When Israel was a child, I loved him, and out of Egypt I called my son.

This passage and those that follow clearly indicate that the "son" refers to Israel during its exodus from Egypt (such as in Exodus 4.22, where Israel is again referred to as God's son). This "prophecy" refers to a past event. The author of Matthew, who would have us believe that Hosea 11.1 predicts a future event, is again very brazen in his distortion.

These are only two examples out of many similar cases. Time and again, Old Testament passages are distorted, misinterpreted and quoted out of context in the attempt to manufacture prophecies for Jesus.

Christians sometimes counter these objections by arguing that the cited Old Testament passages have a double meaning: one for the time in which they were written and another long-range, esoteric meaning. But this ruse is obviously a feeble attempt to escape critical evaluation. If, when we object to an alleged prophecy, the Christian replies that the New Testament writer knew what he was doing even if we do not, we then leave the realm of reason and enter the domain of faith. The Christian asks us to accept the legitimacy of these prophecies on faith, on the testimony of the person who uses them as prophecies. This permits the New Testament writers to extract any Old Testament passage at will, distort it beyond recognition, and then claim the sanction of divine inspiration. In this event, prophecy is reduced to arbitrary decree and thus loses its argumentative impact.

In addition to distorted prophecies, there are also many mistaken and unfulfilled prophecies in the Bible. It is rather embarrassing for Christians to admit that, according to the Bible, Jesus was fond of predicting the end of the world as we know it within the lifetime of his followers. For instance, Matthew 24. 29-34 reads, in part:

Immediately after the tribulation of those days the sun will be darkened, and the moon will not give its light, and the stars will fall from heaven . . . then will appear . . . the Son of man coming on the clouds of heaven with power and great glory. . . . Truly, I say to you, *this generation will not pass away till all these things take place.* (Emphasis added.)

Jesus mistakenly taught that the people of his generation would see the advent of the kingdom of God, a teaching that is reflected in many other passages as well. Matthew 4.17 ("Repent, for the kingdom of heaven is at hand.") and Mark 9.1 ("Truly I say to you, there are some standing here who will not taste death before they see the kingdom of God come with power.") are typical examples. (Cf. Matthew 10.7, 10.23, 16.28, 23.36; Mark 1.15, 13.30; Luke 9.27, 21.32.)

After the death of Jesus, his followers mistakenly predicted his imminent return. Here is a random selection:

Hebrews 1.2: ". . . in these last days he [God] has spoken to us by a Son, whom he appointed the heir of all things."

I Corinthians 7. 29: "I mean, brethren, the appointed time has grown very short; from now on, let those who have wives live as though they had none. . . ."

I Peter 4.7: "The end of all things is at hand. . . ."

I Peter 1.20: "[Jesus] was made manifest at the end of the times for your sake."

James 5.8: "Establish your hearts, for the coming of the Lord is at hand." (Cf. Hebrews 9.26, 10.37; I Timothy 6.13-14; I Thessalonians 4.15; 2 Peter 3. 12-14; I John 2.18; Revelations 1.1, 3.11, 22.7.)

In conclusion, the Bible shows no traces whatsoever of supernatural influence. Quite the contrary, it is obviously the product of superstitious men who, at times, were willing to deceive if it would further their doctrines. Some people may wish to revere parts of the Bible as good literature or as a source of inspiration and comfort (and even these are questionable), but these have no bearing on the veracity of the biblical record. From the standpoint of atheism, any appeal to the Bible as evidence of supernaturalism must be dismissed as irrational.

II

Miracles

What is a miracle? Some theists define it as divine intervention in the natural course of events. This definition presupposes the existence of a god, and since it requires that one first believe in a supernatural being before one can believe in a miracle, it is useless for establishing the existence of a god. The Catholic philosopher R. P. Phillips defines a miracle in this manner, and he admits that, on this basis, an appeal to miracles lacks argumentative force:

> It would evidently be absurd to argue with an atheist or a thoroughgoing Agnostic as to the possibility of miracle. As he does not acknowledge the existence of God, to discuss whether God can work miracles would be a waste of time ... unless miracles are acknowledged to be possible they cannot be adduced as evidential facts, so that the fundamental theses of Natural Theology and of Theism are presupposed by the discussion of miracle, and cannot be proved by it.[26]

Another definition of a miracle is any event so unusual that it can be explained only with reference to a supernatural power. Thus if we were to observe an exceptionally strange occurrence, such as an iron bar floating on water, we might conclude that a supernatural being is at work.

211

This kind of argument mistakenly assumes that positing a god somehow explains an unexplained event. The theist observes the "floating iron," thinks, "How amazing! How is it possible?"—and then provides himself with the solution: "An unknowable power must be responsible." But this explains nothing. One cannot answer the question, "How is it possible?" with the response, "An unknowable being using unknowable means did it."

Contrast the preceding approach with that of a rational man. If a scientist observes something that he cannot explain in terms of presently known physical laws, he will investigate the matter thoroughly to determine if his interpretation is correct and if he is aware of all relevant factors. If he concludes that the phenomenon cannot be explained with reference to presently known scientific principles, he will search for a principle that will explain it. And, if he is unsuccessful in this attempt, he will simply admit that there is something that he cannot explain within his present context of knowledge, something that requires further investigation. Underlying this entire process is the knowledge that, since contradictions cannot exist in reality, the presence of a contradiction in one's thinking constitutes proof of an error. The scientist is also aware that this contradiction will not disappear by attributing the occurrence to an act of god; he realizes that such an inference is not only unjustified, but that it explains nothing, that it is an evasion rather than an explanation.

Since the positing of a god explains nothing, one cannot infer the existence of a god from an unusual event as a causal explanation. Regardless of the phenomenon involved, it is *never* rational to jump from the statement, "x is unexplained" to the statement, "Therefore, a supernatural power must have caused x." Explanations, by their very nature, must fall within the realm of natural causality. To posit the supernatural as an explanation is to posit the unknowable as an explanation, and this is nothing more than an exercise in futility. (The issue of "god" as an explanatory concept is discussed in the following chapter.)

A third definition of a miracle (closely related to the preceding) is any event that cannot be subsumed under natural laws. Here, of course, the problem is that one is never justified in claiming that a given occurrence falls outside the realm of natural law. Such an assertion, even if it made sense, would require omniscience. All that one may say is that an event cannot be explained with reference to *presently* known laws, but this does not mean that the event cannot be explained with reference to principles as yet unknown. No man can lay claim to omniscience, and no man can claim to possess a noncontextual and unalterable knowledge of all physical laws. While one may assert that something is presently unexplained, one may never conclude that something is inherently unexplainable.

This brings us to a crucial point that has not been sufficiently emphasized by critics of the supernatural. The controversy between naturalism and supernaturalism is not a contest between two rival modes of explanation; it is not a matter of which provides a better explanation. Rather, it is an issue of explanation versus no explanation whatsoever. It is an issue of the knowable versus the unknowable.

In order to move from an alleged miracle to the existence of the supernatural, one must move from the presently unknown to the forever unknowable. And, for reasons that should already be apparent, this inference cannot be justified under any circumstances. The attempt to argue from a supposed miracle to the existence of god is thus doomed to failure as a matter of principle.

Why do people claim to have witnessed miracles? John Hospers has some interesting remarks on this subject:

> It is interesting to observe . . . that people are quick to accept as a miracle any unusual event, or an event that goes contrary to natural probabilities, as long as it works in their favor. A hundred people are killed in an airplane accident, but one survives. "It's a miracle!" say the survivor and his family. What the families of the non-survivors had to say about the

matter is usually not recorded. . . . In general, people
who already have some kind of theistic belief are apt
to call miraculous any event that is unusual, whose
causes they do not fully know, and that works in
their favor . . . what people call a miracle depends
very much on what they *want* to believe, more than
on what the facts of the case are.[27]

Because our lives lack such colorful events as seas parting, the
sun standing still and burning bushes that talk, most Christians
prefer to discuss miracles recorded in the past. Jesus, for
example, is reported by a number of people to have performed
miracles; so it seems reasonable, at least from the Christian
viewpoint, to accept the veracity of their testimony.

Before discussing the philosophical problems involved here,
we can make a few general observations concerning the purported miracles of Jesus. We should first note that none of the
Gospel writers were eyewitnesses to the events that they
describe, but even if the authors had been personal friends of
Jesus, their reports would be no more credible. To cast doubt
on the trustworthiness of the Gospel writers is not necessarily
to impugn their integrity (although this may be a factor in some
cases); rather, as Thomas Huxley observed, "when we know
that a firm belief in the miraculous was ingrained in their minds,
and was the presupposition of their observations and rea-
sonings," the New Testament writers simply cannot be accepted
as reliable witnesses. It is doubtful that anyone, even the most
devout Christian, actually believes that as mankind advanced in
knowledge, the frequency of miracles coincidentally tapered
off. Stories circulated about Jesus after his death, stories not
unlike those reported of other men, and the uncritical mind of
the early Christian saw no particular reason why these stories
should be questioned. As man progressed, as his thinking
became more logical, he became more selective in his beliefs.
And, not surprisingly, the number of reported miracles
diminished.

214

The Gospels themselves contain some clues which suggest that the stories of Jesus as a miracle worker evolved after his death. For example, the Gospel of Mark reports that when Jesus traveled through his native country, "he could do no mighty work there . . . because of their unbelief" (6. 5-6). These were the people who knew Jesus best, and if they later denied reports of his supernatural power, a rejoinder was readily available: these people never saw Jesus perform miracles because they lacked faith.

Another possible indication is the silence that Jesus is reported to have enjoined on some of those he cured. For example, after curing a leper, Jesus is said to have done the following:

> And he sternly charged him, and sent him away at once, and said to him, "See that you say nothing to any one. . . ." (Mark 1. 43-44)

Once again, if rumors of miraculous power circulated about Jesus after his death, and if people complained that they were unaware of this power while Jesus was alive, here was an explanation: the miracles were unknown simply because Jesus had commanded silence. "The silence repeatedly enjoined on these occasions," writes Loisy, "was the explanation, naive enough, but indispensable, of why . . . [the miracles] had not been heard of before."[28]

If one compares reports of miracles from the so-called synoptic Gospels (Matthew, Mark and Luke), one will find that, as one moves from the earlier to the later Gospels, some of the miracles become more exaggerated. Consider the following passage from Mark, the earliest Gospel:

> That evening, at sundown, they brought to him all who were sick or possessed with demons. . . . And he healed many who were sick with various diseases, and cast out many demons. . . . (1. 32-34)

215

Now compare the same incident as reported by the two later Gospels, Matthew and Luke (who probably took the original account from Mark and amended it). Here is Matthew:

> That evening they brought to him many who were possessed with demons; and he cast out the spirits with a word, and healed all who were sick. (8.16)

And here is Luke:

> Now when the sun was setting, all those who had any that were sick with various diseases brought them to him; and he laid his hands on every one of of them and healed them. (4.40)

According to Mark, all were brought to Jesus and many were healed; according to Matthew, many were brought and all were healed; and according to Luke, all were brought and all were healed. The miracle keeps getting better all the time. As A. Robertson observes, "We are witnessing the progressive growth of a legend."[29]

Any alleged miracles that are recorded as history are subject to the same criticisms made at the beginning of this discussion. Moreover, the Christian encounters a problem of selectivity. On what basis can he believe in the miracles of Christianity and yet deny the reported miracles of other religions? How does one distinguish historical miracles that are worthy of belief from those that are not? Or, to push the point further, after one has conceded the validity of recorded miracles, how does one distinguish historical fact from mythological fancy?

This brings us to a major objection to historical miracles which was initially presented by David Hume in *An Inquiry Concerning Human Understanding:* namely, "that no testimony for any kind of miracle has ever amounted to a probability, much less to a proof. . . ."[30] Here is a condensation of Hume's argument by Professor Flew:

216

The basic propositions are: first, that the present relics of the past cannot be interpreted as historical evidence at all, unless we presume that the same fundamental regularities obtained then as still obtain today; second, that in trying as best he may to determine what actually happened the historian must employ as criteria all his present knowledge, or presumed knowledge, of what is probable or improbable, possible or impossible; and, third, that, since *miracle* has to be defined in terms of practical impossibility the application of these criteria inevitably precludes proof of a miracle.[31]

In other words, without rational standards with which to sift nonsense from possible fact, without a means to separate the possible from the impossible, there could be no study of history for man. And since a miracle, by definition, does not conform to rational standards, it is absurd to speak of a "historical miracle"; it is a contradiction in terms. If one admits the veracity of historical miracles, one has abandoned rational guidelines; if one abandons these guidelines, however, one cannot speak of *anything* as being historical—including miracles—since one has destroyed one's tool of discrimination. Therefore, as Hume asserted, "we may establish it as a maxim, that no human testimony can have such force as to prove a miracle, and make it a just foundation for any such system of religion."[32] Such is the inescapable dilemma that theists must face, a dilemma that must result from any attempt to "prove" miracles (which means: demonstrate through a process of reason the existence of that which, by its very nature, contra- dicts reason).

Since no testimony can establish the occurrence of a miracle, any explanation of an event through natural means, regardless of how unlikely it may seem, will always have a greater degree of probability in its favor than will an appeal to supernatural forces. This principle, which is essentially an application of

Occams's razor (the principle of parsimony) to explanation, was proposed by Hume:

> When any one tells me, that he saw a dead man restored to life, I immediately consider with myself, whether it be more probable, that this person should either deceive or be deceived, or that the fact, which he relates, should really have happened. I weigh the one miracle against the other; and according to the superiority, which I discover, I pronounce my decision, and always reject the greater miracle. If the falsehood of his testimony would be more miraculous, than the event which he relates; then, and not till then, can he pretend to command my belief or opinion.[33]

Thomas Paine presents this same basic point in a more straightforward manner:

> If . . . we see an account given of such miracle by the person who said he saw it, it raises a question in the mind very easily decided, which is, is it more probable that nature should go out of her course, or that a man should tell a lie? We have never seen, in our time, nature go out of her course; but we have good reason to believe that millions of lies have been told in the same time; it is, therefore, at least millions to one, that the reporter of a miracle tells a lie.[34]

We have seen that an appeal to miracles is incapable of demonstrating or in any way supporting the belief in a supernatural being. Miracles, as many Christians freely admit, must be accepted as articles of faith. And this is where the Christian and the atheist part company.

PART THREE:
THE ARGUMENTS
FOR GOD

To explain the unknown by the known is a logical
procedure; to explain the known by the unknown is
a form of theological lunacy.

—David Brooks,
The Necessity of Atheism

8.
Natural Theology

I
The Final Appeal

The prospects for the Christian are dim. His deity, wavering between incoherency and agnosticism, cannot be rescued by an appeal to faith or revelation. But it is unlikely that the persistent theist will surrender at this point. He may admit that the traditional concept of God is nonsense, but insist that some supernatural being—regardless of its specific characteristics—can be known to exist through reason. There is, he may argue, evidence in nature of a supernatural force, a power that transcends natural laws. While we may not know the attributes of this being (and therefore have no clear concept of it), we do know that there is some kind of supernatural being, whatever it is. And this is what is meant by the word "god."

Natural theology attempts to infer the existence of a supernatural being from natural phenomena which allegedly cannot be explained within the context of the natural universe itself. Using facts of nature as his starting point, the theist attempts to demonstrate the existence of a god without recourse to faith or

221

revelation. Reason, it is claimed, is sufficient to establish the existence of a god.

We have now returned to "god" with a lower case "g." If valid, the arguments of natural theology will verify supernaturalism in some form, but they cannot establish the existence of a creature with the muddled and contradictory attributes of the Christian God. The best that natural theology can do for Christianity is to provide a foundation for rational theism, but it cannot erase the contradictions inherent in the Christian notion of God.

By examining natural theology, we are looking for some evidence, however slight, for the existence of a being that exists beyond the framework of the natural world. In other words, having dispensed with Christianity specifically, we are now concerned with the grounds for theistic belief in general. Are there rational reasons for believing in the existence of any kind of supernatural being, regardless of what its specific characteristics may be? If the general arguments for theism collapse, *atheism*—in the widest sense of the term—will be firmly established.

Natural theology has fallen into disrepute in recent decades, although it does enjoy an occasional resurgence. Liberal Protestants concede the invalidity of rational demonstration for a god, but Catholics (along with some fundamentalist Protestants) continue to defend natural theology. Catholic theology has a rigid philosophic structure based heavily on Aquinas, and to deny the validity of natural theological proofs would destroy this structure at its roots. To find a rigorous defense of arguments for the existence of a god, one needs only to consult the nearest text on Thomistic philosophy.

Having eliminated any possible escape to faith and revelation, we are now prepared to examine the various attempts to construct a rational theism in any form. Unlike many books on religion, this discussion of natural theology comes at the end of the chapters dealing with the philosophical aspects of theistic belief. This was done with two purposes in mind. First, we were able to eliminate Christian theism through an analysis of its

222

concept of God. Since the Christian God is a mass of unintelligible characteristics, it is impossible—in principle—rationally to demonstrate its existence. The Christian cannot even make sense out of the statement, "God exists," much less demonstrate the existence of this unintelligible being.

Second, by debunking appeals to faith and revelation, we have forced the theist to play his game solely in the court of reason. Some theists enthusiastically set out to rationally demonstrate the existence of god and, when pushed into a corner, fall back on an appeal to faith or revelation. By blocking these exits prior to this discussion, we have prevented the theist from utilizing these evasive maneuvers.

Either god stands on reason or he does not stand at all. This basic principle cannot be compromised: to surrender it by an inch is to surrender it in total.

II

The Conditions of Proof

Before discussing specific arguments, we must lay some initial groundwork; we must specify some general conditions to be met by the theist before he begins his argumentation.

(a) Arguments for the existence of god cannot contain theistic presuppositions. The theist cannot assume as true something that requires demonstration.

This fallacy (known as "question begging") is most often encountered among philosophically untrained theists. For example, when confronted with an atheist, this believer will exclaim: "But if a god doesn't exist, what caused the universe?" Or: "If you don't believe in god, how can you account for the magnificent design in nature?"

The fallacy in these questions should be obvious. Granted, *if* we first admit that the universe requires a causal explanation or that the universe exhibits design, then the inference to a first cause or master designer follows automatically. But these are not the issues of debate between theists and atheists. The question is not, "What is the cause of the universe?" Rather, we must ask, "Does the universe require a causal explanation?" Similarly, the question is not, "What is responsible for the design in nature?" Rather, we must first ask, "Does nature exhibit design?"

The failure of the theist to grapple with these basic questions results in immense confusion. God is posited as the solution to a metaphysical problem, but no consideration is given to whether a problem exists in the first place. The problem is constructed in such a way that any solution in natural terms is unacceptable, thus clearing a path for the supernatural.

To prove a supernatural "first cause," the theist must demonstrate—not assume—that the universe requires a causal explanation. To prove a supernatural designer, the theist must demonstrate—not assume—that the universe exhibits design. And likewise for any other arguments. Failure to establish these fundamental issues totally invalidates any supposed proofs derived from the assumed "problems."

(b) The existence of a supernatural being must be decided solely on the basis of evidence and arguments; there is no room for an appeal to faith.

This is essentially the same point made earlier, but it requires special emphasis. Though rarely made explicit, there is an undercurrent in some theistic writing which suggests that the theist somehow perceives a force in arguments which is inaccessible to the atheist—and that "faith" is a necessary prerequisite for this insight. While the arguments for god may not be strictly valid (and therefore will not convince a nonbeliever), the theist argues that one will "see" the force of these arguments—the many evidences of god in nature—if one first believes on faith.

The contemporary philosopher Stephen Toulmin defends an approach similar to this in the following passage from *Reason in Ethics:*

> The existence of God . . . is not something to demand *evidence for;* nor is the sentence, "God exists," one to be believed if, and only if, the evidence for its

truth is good enough. The very last question to ask about God is *whether* He exists. Rather, we must first accept the notion of "God": and then we shall be in a position to point to *evidences of* His existence.[1]

This astonishing passage has disastrous implications. The absurdity of Toulmin's distinction between "evidence for" and "evidence of" becomes clear if, instead of a debate between a theist and an atheist, we imagine a debate between an elf-believer and a nonbeliever.

Elf-Believer (EB): "There is a magic elf on my head."

Skeptic (S): "I don't see anything."

EB: "Of course not, he's invisible."

S: "I don't feel anything either."

EB: "That's because he is not composed of matter. He's magic, remember."

S: "But why should I even accept your notion of an elf at all? What is your elf like, and what is the evidence for its existence?"

EB: "The existence of my elf is not something to demand evidence for. The very last question to ask about my elf is whether he exists. Rather, we must first accept the notion of my invisible elf, and then we shall be in a position to point to *evidences of* his existence."

The irrationality of this approach is obvious. In order to function as grounds for belief, evidence must precede the acceptance of an idea. It makes no sense to accept the idea first and then search for evidence to support it. This is rationalization, not rationality.

Suppose, for the sake of argument, that the skeptic in our dialogue agrees to accept the notion of an invisible elf prior to demanding proof. What would be the nature of "evidences of" the elf's existence?

S: "All right, I'll agree to accept your elf in the absence of evidence, but you will have to tell me more about him since I don't even know what I am to have faith in."

EB: "My elf is the cause of all rain."

S: "What are, as you put it, the *evidences of* his existence?"

EB: "Every time it rains you are seeing my elf in action. What more evidence could you ask for?"

This dialogue is analogous to the theist who uses "evidence" in the same way. He will first ask the atheist to accept the idea of god—*e.g.*, a creator of the universe who is responsible for its orderliness—and he will then point to the facts that the universe exists and that the universe exhibits order. These facts will constitute his "evidences of" god—evidence that he has defined into existence.

Here we see the consequence (and perhaps the motivation) of insisting that the idea of god be accepted prior to the consideration of evidence. This allows the theist to virtually manufacture his evidence to meet desired specifications.

Since this style of argumentation displays a felt need to rationalize faith, an analysis of it falls more within the province of psychology than philosophy. For the present purpose, the above use of "evidence"—or any evidence that claims some privileged status—may be dismissed from serious consideration. We shall concern ourselves only with evidence *for* the existence of a supernatural being. If none exists, the atheistic position is fully established.

(c) A distinction must be drawn between "rational theism" and "rational theists." The possibility of "rational theism" depends solely on the possibility of demonstrating the existence

226

of a supernatural being. A "rational theist" is one who is *motivated* to believe in god because he believes that god's existence can be established through reason.

The "rational theist" must base his belief on the supposed validity of rational arguments. If these arguments are shown to be invalid, he must then relinquish his belief in god. In other words, the validity or invalidity of theistic arguments must make a difference to the "rational theist."

Many times in the past, before knowing better, I would engage in arguments with theists who claimed to have a rational foundation for their belief. After several painstaking hours of pointing out flaws in the proposed arguments, I would receive some form of the following comment: "Well, it really doesn't matter if these proofs are invalid, because I have faith in the existence of god anyway."

The theist who resorts to this approach has no claim to rationality—only to lack of integrity. For this believer, any rational demonstration of god would be irrelevant; such demonstration would be, so to speak, a happy coincidence, a useful tool against nonbelievers.

Before discussing any theist's claim to rationality, the following question must be asked: "If your arguments are shown to be incorrect, will you relinquish your belief in god?" If the answer is "no"—as it often is—then any further discussion with this person is a waste of time. Any claim to rationality or concern with truth is mere pretense on his part, since he is indifferent to the validity of his arguments. This, to put it mildly, is hypocrisy.

Of course, the motivation for offering an argument does not affect the worth of the argument *per se.* A perfectly sound argument may be given for the most insincere or hypocritical reasons. The possibility of "rational theism," therefore, is independent of the existence or nonexistence of "rational theists." I have stressed this psychological maneuver of paying lip service to reason only as a guideline to sort the sincere from the insincere "rational theists" in specific situations.

III
"God" as an Explanatory Concept

Most arguments of natural theology follow the same basic pattern. Each begins with a natural phenomenon—a fact, according to the theist, that requires an explanation. But this fact, he argues, cannot be explained in terms of other natural phenomena; therefore, we must posit the existence of the supernatural, a realm unrestricted by natural law, as an explanation.

In this way the theist claims to move from nature, an observed fact of reality, to something that lies beyond nature. The concept of the supernatural functions as an explanation; it allegedly explains something that cannot otherwise be accounted for. Without the supernatural, the natural universe (or some aspect of it) is reduced to "mere unintelligible brute fact."

The defender of natural theology thus postures as a champion of reason; theism, he maintains, explains the universe and places it within the grasp of man's comprehension. Atheism, on the other hand, renders the universe unintelligible. Since the atheist denies the possibility of explaining the natural universe, he must content himself with an inexplicable cosmos.

This portrayal, however, is a reversal of the truth. It is the theist, not the atheist, who denies to man the possibility of understanding nature. It is the theist, not the atheist, who renders the universe unintelligible. Let us examine this issue in more detail.

To state that the universe is *intelligible,* in this context, means: (a) the universe requires an explanation; (b) this explanation is possible for man. To state that the universe is *unintelligible* means: (a) the universe requires an explanation; (b) no such explanation is possible for man.

The theist claims to adopt the first of these positions, but he actually argues that an explanation of the universe, while required, cannot be grasped by man's consciousness. He therefore reduces the universe to unintelligibility.

228

Consider the nature of an explanation. An explanation builds a conceptual bridge from the known to the unknown, linking the unexplained to the context of one's knowledge. A new idea must be integrated within one's conceptual hierarchy in order to qualify as knowledge. An idea that cannot be so integrated exists in a conceptual vacuum; it cannot be comprehended because one lacks the conceptual framework necessary for comprehension.

The process of explanation consists essentially of *integrating* a new idea or concept within the context of one's present knowledge. Because men differ with regard to their context and scope of knowledge, an explanation is relative to the person seeking it. What is a satisfactory explanation for one man may not be satisfactory for another. For example, we simplify our language when explaining something to a child in order to compensate for his limited sphere of knowledge. Also, a scientist may understand an explanation that explains nothing to a layman who lacks the required technical background. An explanation must provide understanding, and one cannot understand something that lies beyond one's conceptual frame of reference.

While the particulars of knowledge differ among men, all men gain knowledge within one broad context: the context of the natural, knowable universe. Removed from this framework, knowledge is impossible and explanation is unintelligible.

Recall that the supernatural cannot be grasped by man's consciousness. When the theist posits a supernatural being, he is not merely positing the presently unknown that may be grasped with a greater degree of knowledge. The theist is positing the *unknowable*, that which is beyond man's comprehension, that which man will never be able to understand regardless of his degree of knowledge. Since the supernatural must remain forever outside the context of man's knowledge, a "supernatural explanation" is a contradiction in terms. One cannot explain the unknown with reference to the unknowable.

The theist initially constructs a gap between the universe and man's knowledge by claiming that the universe requires an explanation. Then, by stipulating that this explanation cannot be given in terms of natural (*i.e.*, knowable) phenomena, he proclaims that this gap can never be bridged, that any attempt to account for the universe within the context of man's knowledge is doomed to failure. Therefore, he argues, we must turn to the supernatural and the unknowable.

The supernatural, however, does not build a conceptual bridge from the unknown to the known; it sabotages not only the bridge, but the very possibility of ever constructing such a bridge. According to the theist, we can never link that which requires an explanation (the universe or some natural phenomenon) to the context of knowledge available to man. To say that god is responsible for the universe is to say that the explanation of the universe is unknowable to man—or, in other words, that no explanation is possible. *To posit the supernatural explains nothing; it merely asserts the futility of explanation.*

Thus the universe, for which the theist originally demanded an explanation, is now admitted by this same theist to be beyond man's comprehension. According to the theist, the universe requires an explanation which man can never understand. And this renders the universe unintelligible in the full meaning of the term.

The atheist does not face this problem. For the atheist, the universe—the totality of existence—is a metaphysical primary and, as such, cannot require an explanation. The natural, knowable universe provides the context in which all explanations are possible, so to demand an explanation for the universe itself is epistemologically absurd. Corliss Lamont, in *The Philosophy of Humanism*, makes this point as follows:

> In specific scientific explanations as well as in ultimate philosophical questions a stage frequently ensues when it is profitless to keep on asking "Why?" At such a juncture we have to say: "Things are simply constructed this way or behave this way." The speed of light is what it is; the law of gravitation operates as it does; and the number of protons and electrons in each type of atom is what it is. In none of these

instances can an intelligible answer be given as to *why*. . . . In science as well as in philosophy, then, we eventually hit rock-bottom in the pursuit of certain inquiries.[2]

Since the atheist does not accept the premise that the universe requires an explanation in the first place, since he rejects premise (a) stated earlier, he does not contend that the universe (*i.e.*, an explanation for its existence) is either intelligible or unintelligible. Rather, he argues that the concept of "explanation"—and hence the notion of "intelligibility"—is not applicable to the universe as a whole. Man cannot explain the existence of nature, because any attempted explanation logically presupposes the existence of nature. If removed from the framework of the natural universe, the concept of explanation is stripped of its meaning. The universe does not exist for a reason at all; it simply exists.

Of course, the atheist does believe that the universe is intelligible in another sense—namely, that the facts of reality are knowable. And, furthermore, we can explain the existence and actions of particular entities with reference to the existence and actions of other entities which act as causal antecedents. But all of this occurs within the context of the natural universe. The concept of "explanation," if lifted from this framework, no longer serves any function.

The theist digs his own hole from which there is no escape. He creates a problem by demanding an explanation for the natural universe, but now, having destroyed the context in which explanation is possible, he denies to himself the possibility of ever solving his own problem. After asserting that the natural universe requires an explanation, the theist goes on to offer an "explanation" in terms of the supernatural, which, by his own admission, man can never understand.

All arguments of natural theology fail, and though they vary in details, they fail for the same basic reason. The structure of each argument entails an inference from the natural to the supernatural—which, in terms of human knowledge, means an inference from the knowable to the unknowable. This supposed inference hinges on a single point: that the concept of a supernatural being *explains* the previously unexplained. If these arguments are to be valid, the concept of god must serve an explanatory function; it must provide an answer to the problem which it sets out to solve.

As we have seen, however, the concept of god actually negates the possibility of explanation. To say that god is responsible for phenomenon x is to say that some unknowable being "caused" x through some unknowable means. This obviously is not an explanation; rather, it is a concession that, in the opinion of the speaker, phenomenon x is totally *inexplicable*.

If a child asks his father how a magician made a dove disappear, and the father replies, "It's magic," we would hardly accept this as an explanation. Yet the theist attempts the same kind of maneuver. To his own question, "How do we explain natural phenomena?" the theist replies, "It's supernatural"—which, when translated, means: "It's unknowable."

Just as "magic" is not an explanation, so the "supernatural" is not an explanation, but is a concession that no explanation is possible. Because the concept of god has absolutely no explanatory power, it can never be inferred from nature as an explanation for natural phenomena. If, as the theist claims, the existence of the universe (or some aspect of it) requires an explanation, the positing of a supernatural being does not provide it.

Because the supernatural is totally lacking in explanatory power, the naturalistic position is impregnable, and insufficient appreciation of this point sometimes results in undeserved charity toward the theistic position. For example, in his brilliant *God and Philosophy*, Antony Flew bases his atheism on what he calls "The Stratonician Presumption" (after Strato of Lampsacus, *circa* 269 B.C.): this is "the presumption that the universe is everything there is; and hence that everything which can be explained must be explained by reference to what is in and of the universe."[3] In other words, as Flew explains in *An Introduction to Western Philosophy*, "all the phenomena of the universe can and must be explained without reference to any principle or principles in any sense 'outside', or 'beyond.' "[4]

Thus far I am in complete agreement with Flew, but in defending his position, he writes:

> The reason why atheist naturalism must have at least this initial priority over theism is that it is the more economical view. The theist as such postulates more than the atheist; and, in consequence, the onus of proof must rest on him.[5]

This is, Flew explains, the application of Occam's razor to the controversy between naturalism and supernaturalism. Naturalism has the edge because it provides the simpler, more economical explanation of the two. Thus:

> natural theology will surely have to accept the Stratonician Presumption as its starting-point. Of course in so doing it will be accepting this only as a defeasible presumption, and one which it aims by its own arguments to defeat.[6]

Again, in *God and Philosophy*, Flew writes of his Stratonician Presumption that it is "defeasible of course by adverse argument."[7] This is where I must take issue. Flew is quite right in insisting that the natural universe must constitute the starting point of our inquiry, and he is correct in pointing out that the burden of proof falls solely on the theist. But Flew is wrong, or at least misleading, when he grants to theism the theoretical possibility of gaining a foothold by dislodging naturalism through argumentation. There is no such possibility, even in principle.

Naturalism has the priority over supernaturalism, not because it is the more economical of two explanations, but because it is the only framework in which explanation is possible. Returning to the point that was made earlier in our discussion of miracles: the contest between naturalism and supernaturalism is not a battle between two rival modes of explanation, in which naturalism is selected because it is a better or more economical mode of explanation. Rather, naturalism is selected because it is the only *possible* method of explanation. Naturalism is the only context in which the concept of explanation has meaning.

Once the theist removes himself from the framework of natural causality and the general principles or "laws" by which man comprehends the universe, he forfeits his epistemological right to the concept of explanation and precludes the possibility of explaining anything. In the following two chapters, we shall examine some arguments for the existence of a god, and we shall see how the concept of god fails to explain the very problems for which it is posited. The theist manufactures pseudo-problems that he challenges the atheist to solve, and that, in the final analysis, the theist himself is unable to solve.

It has been said that few people doubted the existence of god until philosophers attempted to prove it. In considering the forthcoming arguments, we shall understand why.

9.
The Cosmological Arguments

Cosmology is the branch of philosophy that deals with the origin and structure of the universe. A cosmological argument attempts to demonstrate the existence of god by applying philosophical or scientific principles to a basic fact of the universe—a fact, it is claimed, that cannot be explained without reference to a supernatural being. Three cosmological arguments are commonly used today: the first-cause argument, the contingency argument, and the entropy argument.

I

The First Cause Argument

The first-cause argument is perhaps the most popular of the cosmological proofs. It has been used extensively by theologians of all denominations, as well as by laymen. Considering the

THE ARGUMENTS FOR GOD

wide attention that this argument has received, and considering the many times that it has been refuted in the past, it seems repetitious to discuss it here. But the first-cause argument has survived, complete with ambiguities and fallacies, which makes it necessary to refute it once more—hopefully for the last time.

The first-cause argument has two major variations. As used by many theists, especially laymen, the first-cause argument serves to defend the idea that "In the beginning God created the heavens and the earth." Although philosophy is not sophisticated enough to demonstrate a six-day creation—or to prove that the omnipotent deity, apparently weary, "rested on the seventh day from all his work which he had done"—we can, claims this theist, at least demonstrate, philosophically, that a creation occurred. There was a "beginning" when god caused the universe to exist.

According to this version of the first-cause argument, we must posit a *temporal* first cause, *i.e.*, a first cause in *time*. In considering a causal sequence extending over a period of time, we must finally reach a first cause—an uncaused cause that started everything going.

A more detailed statement of this argument is the following: Every existing thing has a cause, and every cause must be caused by a prior cause, which in turn must be caused by a still prior cause, and so on, until we reach one of two conclusions: (a) either we have an endless chain of causes—an infinite regress, or (b) there exists a first cause, a being that does not require a causal explanation.

According to this argument, an infinite regress of causes is impossible. Without a first cause, there could be no second cause; and without a second cause, there could be no third cause, and so on ad infinitum. We would then reach the absurd conclusion that nothing presently exists. But since things do exist, we must reject an infinite regress and conclude that a first cause exists, a cause which we call "god." (With slight alterations, this argument may be used to "prove" the existence of a first cause of motion or a first cause of change. However, these are simply variations of a basic theme and do not merit separate consideration.)

This causal argument rests on two main assumptions: that the universe as a whole requires a causal explanation, and that we cannot provide an adequate explanation within the context of the universe itself. Therefore, we must posit a *transcendent* first cause, a being that transcends natural cause-effect relationships.

Since the universe is not causally self-sufficient, we need to reach beyond the universe to account for the basic fact of the universe: the fact that it exists. If the atheist denies the existence of a supernatural being, how can he explain the existence of the universe? Surely it cannot just "happen" to exist; there must be a causal explanation.

Before we discuss the supposed mystery of existence, it is necessary to make some preliminary remarks concerning this argument.

(1) Even if valid, the first-cause argument is capable only of demonstrating the existence of a mysterious first cause in the distant past. It does not establish the *present* existence of the first cause. On the basis of this argument, there is no reason to assume that the first cause still exists—which cuts the ground from any attempt to demonstrate the truth of theism by this approach.

This objection alone demolishes the temporal version of the causal argument, but it is not the only objection that can be raised in this context. For example, this argument cannot establish that the first cause was (or is) alive, nor can it establish that the first cause was (or is) conscious. And an inanimate, unconscious god is of little use to theism.

In fact, even if we were to accept this argument, the most that it can possibly demonstrate is that something has existed which is itself uncaused. And as one philosopher has pointed out, "somebody believing in the eternity of atoms, or of matter generally, could quite consistently accept the conclusion."[1]

(2) The theist may object to this last remark, claiming that not only must there be a first cause, but this first cause cannot be part of the natural universe. The universe does not explain the reason for its own existence, but a supernatural first cause does provide us with an explanation. This transcendent first cause, therefore, explains the previously unexplained.

Assuming for the moment that the universe requires a causal explanation, does the positing of a first cause provide us with that explanation? How does the concept of god function as an explanatory concept in this instance? A supernatural first cause, a god, supposedly caused the universe to exist. Consider the nature of this "explanation." Does it provide one with a conceptual grasp of the issue being considered? Does it provide a causal explanation in any meaningful sense? No, it does not.

To posit god as the cause of the universe still leaves two crucial questions unanswered: *What* caused the universe? *How* did it cause the universe? To say that a god is responsible for the existence of the universe is vacuous without knowledge of god's nature and the method used in creating existence. If god is to serve as a causal explanation, we must have knowledge of god's attributes by virtue of which he has the capacity to create matter from nonexistence, and knowledge of the causal process involved in creation, by virtue of which god is designated as a cause.

If, as the theist asserts, the existence of the universe requires a causal explanation, the positing of a transcendent first cause or god does not provide us with this explanation. The theist's solution consists of saying: An unknowable being using unknowable methods "caused" the universe to snap into existence. This, remember, is offered as an explanation, as a rational solution to an apparent problem. This is supposed to resolve one's intellectual doubts about the mystery of existence.

To say that god caused the universe to exist is to argue that man can never comprehend the existence of the universe. The theist demands a causal explanation of the universe and then fails to provide an explanation. Even if a supernatural being did exist, the "problem" of existence would be as puzzling as before. After all, how did it create existence from nonexistence? "Somehow" is not an explanation, and "through some incomprehensible means" is a poorer explanation still. The theist is trapped in a dilemma of his own making—the "mystery" of existence—and he must confront an unintelligible universe.

(3) Are the premises of the first-cause argument true? Does the universe require a causal explanation?

In considering the causal argument as a whole, one contradiction immediately stands out. The first premise of this argument states that everything must have a cause, and the conclusion asserts the existence of an uncaused supernatural being. But if *everything* must have a cause, how did god become exempt? Professor John Hospers points out the contradictory nature of the first-cause argument:

> . . . the causal argument is not merely invalid but self-contradictory: the conclusion, which says that something (God) does not have a cause, contradicts the premise, which says that everything does have a cause. If that premise is true, the conclusion cannot be true; and if the conclusion is true, the premise cannot be. Many people do not at once see this because they use the argument to get to God, and then, having arrived where they want to go, they forget all about the argument . . . if the conclusion contradicts its own premise, we have the most damning indictment of an argument that we could possibly have: that it is self-contradictory.[2]

In *The Necessity of Atheism*, David Brooks makes a similar criticism:

> By predicating a First Cause . . . the theist removes the mystery a stage further back. This First Cause they assume to be a cause that was not caused and this First Cause is God. Such a belief is a logical absurdity, and is an example of the ancient custom of creating a mystery to explain a mystery. If everything must have a cause, then the First Cause must be caused and therefore: Who made God? To say that this First Cause always existed is to deny the basic assumption of this "Theory." Moreover, if it is rea-

sonable to assume a First Cause as having always existed, why is it unreasonable to assume that the materials of the universe always existed? To explain the unknown by the known is a logical procedure; to explain the known by the unknown is a form of theological lunacy.[3]

The contradiction in the causal argument stems from its basic flaw: its demand for a causal explanation of the universe, the totality of existence.

When one asks for the cause of something, whether it be an entity or event, one is asking for the entity or action of an entity (prior event) that caused it. Causal explanation is possible only within the context of existence. Nathaniel Branden writes:

> Within the universe, the emergence of new entities can be explained in terms of the actions of entities that already exist. . . . All actions presuppose the existence of entities—and all emergences of new entities presuppose the existence of entities that caused their emergence. All causality presupposes the existence of *something that acts as a cause.* To demand a cause for all of existence is to demand a contradiction: if the cause exists, it is part of existence; if it does not exist, it cannot be a cause. . . . Causality presupposes existence, existence does not presuppose causality. . . . Existence—not "God"—is the First Cause.[4]

This passage demonstrates that the causal argument drops the epistemological context that gives meaning to the concept of causality. "What caused the universe?" is an absurd question, because before something can act as a cause, it must first exist—*i.e.*, it must first be part of the universe. The universe sets the foundation for causal explanation and cannot itself require a causal explanation.

The primacy of existence is illustrated in science by the principle that matter can neither be created nor destroyed. J. S. Mill hinted at the above objection to the causal argument when he stated that, "As a fact of experience . . . causation cannot legitimately be extended to the material universe itself, but only to its changeable phenomena. . . ."[5] Chapman Cohen, a noted English atheist, commented that discussing causality outside the context of the universe "is like discussing a bird's flight in the absence of an atmosphere."[6]

The universe, then, has always existed and always will exist. Some theists find this difficult to accept, and they argue that god makes the universe easier to understand. Yet, while the theist complains of difficulty accepting the notion of an eternally existing universe, consider his alternative. We must conceive of a supernatural, unknowable, eternally existing being, and, moreover, we must conceive of this being creating matter from the void of nonexistence. It is strange that those who object to the idea of eternal matter display little difficulty in accepting the creation of something out of nothing. While the idea of an eternal universe may be initially difficult for some people to assimilate, the theist's alternative is an exercise in fantasy.

Until the theist is able to discuss causality in terms of nonexistence, his demand for a cause of the universe will remain nonsensical—and he will be unable to escape the contradictory nature of the causal argument.

(4) Where does the atheist stand on the possibility of an infinite regress of causes? Is such a thing possible?

To clarify this issue, it is helpful to distinguish between a "first cause" and a "causal primary." A first cause, in the context of the present discussion, refers to being which is uncaused, but which caused the universe to exist at some point in time. For reasons already presented, this notion is logically absurd.

A causal primary, on the other hand, is the metaphysical basis for the concept of causality. It does not require explanation, because it makes explanation possible; it is the basis of all causal interactions. Existence, the causal primary, is presupposed by all causal processes—all motion and change—and therefore must be regarded as existing eternally.

While there must be a causal primary for there to be causality, there is no need for a first cause in time. There is no reason why a succession of changes cannot proceed infinitely into the past. As long as we remember that existence had no beginning in time, there is no problem in grasping that change, a natural corollary of existence, had no beginning as well.

But, the theist may argue, without a first cause of change, there would be no second cause, third cause, or presently existing causes. But since causal processes are presently occurring, there must have been a first cause in time.

This rejoinder is partially correct. Without a first cause, there cannot be a second cause, third cause, and so on. In other words, without a first cause, we cannot assign a numerical designation to each causal process. This does not entail, however, that causal interactions could not presently exist.

In order to assign a numerical designation (such as second, tenth, one thousandth) to any causal process, one must presuppose the existence of a first cause. After all, to call something the tenth cause means that there were nine causes preceding it, so there must have been a first cause in this series. Consequently, this tactic, since it relies on the prior acceptance of a first cause, must be rejected as blatant question begging.

From the fact that causal series extend infinitely into the past, it follows that we cannot assign sequential numbers to each causal process. But it does not follow from this that causality cannot occur. The issue of numerical designations is irrelevant to causality.

In the final analysis, the temporal version of the first cause argument must be rejected as muddled, contradictory and, at times, simply irrelevant. The case for rational theism must look elsewhere for support.

II

The Sustaining First Cause

A second version of the first-cause argument, though not generally used by laymen, is popular among philosophical theists (and Thomists in particular). These theists do not maintain that an infinite regress of temporal causes is impossible;

242

indeed, even Aquinas conceded the philosophical possibility of an eternally existing universe. These theists defend another kind of causal argument, one that views causality in a hierarchical sense.

According to this argument, god is not the cause of the universe in the sense that a father is the cause of his son, because the present existence of the son does not depend on the continued existence of the father. The father may die, but the son will remain—just as, if a first cause in time ceased to exist, the universe would remain.

This argument contends that god is the cause of the universe in the same way that "the activity of the pen tracing these words on the page is here and now dependent on the activity of my hand, which in turn is here and now dependent on other factors."[7] We must posit a sustaining first cause, a being who acts as a kind of metaphysical underpinning for existence. The universe is presently dependent on this cause; if the cause ceased to exist, so would the universe.

This conception of causality will seem foreign to anyone not versed in the metaphysics of Aristotle and Thomas Aquinas, so it is best to allow the proponents of this argument to speak for themselves. Here is part of the formulation by Aquinas:

> In the world of sense we find there is an order of efficient causes. There is no case known (nor indeed, is it possible) in which a thing is found to be the efficient cause of itself, because in that case it would be prior to itself, which is impossible. Now in efficient causes it is not possible to go on to infinity . . . if in efficient causes it is possible to go on to infinity, there will be no first efficient cause, neither will there be an ultimate effect, nor any intermediate efficient causes, all of which is plainly false. Therefore it is necessary to admit a first efficient cause, to which everyone gives the name of God.[8]

This argument begins with the observation that "there is an order of efficient causes." This is the premise on which the argument depends. In explaining the meaning of "order" as Aquinas uses it, F. C. Copleston writes:

> ... when Aquinas talks about an "order" of efficient causes he is not thinking of a series stretching back into the past, but of a hierarchy of causes, in which a subordinate member is here and now dependent on the causal activity of a higher member. ...
>
> We have to imagine, not a lineal or horizontal series, so to speak, but a vertical hierarchy, in which a lower member depends here and now on the present causal activity of the member above it. It is the latter type of series, if prolonged to infinity, which Aquinas rejects. And he rejects it on the ground that unless there is a first member, ... a cause which does not itself depend on the causal activity of a higher cause, it is not possible to explain the ... causal activity of the lowest member.
>
> ... Suppress the first efficient cause and there is no causal activity here and now ... The word "first" does not mean first in the temporal order, but supreme or first in the ontological order.[9]

Because of its complex Thomistic background, this argument is rather difficult to discuss in a nontechnical manner. The interested reader may consult other sources if he wishes to pursue it at length. We shall discuss only a few general points.

(1) This argument avoids a major pitfall of the temporal causal argument. If the premises are true, and the conclusion validly follows, the theist has established the *present* existence of a first cause—something the previous version was incapable of.

Not all of the previous problems have been surmounted, however. Even if valid, this causal argument cannot demonstrate the existence of a living, conscious being, so it is of limited value at best.

(2) A major problem with this argument, put simply, is understanding it. What does it mean to say that there is a hierarchial structure of causes existing in the universe?

Aquinas is of no help here. After carefully examining the original intent of this argument, Anthony Kenny concludes that Aquinas believed in an intimate correlation between the activity of the "heavenly bodies" and the activity of man. Man is inexorably intertwined, so to speak, with the rest of the universe. Therefore, the causal series on which Aquinas based his argument "is a series whose existence is vouched for only by medieval astrology." Whereas other cosmological arguments begin with facts about the universe, this one, asserts Kenny, "starts from an archaic fiction."[10]

Despite this medieval framework, however, modern theologians have attempted to salvage the causal argument. A common illustration of hierarchical causality (similar to one suggested by Aquinas) is a hammer in the process of driving a nail into a block of wood. Here we have series of causal interactions—the arm moving the hammer, the hammer driving the nail, etc.—and without a starting point of motion, an apex of the series, none of the subordinate causes would occur.

It is not at all clear how this illustration (or any similar to it) is supposed to apply to the universe. The causal series in this example terminates with the man who is holding the hammer, and there is no indication that any similar series permeates nature. At this point, some theologians appeal to the interdependence of natural phenomena. Here is an example from *Modern Thomistic Philosophy* by R. P. Phillips:

> ... life is dependent, *inter alia,* on a certain atmospheric pressure, this again on the continual operation of physical forces, whose being and operation depends on the position of the earth in the solar system, which itself must endure relatively unchanged.[11]

This example is of no help. While it is true that there is causal interdependence among various aspects of the universe, this interdependence can be explained solely with reference to causal processes extending across a span of time. Moreover, this causal interdependence always occurs within the context of the natural universe, whereas the theist wishes to move from the natural to the supernatural. Matter and energy are the basic constituents of the natural universe—the framework in which causal dependence occurs—but the theist wishes to make these components themselves causally dependent upon some supernatural agency. This is a far cry from an illustration that appeals to common facts about the universe.

Finally, in explaining the meaning of a hierarchical series of causes, James Ross has suggested the following:

> . . . in a stack of bricks the one which holds up the top one exercises its causality in holding the top one where it is only by virtue of the fact that the bricks under it are holding it up, and so on down through the whole stack. Such an ordering of causality is an essential ordering. [12]

This illustration is more successful than the previous attempts. Here we do have a structure of causal relationships in which each cause (*i.e.*, each brick) depends on the existence of a previous cause (*i.e.*, a lower brick). Unless there were a first brick, a foundation for the series, the stack would collapse.

While this example clarifies the notion of hierarchical causality, it has no applicability to the natural universe. If the universe consisted of solid chunks of matter, each resting against the next, then this analogy might serve some purpose. Perhaps we could infer a basic brick of the universe, and perhaps we would choose to call this brick "god." In the context of the present universe, however, the above illustration is useless.

Antony Flew correctly notes that the hierarchical first-cause argument retains its superficial persuasiveness only as long as we "continue to think in the familiar terms of temporally successive links in causal chains. . . ."[13] After we remove the concept of causality from this context, we cannot assume that there is an "order" of causes in the universe. The theist must demonstrate, not assume, that such an order exists. Before he can accomplish this, however, he must explain what he means by hierarchical causality. If we are told that Atlas supports the world on his shoulders and thereby "sustains" it, we at least get a rough idea of what is meant by "sustains." But when the theist tells us that god sustains the universe, or when he tells us that god is the first cause of a mysterious hierarchy, we are not presented with an intelligible explanation of the subject being discussed.

(3) Like all cosmological proofs, this first-cause argument attacks the primacy of existence. According to the theist, the continuing existence of the natural universe requires a causal explanation, and he offers "god" as his explanation. We have already discussed the inability of "god" to function as an explanatory concept, so there is no need to repeat it here. Similarly, this argument shares the same basic flaws as the previous first-cause argument: the premise, which states that everything must have a sustaining cause, contradicts the conclusion, which posits an uncaused god. If the theist has no difficulty accepting an uncaused god, why does he complain when asked to accept an uncaused universe? There is absolutely no evidence to suggest that the natural universe is in any way dependent upon some supernatural agency. On the contrary, the concept of causality makes sense only *within* the context of the natural universe, and to demand a cause of the universe is nonsensical.

The argument for a sustaining first cause is similar in many respects to the so-called contingency argument for the existence of god. Thus, many of the forthcoming comments concerning the contingency argument will pertain to the present discussion as well.

III

The Contingency Argument

The contingency argument is generally considered to be the most sophisticated of the cosmological proofs for the existence of a god. Its structure is similar to the causal argument, but it attempts to establish the existence of a "necessary being" rather than a first cause.

The classical statement of the contingency argument—the third of the "Five Ways" of Aquinas—is so drenched in Thomistic metaphysics that the modern reader often finds it difficult to understand. Because there are technical problems entailed by Aquinas's presentation, we shall consider a simplified version of this argument. In a celebrated debate with Bertrand Russell, the Catholic philosopher F. C. Copleston summarized the contingency argument as follows:

> First of all . . . we know that there are at least some beings in the world which do not contain in themselves the reason for their existence. For example, I depend on my parents, and now on the air, and on food, and so on. Now, secondly, the world is simply the real or imagined totality or aggregate of individual objects, none of which contain in themselves alone the reason for their existence. . . . since objects or events exist, and since no object of experience contains within itself the reason of its existence, this reason, the totality of objects, must have a reason external to itself. That reason must be an existent being. Well, this being is either itself the reason for its own existence, or it is not. If it is, well and good. If it is not, then we must proceed farther. But if we proceed to infinity in that sense, then there's no explanation of existence at all. So, I should say, in order to explain existence, we must come to a being which contains within itself the reason for its own existence, that is to say, which cannot not-exist. [14]

248

Copleston is clearly searching for an "explanation of existence." According to his argument, nothing within the natural universe is capable of explaining its own existence; nothing exists necessarily. Rather, everything within the universe depends on something else for its existence; everything is contingent. But, he argues, if we are to explain the fact of existence, we cannot be content with an infinite series of contingent beings. Instead, we must posit the existence of a being who exists independently of all other beings, a being who exists necessarily, a being who cannot not-exist.

> ... if there were no necessary being, no being which must exist, and cannot not-exist, nothing would exist. ... Something does exist; therefore, there must be something which accounts for this fact, a being which is outside the series of contingent beings.[15]

The contingency argument echoes the familiar strain of the cosmological arguments: Why existence rather than nonexistence? When Russell objected to the contingency argument on the basis that "the concept of cause is not applicable to the total," and, therefore, "the universe is just there, and that's all," Copleston replied, "Why something rather than nothing, that is the question."[16]

As we have seen, this last question is epistemologically absurd. If one drops the context of existence, one abandons the possibility of explanation. The question "Why?" demands a causal explanation, and the concept of causality presupposes something that acts as a causal agent. Copleston's question is loaded with theistic presuppositions; to grant it legitimacy is to concede that existence is not a causal primary. Yet, this is the central issue. How can the theist hope to make sense of causality divorced from existence?

The contingency argument thus shares the fallacy common to all cosmological arguments: it ignores the context, the conceptual framework, from which the concepts of "explanation" and "causality" derive their meaning. These concepts have no meaning if removed from the context of existence, and the theist's demand for a cause or explanation of the universe reduces to nonsense.

It is interesting to examine the methodology employed by Copleston in the contingency argument. Is he claiming, as an experienced fact, that the universe is contingent upon something else for its existence? This appears to be the case when he states that "at least some beings in the world . . . do not contain in themselves the reason for their existence." Copleston then offers the dependency of man as an illustration of contingency, which presumably can be verified by any impartial observer. Yet, just a few sentences later, Copleston states that "*no* object of experience contains within itself the reason of its existence." He has made a transition from specific instances to a generalization without any attempt to justify this move.

While we do observe the causal dependency of specific entities within the universe, we do not observe a similar dependency with regard to matter itself. We do not observe the creation or annihilation of matter, so the claim that the universe as a whole is contingent cannot be supported by factual evidence. On the contrary, empirical evidence points to matter as a metaphysical primary, which cuts the ground from under any attempt to establish the contingency of the universe by empirical means.

Copleston argues that, because specific entities within the universe depend upon other factors for their existence, the universe as such—the totality of existence—must also depend upon something else, namely, a "necessary being." If we add up a number of contingent entities, the sum total—the universe—must also be contingent.

However, Copleston has *not* established that *everything* within the universe is dependent upon something else. On the contrary, the existence of matter is unconditional—there is nothing else for it to depend on. The contingency argument is made plausible only by the ambiguity when we say that something has ceased to exist.

It is true that man would cease to exist if the Sun moved away from the Earth, but this does not mean that man would collapse into nonexistence, that the constituent elements of his body would completely disappear. Rather, the chemical composites that form the entity "man" would decompose, and the functions of this entity (such as respiration and consciousness) would cease to exist. Functions of the human body cannot exist apart from the body, and the sustenance of man's body depends upon the fulfillment of specific conditions (such as food and temperature). When we say that a man ceases to exist, we mean that a particular molecular composition and its corresponding attributes no longer exist. We do not mean that the material components of the entity man disappear into nonexistence.

At the risk of sounding Aristotelian, we may say that the entity "man" represents a certain form of existence, and this form is contingent upon causal conditions; but the substance of man, the irreducible atomic consituents that comprise man, do not depend upon anything. They do not risk disappearance, nor do they exist because something else exists; they simply exist.

A major flaw in the contingency argument lies in its artificial dichotomy between necessary and contingent existence. To say that something exists contingently makes sense only within the sphere of volitional action. So, for example, we might say that a building exists contingently, meaning that, if certain men had decided to act differently, the building would never have been constructed. With this exception, however, the idea of contingent existence has no application. Everything exists necessarily.[17]

In using the distinction between necessary and contingent existence as part of his argument, the theist smuggles in a crucial premise. He assumes that there are, in effect, two kinds of existence: deficient and sufficient. He then argues that the universe is metaphysically deficient, that it does not exist necessarily, so we must infer the existence of a transcendent necessary being. Thus, in his original distinction between necessary and contingent existence, the theist assumes beforehand that natural existence requires an explanation.

In using the necessary-contingent dichotomy in his argument, the theist is asking that a major point of controversy be conceded to him without argument. If the dichotomy is challenged, the contingency argument can go nowhere. If one rejects the notion of contingent existence (in the sense here described),

251

there is no reason to posit a transcendent, necessary being. As Copleston puts it, "if one refuses even to sit down at the chess-board and make a move, one cannot, of course, be checkmated." [18]

Finally, we should mention the underlying dogma of the contingency argument: the so-called "principle of sufficient reason." According to this principle, there must be a sufficient reason, an explanation, for the existence of everything. Many theists accept this principle as axiomatic, claiming that it is an essential ingredient of rationality. But, as we shall be further from the ... is false; not everything ... emphasized, the natural ... explanation is possible, so the concept of explanation cannot legitimately be extended to the universe as a whole. Even the advocate of sufficient reason cannot adhere to this principle consistently: after applying it to the universe, the theist attempts to offer god as an exception to the principle, usually under the guise that god is his own sufficient reason for existing. But if god can be his own sufficient reason, there is no basis on which to argue that the universe cannot likewise be its own sufficient reason, in which case there is no need to posit god in the first place.

This discussion has touched on only a few objections to the contingency argument, but since the preceding remarks are adequate to point out its ambiguities and its theistic presuppositions, there is no need to belabor minor details. The contingency argument is among the most confusing and irrational of the alleged proofs for god. More than any other, it explicitly attacks the primacy of existence. And this opens the door for epistemological chaos.

IV

The Entropy Argument

Entropy, a word coined by the German physicist Rudolf Clausius (1822-1888), refers to the unavailability of energy in a closed system (*i.e.*, a system that does not permit the escape or

252

transfer of energy). The units of entropy are calories per degree Celsius, arrived at, roughly, by dividing the heat energy of a system by the temperature of the hottest object in the system. More simply, entropy pertains to the degree of randomness or disorganization is a closed system; maximum entropy would be a state of perfect equilibrium.

Since the latter part of the nineteenth century, some theologians and physicists have used the entropy concept coupled with the Second Law of Thermodynamics as a kind of modern cosmological argument for the existence of a god. Briefly, the Second Law of Thermodynamics states that, in a closed system, entropy tends toward a maximum; there is an increase in randomness, a tendency toward equilibrium and, consequently, a decrease of available energy.

For example, heat is caused by the movement of molecules; the faster the average movement of the molecules, the hotter the object. If a hot object is brought into contact with a cold object, there will be a transfer of heat from the hot object to the cold object caused by the collision of molecules. As the faster molecules collide with the slower ones, there is an overall leveling of the temperatures as the faster molecules decrease in velocity and the slower molecules increase in velocity. The net result of this will be an equalization of temperatures as the two objects approach equilibrium. This is called an increase in entropy.

Clausius proposed a forerunner of the entropy argument when he predicted the eventual "heat-death" of the universe, which asserted (in the words of Arthur Koestler) "that the universe is running down like clockwork affected by metal fatigue, because its energy is being steadily, inexorably degraded, dissipated into heat, until it will finally dissolve into a single, shapeless, homogeneous bubble of gas of uniform temperature just above absolute zero, inert and motionless. . . ."[19]

Since, according to this view, the universe is "running down," it was only a matter of time until someone suggested that the universe must have been "wound up," energetically speaking, at some time in the past. And who did the winding? It is at this point that we have god, the great energy winder, thrust upon us as an explanation. "The universe as we know it, by the aid of modern science," writes David Trueblood, "could not have originated without the action of a creative Source of energy outside itself. . . ." Therefore, "Science, instead of undermining belief in God, today becomes the first witness."[20]

A recent statement of this argument was made by John Robbins in *The Intercollegiate Review:*

> . . . if the existence of the eternal personal tran-
> scendent God is denied, then there is no alternative
> but to maintain that the material universe has existed
> infinitely backwards in time, and will exist infinitely
> forwards. . . . But if the physical universe has existed
> for an infinite amount of time, there could be no
> order, no complexity, nothing except evenly distri-
> buted atoms in space. Infinite time, coupled with the
> Second Law of Thermodynamics, must yield infinite
> randomness, i.e., zero organization. There could cer-
> tainly be no stars and planets, and most certainly no
> men.[21]

Two fallacies are obvious in this argument, even to the person unfamiliar with physics. First, Robbins wishes to make some mysterious creature responsible for a primordial state of minimum entropy, from which he claims the universe is now running down. But even if this were true, how does Robbins arrive at the dubious attributes of eternal, personal and transcendent? At best, the entropy argument is capable only of demonstrating the existence of some primitive energy source, and this source need bear no resemblance to the Christian God.

Second, Robbins, like most advocates of the entropy argument, is inconsistent. Is the Second Law of Thermodynamics an inexorable law of nature? Yes, according to Robbins, because it "has never been contradicted." Never? Then what prevented his eternal, personal and transcendent god from suffering a gruesome heat-death? If the Second Law is not applicable to god, it is not inexorable. If this is so, on what grounds can the theist assert that the Second Law applies to the entire universe and cannot, under any circumstances, be contradicted?

The universe has not "run down"; on this, theists and atheists can agree. Thus, the question arises: "Why?" The theist, true to the style of primitive man who explained lightning by inventing a lightning god, posits an anti-entropic god. Rather than re-examine his application of the Second Law of Thermodynamics, the theist prefers to argue that it applies without exception—and he then posits an exception to it *as an explanation*. But positing god, for this or any other problem, is not an explanation. It is an evasion, and a poor one besides. If the theist cannot solve the entropy problem, a simple "I don't know" would be much more honest.

Reconciling the Second Law of Thermodynamics with the present state of the universe is not as hopeless as theists like to pretend. To begin with, the Second Law is a statement of statistical probability, and there is nothing inherently contra-dictory in supposing that a closed system can decrease in entropy or fluctuate between increasing and decreasing entropy states. But this probability, while metaphysically possible, is extremely unlikely, so it is usually ignored in practical applications.

More importantly, however, the Second Law pertains only to closed systems, which, according to many physicists, renders it inapplicable to the universe as a whole. Professor Grünbaum, a physicist, writes:

> An inherent limitation on the applicability of the . . . entropy concept to the entire universe lies in the fact that it has no applicability at all to a *spatially* infinite universe. . . . [22]

Professor E. A. Milne, commenting on another physicist's acceptance of the heat-death thesis, writes:

> Jeans's own studies in the realm of the second law of thermodynamics were all concerned with the kinetic theory of gases, in which the specimen under dis-cussion is supposed walled around in a finite vessel;

and to such systems the notion of a heat-death is applicable. But by no means is the same result to be predicted of the whole universe. [23]

Finally, according to Landau and Lifshitz, authors of *Statistical Physics*:

> . . . in the general theory of relativity the universe as a whole must be regarded not as a closed system, but as one which is in a variable gravitational field. In this case the application of the law of increase of entropy does not imply the necessity of statistical equilibrium. [24]

Since the concept of entropy can be defined only with reference to closed systems, it cannot legitimately be applied to the universe as a whole. The theist takes a scientific principle derived from a specific context, and attempts to shift this context in order to manufacture a need for god. In the name of science, the theist posits a "god of the gaps," a god who allegedly fills in the gaps of human knowledge. But gaps of knowledge eventually close, leaving god without a home.

The entropy argument is a cosmological argument draped in scientific jargon—but an invalid argument, even when presented in scientific terms, is still invalid.

10.
The Design
Arguments

The label "design argument" includes a family of arguments which differ in details, but which share a common approach: each attempts to infer the existence of a divine intelligence, a master planner, from alleged evidences of planning in nature. If it can be shown that nature exhibits design, we must conclude that nature had a designer with intelligence and immense power. And this seems to be an excellent candidate for a god.

The design argument has more appeal than the cosmological proofs, probably because it seems more straightforward and forceful at first glance. If we accept the premise that the universe displays planning, the inference to a master designer follows with irrefutable logic (unlike the premise of the first-cause argument where, even if we accept the basic premise of existence—which we must—the inference to a first cause does not follow automatically).

Of course, the problem with any version of the design argu-ment is that the theist must demonstrate that the universe displays intelligent planning. This is the crux of the argument, and this is what needs to be proven. For this reason, the so-called argument *from* design is perhaps better described, as Antony Flew suggests, as the argument *to* design—*i.e.*, as an argument to demonstrate the presence of design in the first place.

We shall now examine three common versions of the design argument, and we shall see how each argument totally fails to make its case.

I

The Teleological Argument

The teleological argument (from the Greek *telos* meaning "end" or "goal") attempts to establish that natural entities act in such a way as to achieve ends or goals, and that these ends cannot be the result of blind chance. Therefore, we must conclude that these entities fall under the direction of an intelligence, god, who prescribes these ends, just as human beings prescribe ends on a lesser scale. A succinct statement of this argument is found in the classic formulation by Thomas Aquinas:

> We see that things which lack knowledge, such as natural bodies, act for an end, and this is evident from their acting always, or nearly always, in the same way, so as to obtain the best result. Hence it is plain that they achieve their end not by chance, but by design. Now whatever lacks knowledge cannot move towards an end, unless it be directed by some being endowed with knowledge and intelligence; as the arrow is directed by the archer. Therefore some intelligent being exists by whom all natural things are directed to their end; and this being we call God.[1]

Aquinas follows the metaphysics of Aristotle in many respects, but this argument runs against the grain of Aristotle's thought. While Aristotle applied the idea of final causation (*i.e.*, explanation in terms of ends) to nature, he regarded these ends as inherent in nature, rather than as being imposed by an external agent. According to Aristotle, each entity tends to develop in the direction of its natural end—such as with an acorn which, under a given set of circumstances, will naturally grow into an oak tree.[2] For Aquinas, however, the fact that acorns continue to grow into oaks, the fact that nature exhibits regularity, constitutes evidence of divine guidance. Apparently, without the assistance of god, nature would degenerate into chaotic randomness.

(1) Let us grant the premises of this argument and see where it leads. Order is exhibited in nature; order requires a designer; therefore, god exists. Surely, the wondrous regularity of nature—where acorns grow into trees and planets revolve around the sun—cannot be the result of mere chance. There must be a master planner at work.

It is now up to the theist to answer the question: Who designed god? Surely, nothing as complex and intricate as a supernatural intelligence can be the result of mere "chance." Therefore, there must be a super-designer who designed god. But a super-designer would require a super-super-designer, and so on *ad infinitum*. Thus, by the premises of the teleological argument, we are led to an infinite series of transcendental designers—a "solution" that leaves much to be desired. If an orderly universe requires explanation, the positing of a god does not provide it.

(2) According to Aquinas, natural bodies "act for an end" in the sense that, given the same circumstances, they will always act in the same way. (His statement that they "obtain the best result," aside from being irrelevant, is simply false. Do the bacteria which cause malaria, typhoid and other diseases "obtain the best result"? For whom?)

The crux of the teleological argument—and its fundamental

error—lies in the assumption that order presupposes conscious design (where "order" refers to the regularity in nature). This is demonstrably false. It is true that order exists in the universe, that there is regularity in nature, that entities will behave in the same way under the same circumstances—but it is *not* valid to infer from this the existence of any master designer. On the contrary, order is simply the manifestation of causality, and causality is a derivative, a logical corollary, of the Law of Identity.

To exist is to exist as something, and to be something is to possess specific, determinate characteristics. In other words, every existing thing has identity: it is what it is and not something else. To say that something has determinate characteristics is to say that it has a limited nature, and these limits necessarily restrict its range of possible actions. The nature of an entity determines what it can do in a given set of circumstances. In *An Introduction to Logic*, H. W. B. Joseph writes:

> ... to say that the same thing acting on the same thing under the same conditions may yet produce a different effect, is to say that a thing need not be what it is. But this is in flat conflict with the Law of Identity. A thing, to be at all, must be something, and can only be what it is. To assert a causal connection between 'a' and 'x' implies 'a' acts as it does because it is what it is; because, in fact, it is 'a.' So long therefore as it is 'a,' it must act thus; and to assert that it may act otherwise on a subsequent occasion is to assert that what is 'a' is something else than the 'a' which it is declared to be.[3]

It is a mistake to confuse "order" with "design." If there is design in nature, there must be a designer, but the same is not true of order. Order does not presuppose an orderer; it is simply entailed by the nature of existence itself.

(3) Exactly what does the theist imagine the universe would be like if it was not guided by a master planner? What would a

disordered universe be like? What would an acorn do?—grow into a stone, perhaps, and then into a theologian? If an acorn did grow into a stone, it would have to possess qualities radically different from what we now designate by the term "acorn," in which case it would cease to be an "acorn" in any meaningful sense.

Once we accept the fact of existence, we must also accept the fact that things are what they are (identity), and that they behave as they do in virtue of what they are (causality). The theist's choice between chance and design is a false alternative. Because the order of nature is not a result of planning, it does not follow that it is the consequence of mere "chance." Metaphysically speaking, there is no such thing as "chance." Occurrences do not "just happen" inexplicably, without causes. We speak of "chance" when we are unaware of all relevant factors, such as when we say that the result of a coin toss is a matter of chance. But this simply means that, within one's context of knowledge, the outcome of the toss is unknown. Nevertheless, causal conditions are at work, and if we were armed with the necessary knowledge—such as the velocity, height and angle of the toss—a prediction of the result would be possible. The concept of "chance" is epistemological, not metaphysical.

The real alternative facing us in the design argument is between *natural necessity* and supernatural caprice. According to the naturalist, the universe exhibits order because order is one aspect of existence; the two are inseparable. According to the theist, the universe is inherently unstable and chaotic, but god, an unknowable being, somehow glues it together using unspecified and unknowable means. Once again, the choice between naturalism and supernaturalism is a choice between reason and magic.

It is interesting to observe that if an event appears to contravene the order of nature, the theist is the first to proclaim that a natural law has been violated and that this miraculous event is evidence of a supernatural influence. Yet this same theist will appeal to the presence of order and natural law as evidence for god as well. If nature is *not* uniform, this proves the existence of god. If nature *is* uniform, this also proves the existence of god. Whichever way we turn, god gets the credit, which, of course, is remarkably convenient for the theist. In the typical style of theology, all exits are covered, contrary evidence is defined out of existence, and the theist is insulated from attack. This is a clear case of eating one's cake and having it, too.

In the final analysis, the teleological argument has everything backwards. An orderly universe is precisely one in which there is no room for supernatural influence; to admit the existence of order is to eliminate the need for a god. When the French astronomer Laplace was asked by Napoleon why he did not mention God in his writing, Laplace answered, "Sire, I have no need of that hypothesis." And neither does anyone else.

If acorns start growing into theologians, or if women begin turning into pillars of salt, then we may wish to hypothesize about a supernatural influence. But until such time as nature becomes hopelessly unintelligible and unpredictable, we need look no further than nature itself for explanations.

II

The Analogical Argument

The analogical argument from design consists of drawing an analogy between natural objects and man-made artifacts. According to the theist, both of these display the intricate adjustment of various parts, so we are justified in supposing that the natural objects, like the man-made artifacts, are the product of conscious design.

This argument is often associated with William Paley (1743-1805), who popularized it with his famous example of a watch. Suppose, he argues, that one were to find a watch on the ground. How would one go about determining its origin?

> ... when we come to inspect the watch, we perceive ... that its several parts are framed and put together for a purpose, *e.g.*, that they are so formed

and adjusted as to produce motion, and that motion so regulated as to point out the hour of the day; that, if the different parts had been differently shaped from what they are, of a different size from what they are, or placed after any other manner, or in any other order, than that in which they are placed, either no motion at all would have been carried on in the machine, or none which would have answered the use that is now served by it.

... the inference, we think, is inevitable, that the watch must have had a maker; that there must have existed, at some time, and at some place or other, an artificer or artificers, who formed it for the purpose which we find it actually to answer; who comprehended its construction, and designed its use.[4]

Paley extends this illustration to the natural universe, which he contends must also have been designed by a master intelligence.

... every indication of contrivance, every manifestation of design, which existed in the watch, exists in the works of nature; with the difference, on the side of nature, of being greater and more, and that in a degree which exceeds all computation.[5]

Many objects are commonly appealed to as evidence of design in nature, the most popular of which is the human or animal eye. The eye is immensely complex, and each of its many components must function in unison with other components in order to produce vision. With this intricate adjustment of parts, we have the adaptation of means to the end of vision. Therefore, concludes the theist, we must infer the existence of a designer, just as we did in the case of the watch. Similarly, when we observe the many elaborate structures and adaptations in nature as a whole, we must conclude that nature itself is the product of intelligent planning. The blind forces of nature cannot explain such wonders.

263

(1) A number of weak objections have been made against this argument. Some philosophers point out that this argument, even if valid, does not establish the existence of only *one* designer, so it may be used with equal force to prove polytheism. Of course, since our concern is only with the truth of theism generally (*i.e.*, the existence of one or more gods), this criticism is irrelevant.

Philosophers have also maintained that the analogical argument, if valid, only establishes the existence of a master designer, not necessarily an omnipotent creator (such as the God of Christianity). But this objection misses the point. In most cases, the analogical argument does not even purport to establish the existence of an omnipotent creator (especially as used by modern theologians). The primary purpose of the design argument is to establish that the universe is not causally self-contained, that we must look to a supernatural power as an explanation for natural phenomena. To criticize this argument on the grounds that it proves only a designer, not a creator, is a concession, not a criticism.

A similar objection with more to recommend it is that the analogical argument, if valid, does not necessarily point to the existence of a *supernatural* being. It is possible that the designer is a natural creature with superior capacities, in which case the design argument would be incapable of crumbling the naturalistic premise. And, strictly speaking, the designer would not be a "god." (See Chapter 2.)

Finally, it has been suggested that the analogical argument cannot establish the *present* existence of a master designer. Few exponents of the design argument maintain that god personally supervises each natural occurrence. Rather, god is said to have directed natural forces in such a way that they continue to operate on their own accord. On this basis, however, there is no reason to suppose that the master designer is still alive; he may have died some time ago (just as a machine may continue to function long after its manufacturer has died).

(2) An interesting sidelight to this argument is the fact that the objects or events which are offered as evidences of design

are always things which man considers good or desirable. As W. T. Stace explains:

> The argument never selects as proving design those complicated trains of causes which produce blindness in some persons or animals; or the causes which produce, not life, but death. If a city is wrecked by a tidal wave and thousands of its inhabitants are drowned, or any other train of events produces a human disaster, such cases are never chosen as instances which prove design.
>
> But it is obvious that the causes in such cases are just as complex as are the causes which produce valuable things, and that they co-operate with one another and are adjusted to one another to produce the effects which they do produce. . . . Why then are not the evil things chosen as showing design as well as the valuable things?[6]

Most theists assume that the analogical argument, if valid, works in their favor by demonstrating the existence of a benevolent deity. But, as Stace points out, if we admit the desirable aspects of nature as products of design, we must also admit the undesirable aspects of nature as products of design. And this puts the theist in a difficult position How can he justify a god who purposefully inflicts natural disasters upon man? The theist who accepts this design argument must confront the problem of evil head-on (see Chapter 3). The master designer could very well be a demon or mischievous elf.

(3) Paley's design argument is open to a number of more serious objections. To begin with, what does the theist mean when he says that both natural and man-made objects display the adaptation of means to ends? What does the theist mean by "end"?

If, by "end," the theist is calling our attention to the regularity in nature, if he is pointing to the uniform behavior of natural entities, then he is simply pointing to examples of identity and causality which, as previously indicated, are necessary corollaries of existence. There is no argument here; everything, whether man-made or natural, is subject to identity and causality. These characterize all of existence, not merely artifacts. So while it is true that artificial and manufactured objects share the characteristic of resulting in certain ends (in the sense here described), this is irrelevant to whether or not they are the product of conscious intent.

What else might the theist mean by "end"? One basic alternative remains. He may wish to make "end" synonymous with "purpose." When he claims that natural objects display the adaptation of means to ends, he may mean that various aspects of nature cooperate in pursuit of a given purpose. But this is flagrant question begging. It is precisely the existence of purpose in nature that the theist must demonstrate, so he obviously cannot appeal to the "purpose" in nature as one of his premises.

This brings us to a fundamental objection. The inferential process represented in the design argument is the reverse of what actually occurs. We conclude that a watch is the result of design, not because we see "that its several parts are framed and put together for a purpose," but because we know by direct experience that watches are made by men. We do not, as Paley insists, infer that a watch is man-made because we perceive design in it; rather, we infer that a watch is designed because we know it is man-made. As Professor Wallace Matson points out in his excellent critique of the design argument:

> Proponents of the design argument take it for granted that the properties according to which we judge whether or not some object is an artifact, are accurate adjustment of parts and curious adapting of means to ends. But this is not the way we judge, even provisionally, whether something is an artifact or not. This is clear from our being able to tell whether something is an artifact without knowing what it is for or whether its parts are accurately adjusted.[7]

According to Matson, if human visitors on another planet were searching the surface for objects indicating the existence of intelligent life, they would look, not for purpose as such, but for "evidences of machining, materials that do not exist in nature, regular markings, and the like."[8] Similarly, if an archaeologist wishes to determine whether an unknown object is a primitive ax or merely a rock, he does not do so by "determining whether the object can serve a purpose; he looks instead for those peculiar marks left by flaking tools and not produced by weathering."[9] In other words, in order to conclude that an object was designed, we must first establish that it was manufactured. Therefore, in order to conclude that the natural universe was designed, we must first establish that it was manufactured by an intelligent being.

It is here that the defender of the design argument faces his most serious problem. How can he demonstrate that the natural universe was in some way manufactured by an intelligent being? Only one way is open to the theist: he must first demonstrate the existence of an intelligent designer, and then—and only then—he can assert that the universe is the product of design. In other words, *one must first know that a god exists before one can say that nature exhibits design.* And this renders the design argument useless for proving the existence of a god.

The theist will undoubtedly object to his last claim. After all, he may argue, there are many cases where we can have knowledge of design without having prior knowledge of a designer. For instance, suppose that we discovered ancient ruins on another planet; this would convince us that intelligent life existed at one time on this planet. Here we begin with designed artifacts, the ancient ruins, and infer the previous existence of intelligent designers. It seems absurd, then, to claim that we cannot establish the presence of design in nature without prior knowledge of god's existence.

This objection ignores an important difference between evidence of design on another planet and evidence of design in the universe as a whole. We would recognize ruins on another planet only insofar as those ruins resembled, at least to some extent, the methods of man. And our ability to recognize man-made characteristics depends on our ability to identify characteristics that are *not found in nature*. If, for example, a man was to design an object which looked like a natural rock in every respect, then, while this object would in fact be the product of design, another person could not tell this from merely examining the rock. As far as he is concerned, this rock is a product of nature. The closer the resemblance between a designed artifact and a natural object, the more difficult it is to determine that the artifact is in fact a product of design.

We see, therefore, that the characteristics of design stand in contradistinction to the characteristics of natural objects. Thus, if objects on another planet bear marks that are not usually found in nature, we might conclude that these objects were designed by an intelligent being.

Now consider the idea that nature itself is the product of design. How could this be demonstrated? Nature, as we have seen, provides the basis of comparison by which we distinguish between designed objects and natural objects. We are able to infer the presence of design only to the extent that the characteristics of an object differ from natural characteristics. Therefore, to claim that nature as a whole was designed is to destroy the basis by which we differentiate between artifacts and natural objects. Evidences of design are those characteristics *not* found in nature, so it is impossible to produce evidence of design *within* the context of nature itself. Only if we first step beyond nature, and establish the existence of a supernatural designer, can we conclude that nature is the result of conscious planning.

To repeat: unless the theist *first* proves the existence of a god, there is no way, in principle, by which he can demonstrate that the universe exhibits design. Knowledge of god must precede knowledge of natural design, so the design argument has no possibility of success. Appeals to complex and intricate structures, such as the eye, are of no help; the eye does not display characteristics that cannot be accounted for in natural terms, and the similarity between the eye and man-made artifacts is irrelevant. Natural and man-made objects also share the common trait of coloration, but this is no reason to suppose that there exists a master painter-dyer. Paley's design argument must be rejected as a total failure.

III

The Argument from Life

The argument from life is the modern, scientific version of the design argument. It is based on the improbability of life originating from the random movement of atoms. Since, it is claimed, the chance occurrence of the right combination of atoms needed to form even the simplest of living organisms is so remote, life is probably the result of intelligent planning. Theists sometimes use the analogy of an explosion in a print factory creating the *Encyclopedia Britannica* to illustrate the improbability of life originating from nonintelligent causes.

(1) This argument falls prey to what has by now become a familiar difficulty: it assumes that, if life needs explaining, the positing of a god provides that explanation. But this, of course, explains nothing. If god himself is in any sense alive, then he must also be the result of conscious design by a supergod—and so on into our familiar regress.

(2) Most calculations of the probability of life occurring without planning, completely ignore the hierarchical and integrative nature of life. Matson, commenting on one such calculation, writes:

> ... the only thing really proved, granting the calculations, is the fantastic improbability of any protein molecule ever having come into existence all at once as the result of the simultaneous combination of its simple atomic constituents. But no 'materialist'—at least, none since the fifth century B.C.—ever dreamed of anything of this sort.[10]

269

The complex compounds that make life possible are not the result of a sudden combination of atoms (as the print factory example would lead us to believe); rather, they are the result of many intermediate steps and synthesizing processes. Thus, calculations that place the probability of life at fantastic odds can tend to be misleading.

(3) The argument from life again presents us with the false alternative between design and chance. Surely the arrangement of atoms into protein molecules is not a matter of chance, argues the theist, so there must be design. In fact, there is neither; we have with life what we have with every other natural phenomenon: natural causes operating according to natural necessity. If the theist insists that, natural necessity notwithstanding, the existence of life in the universe is extremely improbable, we can grant him this assertion for the sake of argument before discussing the issue of probability. Life may be an extraordinarily unusual occurrence, but what does this prove? Only that an extraordinary occurrence has taken place.

(4) The basic error of this argument lies in its devious use of probability. In a celebrated defense of the argument from life, Lecomte du Noüy explains his application of probability:

... let us define what is understood by the *probability* of an event: it is the ratio of the number of cases favorable to the event, to the total number of possibilities, *all possible cases being considered as equally probable.*[11]

This last phrase is the key; all cases within the realm of logical possibility are considered equally probable. Since the particular arrangement of atoms needed to produce life is only one among many millions of possible arrangements, argues du Noüy, the odds against life are almost infinitely overwhelming, and we must conclude that life is the product of conscious design.

Consider the implications here. According to this use of probability, every event in the universe, when compared with

270

the endless variety of possible alternative events, becomes almost infinitely improbable. W. T. Stace describes the consequences of this view:

> A man walking along a street is killed by a tile blown off a roof by the wind. We attribute this . . . to the operation of blind natural laws and forces, without any special design on the part of anyone. Yet the chances against that event happening were almost infinite. The man might have been, at the moment the tile fell, a foot away from the spot on the sidewalk on which the tile fell, or two feet away, or twenty feet away, or a mile away. He might have been at a million other places on the surface of the earth. Or the tile might have fallen at a million other moments than the moment in which it did fall. Yet in spite of the almost infinite improbability of that happening, we do not find it necessary to suppose that someone threw the tile down from the roof on purpose. We are quite satisfied to attribute the event to . . . the operation of natural forces.[12]

Consider another example. When it rains, the probability that a particular raindrop will fall exactly as it does is, according to du Noüy's use of probability, extremely slight. There are endless ways in which a raindrop may fall, if we consider each possibility as equally probable. Must we then believe in the existence of a rain god, who directs each drop? Does the alleged improbability that a raindrop falls as it does constitute evidence of intelligent planning?

Such an argument for a god of rain is nonsensical, but it is essentially the same as the argument for a god of life. If we regard every conceivable arrangement of atoms at any given moment as equally probable, then the "probability" of life is extremely unlikely. *But, on this basis, the probability of every occurence in the universe is also extremely small.* The "chance" combination of atoms needed to form a simple rock is ex-

THE ARGUMENTS FOR GOD

tremely unlikely, when contrasted with the billions of different "possibilities" open to these atoms. Is it not miraculous that, out of endless possibilities, billions of atoms come together in exactly the right way so as to produce a glob of dirt? Surely, therefore, we must posit a rock god, or a dirt god, to explain such intricate and complex structures.

When applied correctly, the notion of statistical probability can be useful, but du Noüy's application of probability, the application on which the argument from life depends, is absurd. Life is a natural phenomenon, the product of natural forces, and there is no reason whatever to posit a god as the source of life. Life is an extremely complex phenomenon, but so are most natural phenomena. Nature itself is complex, and man has expended tremendous time and energy in an effort to probe its mysteries. As man acquires more knowledge, fewer mysteries remain—and life has long ceased to be regarded by scientists as an inexplicable occurence.

PART FOUR:
GOD: THE PRACTICAL
CONSEQUENCES

When I was a child, I spake as a child, I understood
as a child, I thought as a child: but when I became a
man, I put away childish things.

—Paul of Tarsus
I Corinthians 13.11
(King James Version)

11.
Ethics, Rationality, and Religion

I

Introduction

Among the many myths associated with religion, none is more widespread—or more disastrous in its effects—than the myth that moral values cannot be divorced from the belief in a god. Perhaps the most common criticism of atheism is the claim that it leads inevitably to moral bankruptcy; and perhaps the strongest psychological bond to religion is the conviction, held implicitly by many people, that to abandon theism is to abandon morality as well.

This identification of ethics with religion has no basis in fact, and few theologians care to defend such a position explicitly. It functions, instead, as a kind of underlying assumption, apparently in the hope that if it goes unstated, it will also go unchallenged. However, not only are religion and ethics distinct spheres, but a theological approach to ethics, a moral theory based on divine will, is inimical to human life and happiness—and thus negates the foundation of rational ethics. In this chapter and in the one that follows, we shall examine the basic form of religious morality, as well as its specific content as manifested in Christianity. And we shall see how it is profoundly antilife, especially in terms of its psychological effects.

This discussion is not intended to be an exhaustive study of ethics, nor is it intended to be a complete analysis of religious morality and its many implications. The focus here is on a particular aspect of ethics and religion, an aspect that, in my opinion, has been generally neglected by philosophers: the relation between moral principles and human motivation. More specifically, we shall discuss two divergent approaches to ethics, the rational and the religious, and we shall see how each approach functions in human life and in the attainment of happiness.

When discussing the practical effects of religion, many atheists concentrate on the historical and sociological impact of religious doctrines, such as those of Christianity. These critics point out, and justifiably so, that many Christian beliefs have left disaster in their wake. Some effects are obvious, such as the atrocities of various Inquisitions, whereas others are more subtle, such as the role of Christianity in perpetuating an alliance between church and state. And, of course, we have intense opposition from some religious factions to the legalization of victimless crimes, such as abortion, drug use, prostitution and pornography. These issues, however, are covered thoroughly in other sources, and they shall not concern us here.

I am concerned, not with the social impact of religious morality, but with its personal impact upon the individual believer, an impact registered in terms of happiness and psychological health. As any person raised in a religious background can attest, religious training has a profound psychological influence—and I believe this influence to be overwhelmingly detrimental.

Some clarification may be necessary at this point. I am not recommending atheism as the key to happiness, nor am I suggesting that atheists are necessarily happier than theists. It would be fortunate if the attainment of happiness were that simple, but it is not. Abandoning the belief in god may have very little influence on a person's life one way or the other, and it is clear that atheists are just as capable of moral atrocities as are theists. And it is equally clear that atheism is no safeguard against misery, anxiety and neurosis.

It is necessary to distinguish between the mere belief in a supernatural agency which, theoretically speaking, may have little psychological influence, and the belief in a system of doctrines structured around this supernatural being which, more often than not, claims a heavy psychological toll. Few theists are able to disassociate their belief in god from their other beliefs, particularly in the area of ethics. Christianity, to take an obvious example, entails a wide range of doctrines touching on areas crucially important to human life. The God of Christianity is not an impersonal abstraction; he is intimately involved in human affairs. He offers a scheme of salvation, promulgates moral commandments, and threatens punishment for disbelievers. Christianity is more than theistic belief; it is a way of life. It offers a view of the universe, man's role in the universe, and the requirements for human well-being—thereby impinging on ethics and psychology.

If it is true that Christian doctrines are largely harmful, then atheism is conducive to happiness insofar as it removes definite *obstacles* to happiness. Repeating a theme from Chapter 1, atheism, while not a guarantee of happiness, is capable of clearing the way for the attainment of happiness. Rejecting the Christian view of sex, for instance, can have dramatic psychological consequences, but it does not insure that one will experience a rewarding sexual relationship. Similarly, rejecting the general approach of Christianity to moral principles can eradicate a major source of guilt and self-doubt, but it does not insure that one will be a happy, confident person.

To put this issue in a slightly different way, atheism, as such, is not an answer to anything, but it provides a general context in which answers are possible. Atheism provides one with a clean slate, in effect, and what one does beyond this point is entirely a matter of choice. But under no circumstances should atheism be regarded as a cure-all or as an escape from personal responsibility.

It should also be stressed that the following discussion of

religious morality is not an attempt to dispose of religion through psychological analysis. I am not suggesting, as did Freud, that the belief in a god stems from the longing for a father image; nor am I suggesting, as have other psychologists, that religious belief represents a kind of neurosis. Such generalizations, even if they have some basis in fact, are invariably guilty of oversimplification. Moreover, they are irrelevant with regard to the truth of theism and Christianity. Our primary concern is not with the various motives for belief in theism and Christianity, but with the consequences of these beliefs once they are accepted.

Finally, in response to the severe criticisms of religious morality and Christianity that follow, many people may feel that the overall picture is unbalanced. After all, they may argue, there must be some good things to say about religious morality and Christianity. If there are, however, I have been unable to find them. While some teachings of Christianity appear to have benevolent implications, this benevolence disappears when they are considered within the context of their wider ethical framework. It is doubtless possible to find something good to say, in an extremely narrow sense, about any ethical system, especially concerning some of its precepts. For instance, most moral systems advocate honesty over deceit, but this does not necessarily provide a strong point in favor of an ethical theory. Similarly, most ethical theories advocate some notion of benevolence and good-will among men, but the mere use of a term such as "benevolent" does not guarantee that the theory is, in fact, benevolent.

Considered in terms of its basic approach and precepts, Christian ethics must be condemned in its entirety. This is not to omit the possibility that it may have some good things to say occasionally and that it has had a constructive influence at certain times in history (although, in most cases, the reverse has been true). Rather, to condemn Christian ethics as a whole is to say that, as an ethical system—i. e., as a system of principles to guide man's choices and actions—it totally fails to accomplish what an ethical system should accomplish. Christian ethics is based throughout on falsehood—and this alone is sufficient to guarantee its failure; in addition, it advocates a conception of moral principles and their role in human existence which, by its very nature, works contrary to man's happiness and well-being. Christian ethics is more conducive to misery than to happiness, and it prescribes moral principles that are more accurately described as a code of death rather than a code of life. While ostensibly offering man a reprieve from the suffering in life, Christian ethics, like Christian theology, creates many of the problems that it later offers to solve. And, like theology, Christian ethics fails miserably in its attempt to find a solution.

Since it is difficult to criticize an ethical approach without an approach of one's own that serves as a reference point, it is necessary to discuss my own approach to ethics, so that my objections to religious morality can be viewed in their proper context. To this end I offer the following concept of ethics, generally modeled after various Aristotelian philosophers, as the science of human values.

II
The Science of Ethics

"If one wishes to understand the definition and distinctive nature of a particular science," writes Nathaniel Branden, "the question to answer is: *What are the specific facts of reality that give rise to that science?*" [1] Science, in its most general sense, is the methodology concerned with the discovery of facts and their classification into a coherent, integrated system; and the definition of a particular science is determined by which aspect of reality it seeks to understand. It is within this broad meaning that the various disciplines of philosophy qualify as branches of scientific inquiry. Metaphysics, for example, investigates existence in terms of its most fundamental attributes—characteristics, such as causality, that are common to *all* entities, despite their individual differences. In the words of Corliss

279

Lamont, metaphysics "deals with the lowest common denominators of everything that exists, whether it be animate or inanimate, human or nonhuman." [2] Similarly, epistemology investigates the nature and origin of human knowledge as such, apart from any specialized field of knowledge.

The spheres of philosophy may be viewed as the most basic of scientific inquiries. By dealing with the traits that the particular, more specialized sciences have in common, the branches of philosophy serve as unifying forces, enabling man to integrate the specialized sciences within a systematic framework of knowledge. Thus, metaphysics enables us to relate physics to biology, biology to psychology and so forth; and epistemology enables us to identify the essential characteristics of knowledge common to all fields—whether mathematics, history or biology—and it permits us to apply knowledge gained in one field to another, apparently unrelated, discipline.

In this section, I shall defend the thesis that ethics, while a branch of philosophy, is also a kind of science, specifically, the science of human values. Ethics seeks to discover human values, classify them, and integrate them into a coherent system of principles that is used to guide man's choices and actions. This view of ethics proceeds from a specific application of Branden's question, namely: What are the facts of reality, if any, that give rise to the discipline of ethics? Why should man concern himself with ethical theory in the first place?

The general neglect of this issue by philosophers is responsible for much of the confusion and disagreement that now exist among ethical theorists, who attempt to discuss ethics without considering *why* they are discussing ethics. No philosopher is more keenly aware of the importance of this problem than Ayn Rand, and it constitutes the general framework for her essay, "The Objectivist Ethics":

> What is morality, or ethics? It is a code of values to guide man's choices and actions—the choices and actions that determine the purpose and the course of his life. Ethics, as a science, deals with discovering and defining such a code.

The first question that has to be answered, as a precondition of any attempt to define, to judge or to accept any specific system of ethics, is: *Why* does man need a code of values?

Let me stress this: The first question is not: What particular code of values should man accept? The first question is: Does man need values at all—and why?[3]

Philosophers who fail to consider this issue usually conclude that ethics has no foundation in fact, that the realm of values is forever separated, by logic, from the realm of facts. Ethics, they declare, is concerned with what *ought* to be the case, while science is concerned with what *is* the case; and the normative recommendations of ethics cannot logically be derived from the descriptive statements of science. Consequently, two theories of ethics have enjoyed considerable vogue in the past few decades: emotivism, according to which ethical judgments are mere emotional expressions and therefore lack cognitive content; and subjectivism, according to which ethical judgments have meaning, but this meaning is nothing more than a report of one's personal, subjective preference. Both of these theories and their offshoots uphold the radical cleavage between facts and values, and they have elevated the so-called "is-ought dichotomy" to the status of a modern dogma.

Ethics, according to Rand and other philosophers within the general trend of Aristotelianism, is a normative science; and it is instructive to note that many sciences other than ethics are concerned with ought-judgments. Medicine, for instance, prescribes those actions that must be taken in order to preserve health. A doctor prescribes what *ought* to be done, but this prescription, to be valid, must be based on objective knowledge, such as the facts of human nature discovered through chemistry, physiology, anatomy and so forth. Architecture is another normative science; an architect learns what *ought* to be done in the course of constructing a building; and, as with medicine, his ought-judments must be based on facts.

There is little difficulty in understanding the relationship between "is" and "ought" as displayed in normative sciences. Man has the capacity for choice, and whenever a theoretical principle is applied to the sphere of human action, it becomes necessary to prescribe a course of action, an ought-judgment, if a given goal is to be achieved. A doctor *ought* to do x, *if* he wants to cure his patient. An architect *ought* to do x, *if* he wants his building to stand. Even the purely descriptive sciences, such as physics and astronomy—which have no direct connection with human behavior—require ought-judgments in order to specify correct scientific procedures. A physicist *ought* to do x, *if* he wants his experiment to yield results.

It is important to recognize that both normative and descriptive sciences are concerned primarily with *facts*, with accurately describing the phenomena that fall within their fields of investigation. Before a doctor can accurately prescribe, he must have accurate descriptive knowledge on which to base his recommendations. A normative science is only as good as the facts on which it rests. It is a mistake, therefore, to suppose that normative sciences, because they deal with ought-judgments, differ radically from descriptive sciences in terms of their method; rather, they differ only in terms of the data with which they deal. Both normative and descriptive sciences are concerned with factual knowledge, both are capable of verification, and both are open to such judgments as "valid" or "invalid," "correct" or "incorrect," "true" or "false."

We see, then, that normative and descriptive sciences are identical in that both deal with abstract principles derived from the facts of reality; their difference lies in which aspect of reality they consider, as well as the purpose for which their principles are employed. Descriptive sciences are concerned with "pure" facts and theories; normative sciences are concerned with those facts and theories as they apply to human goals. So, for instance, medicine deals with the facts of anatomy, as those facts apply to the goal of man's health. It is this application of abstract principles to the pursuit of human goals that gives rise to normative sciences and, consequently, to the ought-judgments prescribed by those sciences.[4]

Let us now consider the discipline of ethics—or, as I have previously described it—the science of human values. What are the facts of human nature that generate the need for such a science?

The first relevant aspect of human nature is an obvious one: man is a living entity, a biological organism, who faces the alternative of life or death. And, as Rand has emphasized, it is this conditional nature of life, the alternative between life and death, that generates the concept of "value":

> There is only one fundamental alternative in the universe: existence or nonexistence—and it pertains to a single class of entities: to living organisms. The existence of inanimate matter is unconditional, the existence of life is not: it depends on a specific course of action. Matter is indestructible, it changes its forms, but it cannot cease to exist. It is only a living organism that faces a constant alternative: the issue of life or death. Life is a process of self-sustaining and self-generated action. If an organism fails in that action, it dies; its chemical elements remain, but its life goes out of existence. It is only the concept of "Life" that makes the concept of "Value" possible. It is only to a living entity that things can be good or evil.[5]

Rand does not consider the relation between facts and values to be a serious problem, because, for her, values represent a *kind* of fact (and, in this regard, she follows in the tradition of Aristotelian philosophers). The concept of value expresses the beneficial or harmful relationship of some aspect of reality to a living organism, and to say that something is of value to an organism is to say that it is conducive to the life of that organism. When we say that water is of value to a plant, for example, we mean that water is conducive to the life of that plant. The concept of value, in this instance, signifies the life-serving function of water in relation to the plant, and this relationship is objectively demonstrable. The value judgment involved here is *true*; *i. e.*, it describes an actual relationship. The water will, in fact, further the life of the plant, so to say that water is of value to the plant is to *describe* a fact of reality. Therefore, in this case at least, there is no problem of "deriving" a value from a fact—as if one is dealing with two separate realms—because the value judgment expresses a fact; it is an estimate of a relationship, and this estimate is either accurate or inaccurate, true or false.

If this basic view of values is correct, then any attempt to divorce the realm of values from the realm of facts is fundamentally misguided at the outset. It is a mistake to speak of the facts of physics, biology, psychology, etc., in *contrast* to the realm of values; rather, we should speak of the facts of physics, the facts of biology, the facts of psychology, etc., *and* the facts of value. To claim that the sphere of values cannot be based on or derived from facts, is analogous to claiming that the spheres of physics or biology cannot be based on or derived from facts. Each of these disciplines is concerned, first and foremost, with describing reality. Their difference is not that some are concerned with facts while others are not; all are concerned with describing the same reality, and all employ abstract principles in pursuit of this end. Instead, their difference lies in *which* particular aspect of reality each seeks to investigate.

Like all existing things, animate and inanimate, man has a specific nature; and, like all living organisms, his nature requires a specific means of survival. Unlike other life forms, however, man has the capacity for choice. While other life forms respond to their environment on the automatic level of sensations or perceptions, man's distinctive power of conceptualization permits him to deliberate before acting. He can compare his alternative courses of action, project their consequences, and decide on the action best suited to his needs. In other words, man has the ability to *evaluate* the alternatives confronting him; and the volitional, goal-directed action of man is motivated by his evaluations. What a man values determines how he will act. As Branden puts it, "values constitute man's basic motivational tie to reality."[6]

We thus see that the concept of value applies to man in two different respects. First, there is the objective sense of "value," in which things are *of* value to man—*i. e.*, conducive to his welfare—whether he chooses to recognize them or not. Second, there is the subjective of "value," in which "value" designates the result of an evaluative process; and a man's values, in this case, represent his personal preferences. It is possible, therefore, for a man to *value* things (in a subjective sense) that are not in fact *of value* to him (in an objective sense). Man can pursue self-destructive courses of action; he can pursue goals that are detrimental to his welfare. Nature does not provide him with an automatic means of survival.

> A being who does not know automatically what is true or false, cannot know automatically what is right or wrong, what is good for him or evil. Yet he needs that knowledge in order to live. He is not exempt from the laws of reality, he is a specific organism of a specific nature that requires specific actions to sustain his life. He cannot achieve his survival by arbitrary means nor by random motions nor by blind urges nor by chance nor by whim. That which his survival requires is set by his nature and is not open to his choice. What *is* open to his choice is only whether he will discover it or not, whether he will choose the right goals and *values* or not. He is free to make the wrong choice, but not free to succeed with it. . . .
>
> What, then, are the right goals for man to pursue? What are the values his survival requires? That is the question to be answered by the science of *ethics*. And *this* . . . is why man needs a code of ethics.[7]

If man is to survive, he must have knowledge of those principles of action conducive to survival. And, beyond the level of mere survival, if man is to achieve happiness he must have knowledge of those principles of action conducive to happiness. Man must discover, through a process of reason, the values required for his survival and well-being. To live successfully, man's subjective "I value" must be derived from the objective requirements of his life. Thus, concludes Rand, "Ethics is an *objective, metaphysical necessity of man's survival. . . .*"[8]

Ethics deals with the facts of value as they apply to human action and the achievement of human goals. Like all normative sciences, ethics is concerned primarily with facts—with what is objectively of value to man—and it seeks to apply this knowledge to the realm of human choices and goals. It is this application of values to human action that generates the normative character of ethics, thus giving rise to its various ought-judgments. If x is of value to man (a fact), then man ought to value and pursue x (a normative judgment) if he wants to further his life and well-being (a goal).

Insofar as ethics seeks to discover and systematize factual knowledge of values, it is a science. Insofar as ethics seeks to apply this knowledge of values to human goals, it is a normative science. Insofar as ethics deals with *fundamental* values and goals—those required by the nature of man as such, or by man *qua* man—it is a branch of philosophy.

Like other branches of philosophy, ethics deals with basic concepts, and it attempts to derive the principles of action conducive to fundamental goals. Ethics is concerned with man's life as a whole, and it evaluates particular actions within that context. Ethics enables man to project the long-range consequences of his actions, and to evaluate the desirability of specific actions in terms of their effect on long-range goals.

There is widespread disagreement in philosophy over whether there exists for man an "ultimate value," a supremely important value for which other, lesser values serve as means. An examination of this complex issue would lead us far astray, so, for the purpose of this discussion, I shall posit "happiness" as man's ultimate value. I will not argue that all men actually pursue happiness, nor that all men "ought" to pursue happiness (whatever such an assertion might mean); rather, I shall offer happiness as a hypothetical goal. In other words, *if* a man desires happiness, *then* he ought to be concerned with those conditions, those values, that are conducive to man's happiness.

286

This discussion of ethics, therefore, is directed at those who are concerned with their own happiness and well-being, for these are the people who are in need of a rational code of values to direct their choices and actions. To the extent that a man is unconcerned with his own welfare, he need not bother with ethics. His indifference to principles and long-range goals will bring him misery soon enough.

Ethics, in this view, is concerned with the facts of value as those facts relate to the pursuit of a man's long-range happiness. This is a teleological, or goal-directed, approach to ethical theory, in direct contrast to a deontological, or duty-centered, approach to ethical theory. A simple way of contrasting these approaches is as follows: teleological ethics is concerned primarily with the good, with that which is of value, and it determines what man ought to do within the context of this goal. Deontological ethics, on the other hand, gives priority to what man ought to do, his duty, and it defines the "good" with reference to these moral rules, apart from any goals.

It is impossible to discuss here the many implications entailed by the distinction between teleological and deontological ethics. I shall simply note that it is the normative judgments of deontological ethics, where an "ought" is prescribed without reference to a goal, that cannot be grounded in facts. "One ought to do x." Why? "Because it is morally required, and one ought to do it." This characteristic approach of deontological ethics forever severs values from facts, and it generates the notorious "is-ought dichotomy" that is so widely discussed in contemporary philosophy. To the extent that an ethical theory declares itself indifferent to man's welfare and happiness, it thereby condemns itself.

The preceding discussion of ethics, although brief, is sufficient to point out that ethics, like every normative science, is based on facts; and the normative ought-judgments of ethics are as capable of verification as the normative recommendations of medicine and architecture. As stated previously, however, a normative science is only as good as the facts on which it rests, and a valid science of human values must be rooted in the nature of man as a biological and psychological organism.

Some philosophers fear that positing happiness as an ultimate value will lead to a world of greedy, amoral barbarians, where each man seeks to exploit and trample his neighbor. Bad psychology, however, makes for bad ethics. Just as man is a biological organism with a specific nature, so is he also a psychological organism with a specific nature. And just as any random action will not result in a man's physical well-being, so any random action will not result in a man's psychological well-being. The laws of psychology are as real and binding as the laws of biology; and, just as man is free to pursue a destructive course of action, but is not free to escape its physical consequences, so is he not free to escape its psychological consequences.

The issue of happiness, therefore, cannot be considered apart from the facts of human psychology. Just as a doctor cannot pursue medicine without a respect for the facts of human anatomy, so the philosopher cannot pursue ethics, or discuss what will and will not result in happiness, without a respect for the facts of man's psychology. Those philosophers who object to an ethics of happiness or well-being on the grounds that it permits every person to do as he pleases without regard for the life and property of others, display a shocking disregard for even the rudimentary facts of human psychology. It is for this reason that one good book on psychology, such as Nathaniel Branden's *The Psychology of Self-Esteem*, can do more to advance the science of ethics than any number of modern "analytic" works on ethical theory, which, more often than not, treat the subject of ethics as if it has no connection whatever to human happiness and the business of living.[9]

Before closing this discussion, it should be mentioned that ethics, since it is concerned with fundamental human values, serves as a unifying force that enables man to integrate the various spheres of human action into a consistent pattern. Just as metaphysics provides a transition from physics to biology to psychology, so ethics provides a transition from economics to social theory to politics and so forth. How can one derive, from the principles guiding one's own life, the principles required for dealing with other men? How can one evaluate the relative importance of various alternatives from which one must choose? What is the relationship between economics and politics? None of these questions, or any similar questions, can be answered without reference to fundamental human values and goals, and it is the function of ethics to provide a basic framework from which such answers may be derived.

By providing man with a coherent system of principles, ethics enables man to live as an integrated being. And, in a very real sense, the neglect of ethics results in *disintegration*—both existential and psychological—where individual and social issues are considered without reference to basic principles, where physical coercion becomes the accepted means of social interaction, and where man feels as if he were living in a schizophrenic universe, a vast jigsaw puzzle, where none of the pieces fit together.

III

Normative Ethics and Meta-ethics

In order to understand the differences between the rational and religious approaches to ethics, it is necessary to draw a common distinction between two aspects of ethical theory: normative ethics and meta-ethics.

"Normative ethics" refers to the content, or specific principles, of a moral code, such as the maxims, "One ought to be honest" and "One ought to respect the rights of others."

"Meta-ethics" pertains to the criteria and meaning of ethical terms themselves, such as "value," "moral," and "immoral." What is a value judgment? Can value judgments be justified rationally? What does "moral" mean? What does "immoral" mean? How do we know when to apply these and similar judgments? The answers to these and similar questions fall within the scope of meta-ethics. Put simply, normative ethics tells us what we ought to do, while meta-ethics tells us what we mean by the word "ought." Ethical conflicts may occur in either of these areas.

In the sphere of normative ethics, the disagreeing parties accept the same meta-ethics, but disagree about factual elements of the situation in question or about the interpretation and application of their meta-ethics. As an example of this, consider the doctrinal disagreements among fundamentalist Christians, all of whom accept the Bible as an authoritative source in ethics. While these Christians frequently disagree among themselves over points of detail, they all accept the same meta-ethical foundation. If one Christian could demonstrate that the Bible prohibits a given action, that action would be accepted as immoral by other fundamentalists without further argument, because there is an agreement here concerning the meaning and use of moral terms.

The second kind of disagreement—meta-ethical disagreement—is more basic than the preceding one. Here, one party may concede that, according to his adversary's moral criteria, the action being discussed is "immoral." He does not question the application of the criteria; rather, he questions and demands justification for the use of such criteria to begin with.

This kind of conflict occurs when an atheist argues moral issues with a Christian. If the Christian contends that blasphemy is immoral because the Bible forbids it, the atheist will not deny that the Bible forbids blasphemy. Instead, the atheist will refuse to accept the Bible as a criterion of morality, and he will refuse to accept a concept of "immoral" that means that which is prohibited by the Bible. Thus meta-ethical disagreements focus, not on the application of previously accepted criteria, but on the meaning and use of moral terms themselves.

It has become fashionable among some philosophers to exclude the realm of normative ethics from philosophical inquiry. Philosophy, they tell us, can reasonably investigate the meaning of moral terms, but it cannot, as a discipline, prescribe any particular code of values over any other. Since philosophy represents man's most fundamental kind of rational inquiry, the implication is that normative ethics is excluded from the domain of reason altogether, which surrenders moral issues of substance to religion and faith by default.

From our previous discussion of ethics as the science of human values, it should be clear that both normative ethics and meta-ethics are the proper concern of philosophy and rational deliberation. There is no reason whatever to suppose that philosophers must confine themselves to the analysis of language and concepts while excluding moral issues of substance.[10] It should be noted, however, that many contemporary philosophers focus on meta-ethics (sometimes, unfortunately, at the expense of normative ethics) because they recognize this to be the most crucial aspect of ethical theory. After all, before we can discuss what is good for man, we must agree on the meaning of "good." Before we can discuss whether a given action is moral, we must agree on the use of the term "moral." Most serious conflicts in ethical theory are of a meta-ethical nature, and we shall see that the conflict between rational morality and religious morality is no exception.

Earlier in this chapter, I condemned religious ethics generally and Christian ethics specifically, while stipulating that this did not necessarily imply disagreement with the content of every principle advocated by these approaches. For example, Christianity prohibits theft, and to reject Christian morality is not to suggest that theft merits approval. It is possible for some principles of Christian ethics to coincide with a rational ethics—although many assuredly do not—but any such coincidence does not affect the basic condemnation of Christian ethics. In condemning Christian morality, I am attacking its basic approach to ethical theory, *i. e.*, its meta-ethics, or criteria of ethical standards. *It is Christianity's fundamental view of moral principles and their role in human existence that must be rejected in its entirety.*

We shall now contrast a rational meta-ethics with a religious meta-ethics, and we shall see how these approaches are diametrically opposed, both from a philosophical standpoint and in terms of their psychological impact. And we shall see that this opposition persists despite any occasional and superficial similarity in content.

A rational morality is based on *standards;* a religious morality is based on *rules.* In essentials, rational and religious moral codes are as different as life and death—an analogy that, in this context, is particularly appropriate.

IV

Rational Morality

A rational morality, in essence, is a code of values required by man for his survival, well-being and happiness.[11] The term "rational" is used because such a code must be based on the facts of human value, and only reason can determine what is and is not of value to man. A rational meta-ethics, therefore, is based on man's need for objective values, his need to determine those goals that are conducive to his well-being. To take a simple illustration, food is of value to man, it is instrumental in maintaining his life; poison is not. If man is to survive, he must value food and disvalue poison. Man's evaluations must be based on, and agree with, those things that are actually of value to him.

Just as a rational man is committed to facts and the use of reason, so a rational morality is based on the facts of human value and the role of reason in man's survival. Three aspects of man's nature constitute the foundation of a rational meta-ethics: the fact that man is a conceptual being, the fact that man is a volitional being, and the fact that man is a purposive being.

Man's ability to conceptualize—mentally to abstract, isolate and integrate observed particulars—enables him to think in terms of principles, to project the long-range consequences of his actions, and to be aware of his own cognitive processes and psychological states. It is through conceptual thought that man gains knowledge of his needs, capacities and the external world; and it is through conceptual thought that man gains knowledge of how to exercise his capacities in the external world in order to satisfy his needs.

Volition means that man is the initiator of thought and

292

action, that he has the capacity to generate and sustain a thought process and a physical movement. It should be mentioned that volition, properly considered, does not violate the principle of causality. Volition does *not* mean that man's thoughts and actions are uncaused; it means, instead, that with regard to some thoughts and actions (excluding such things as reflex actions), man acts as a primary causal agent; man is the cause. [12] Volition entails man's freedom to choose among existing alternatives, his choice not being determined by factors beyond his control.

Because man is free to choose his actions, because he is not biologically programmed to act in a given manner, he requires a code of values—a system of principles—to direct his choices. Man's volitional nature necessitates that he choose to think and act in order to survive.

Man's purposive nature means that man is goal-directed, that he is not (and cannot be) bound to perceptual, range-of-the-moment responses. Since man is faced with alternatives, and since he is free to choose among them, if he conceptualizes his choice he must think in terms of a purpose. A value preference (as it applies to and motivates human action) necessarily implies a goal or end—namely, the object, process or state that is valued.

To summarize these three elements: man's conceptual capacity is his ability to think in terms of principles; man's volition necessitates that he think in terms of principles; and man's purposiveness determines the content of those principles.

It is not enough for a man to know only of the abstract role of principles in human survival; one must be able to determine concretely, within the context of one's own life, how to achieve the values required for one's physical and mental well-being. If man is to achieve goals, he must have some method of predicting which actions are conducive to those goals. This is the function of standards. A standard is a principle used to predict the consequences of one's actions.

As a predictive principle, a standard directs a man's choices, thus providing the essential link between action and the acquisition of desired values. A rational morality is one that recognizes the crucial role of standards in human survival, a morality based on man's need to attain values consonant with his nature.

Since it specifies the causal relation between a goal and the action required to achieve it, a standard is best described as a statement of *natural necessity*. The role of natural necessity in human motivation is not a new discovery; it was known by Aristotle in what is now called "practical reasoning," or a "practical syllogism." A general example of this syllogism is the following:

> Mr. Jones wants x.
> In order to obtain x, one must do y.
> Therefore, Mr. Jones ought to (or should, or must) do y.

In this syllogism, the first premise states Mr. Jones's end, or goal, that he wants x. The second premise is a standard that specifies the action necessary to attain goal x, and the conclusion is the concretization of the standard as it applies to the specific case of Mr. Jones. The conclusion is a prescription to act, an ought-judgment, derived from a goal and the action required to achieve it. Implied in the conclusion, "Mr. Jones ought to do y" is the further condition, "if he wants to attain goal x."

Georg Henrik von Wright, an ethical theorist, describes a practical syllogism as a syllogism where "the person who reasons reaches the conclusion that his wants, plus a certain natural necessity, impose upon him the practical necessity of acting in a certain manner."[13] In her article "Causality Versus Duty," Ayn Rand elaborates on this theme:

> Reality confronts man with a great many "musts," but all of them are conditional; the formula of realistic necessity is: "You must, if—" and the if stands for man's choice: "—if you want to achieve a certain goal." You must eat, if you want to survive. You

must work, if you want to eat. You must think, if you want to work. You must look at reality, if you want to think—if you want to know what to do—if you want to know what goals to choose—if you want to know how to achieve them.[14]

Every statement of natural necessity is conditional: one ought to do this, *if* one wants such and such. In rational morality, there can be no "ought" divorced from purpose. A standard presupposes a goal and has relevance only within the context of that goal. Likewise, the application of a standard and the subsequent "ought" have no relevance outside the goal that made them possible.

As the basic method by which man achieves values, standards constitute the meta-ethical foundation of rational morality. It must be remembered that within the framework of a standard meta-ethics, one's goals are primary, and the standards must be derived accordingly; moral principles, in this view, are subservient to human purposes. One does not adopt a moral principle and cling to it through a complete change of context while losing sight of the goal with which it was originally associated.

In other words, it makes little sense to speak of "obeying" or "disobeying" a standard. One does not obey a standard; one adopts and follows it in a given context, for a given purpose. Whether or not one follows a specific standard depends upon the desirability of its goal and one's judgment of the standard's effectiveness in achieving that goal. One's motivation to follow a standard stems from the prior motivation to achieve a particular goal.[15]

This brief discussion is intended only to illustrate the motivational link between rational ethics and human action, and it should not be construed as a definitive presentation of this complex issue. Many important subjects cannot be pursued here, but the relevance of the foregoing remarks will become apparent upon considering the nature of religious ethics.

12.
The Sins
of Christianity

I
Religious Morality

"Religious morality," as the phrase is used throughout this discussion, designates any code of values ultimately derived from the alleged commandments of a supernatural being. This view of morality is clearly presented in the Bible (*e.g.*, the Ten Commandments) and is generally typical of any revealed religion.

Basically, religious morality defends a universal moral order established by god and existing independently of man. Man is born into this moral structure, where he finds that his foremost duty is to obey the dictates of his supernatural lawgiver. Morality, according to this view, serves the purpose of god, not man; and man is required to subordinate himself to the moral code. Obedience is the major virtue, disobedience the major vice.

The most obvious characteristic of religious morality is its authoritarian nature. As soon as the "good" or the "moral" are defined with reference to divine fiat, we are discussing a theory

297

steeped in authoritarianism. And where we have an authority, we have sanctions—and where we have sanctions, we have moral *rules*. Rules, as we shall see, are basic to the meta-ethics of religious morality. Rules are to religious morality what standards are to rational morality.

A rule is a *sanctioned* principle of action. A sanction is a physical or psychological means of coercion or intimidation used for the purpose of motivating obedience to a principle of action. To illustrate these definitions, consider some rules that we encounter every day: traffic laws.

If a posted speed limit did not carry the threat of enforcement by the police, it would not, properly speaking, be a law, or, for our purpose, it would not function as a rule. Laws carry the threat of punishment by the state for disobedience; this is their sanction, and this is why they are designated as rules. The state sanction of punishment exists for the purpose of motivating compliance with the laws.

If speed limits were not enforced, if there were no penalty for ignoring them, then they would function as standards for the goal of traffic safety. One would follow a speed limit, *if* one desired traffic safety (assuming that one considered the speed limit to be a means of attaining it). Failure to observe the posted guideline would presumably result in an increased number of accidents; but the speed limit, as a standard, would not carry an imposed penalty—a sanction—for the fact of disobedience itself.

If one observes the speed limit because one wishes to avoid getting a ticket, one is responding to the limit as a rule. Regardless of whether one sees the limit as a means to traffic safety or whether one desires the goal of traffic safety, one will still obey the limit from fear of the sanction placed upon it. We see, therefore, that one does not follow a rule in the same sense that one follows a standard. One *obeys* a rule and does so because of its sanction.

While a standard appeals to the motive of desiring its goal, a rule appeals to the motive of desiring or fearing its sanction. This is the basic motivational difference between standards and rules.

298

Religion has traditionally appealed to the will of a god as justification for its moral principles. To the question, "Why should I do x?" religion has answered, "Because it is the will of god." To the further question, "Why should I obey the will of god?" religion has answered, "Because he will reward or punish you accordingly, either in this life or in an afterlife."

The power of a supernatural being has thus served as a moral sanction. One obeys a principle, not because one desires its causal result, but because one fears its sanction—in this case, the wrath of god.

The fundamental characteristic of religious morality is that it views every moral principle, in effect, as a traffic law. One is rewarded or punished according to how well one snaps into line with a prescribed set of rules. These rules, when acted upon, do have consequences (as does every human action), but the desirability of those consequences is not the agent's primary motive for acting. Instead, he is motivated to act by the sanction accompanying the rule.

The oldest and crudest form of a rule sanction is the use or threat of physical force. This is manifested in Christianity by the doctrine of hell.

The belief in eternal torment, still subscribed to by fundamentalist Christian denominations, undoubtedly ranks as the most vicious and reprehensible doctrine of classical Christianity. It has resulted in an incalculable amount of psychological torture, especially among children where it is employed as a terror tactic to prompt obedience. Many examples are available, but one should suffice. An English priest named Father Furniss wrote a series of "Books for Children" in the last century which enjoyed a wide circulation among English Catholics well into this century. Dubbed "the children's apostle," Furniss specialized in describing the tortures of hell. Here is an example depicting the torments of a child in hell:

> His eyes are burning like two burning coals. Two long
> flames come out of his ears ... Sometimes he opens
> his mouth, and breath of blazing fire rolls out. But
> listen! There is a sound just like that of a kettle

boiling. Is it really a kettle boiling? No. Then what is it? Hear what it is. The *blood* is boiling in the scalding veins of that boy. The *brain* is boiling and bubbling in his head. The *marrow* is boiling in his bones. Ask him why he is thus tormented. His answer is that when he was alive, his blood boiled to do very wicked things.

Here is another gem:

A little child is in this red-hot oven. Hear how it screams to come out! See how it turns and twists itself about in the fire! It beats its head against the roof of the oven. It stamps its little feet on the floor. You can see on the face of this little child what you see on the faces of all in hell—despair, desperate and horrible.

Hell stands as a constant reminder of the essence of Christianity: God is to be obeyed because, in the final analysis, he is bigger and stronger than we are; and, in addition, he is incomparably more vicious. With the warning, "Obey God or burn in hell," we have a straightforward illustration of a physical sanction, as well as a revealing glimpse into the core of Christianity.

Today many moderate and liberal denominations play down the concept of hell or deny it altogether; nevertheless, their moral codes remained drenched in rules. But without the benefit of hell, what is used as a rule sanction?

The answer lies within the realm of psychological sanctions. Recall that a sanction may be physical *or* psychological. Physical sanctions are usually uncomplicated and easy to detect, whereas psychological sanctions are often complex and subtle, which explains why they are rarely identified.

A psychological sanction is a moral term that is used for the purpose of psychological intimidation, which is intended to motivate compliance with rules. Moral terms, when used in this fashion, function as psychological cue-words—words used to trigger emotions, rather than convey information.

A physical sanction, if successful, causes the emotion of *fear*. A psychological sanction, if successful, causes the emotion of *guilt*. A man motivated by fear may still retain an element of rebelliousness, of determination to strike back given the opportunity. A man motivated by guilt, however, is a man with a broken spirit; he will obey the rules without question. A guilt-ridden man is the perfect subject for religious morality, and this is why psychological sanctions have been extremely effective in accomplishing their purpose.

Religions have long recognized the importance of inculcating a sense of guilt in order to motivate people to obey god's rules. But the feeling of guilt does not automatically follow from the thought of disobeying a supernatural being, even for those who believe in one. Emotions are the consequence of implicit or explicit value judgments, so it was necessary for Christianity to provide the missing evaluative link between the thought of disobeying God and the experience of guilt. This gap was filled nicely by the concept of *sin*.

The notion of sin is perhaps the most effective sanction ever invented. For a Christian, to sin is the worst thing imaginable, and the thought of committing a sin can cause intense guilt. Anyone who comes from a religious background can appreciate the tremendous psychological force of this concept. Sin represents something metaphysically monstrous, something that directly undercuts a man's sense of self-esteem, and this adds to its effectiveness as a manipulative device. Friedrich Nietzsche, in his vitriolic but penetrating attack on Christianity, clearly recognized the function of sin in this context. "Sin," he writes, "... that form *par excellence* of the self-violation of man, was invented to make science, culture, every kind of elevation and nobility of man impossible; the priest *rules* through the invention of sin."[1]

In order to understand fully the nature of sin as a psychological sanction, we must examine the relationship between "sin" and "disobedience to god." Are these notions identical, or do they differ in some respect? The answer to this question becomes apparent upon considering the following statements:

(a) I have disobeyed god, but I have done nothing wrong or evil.

(b) I have sinned, but I have done nothing wrong or evil.

Is statement (a) contradictory? No, not necessarily. Even working from the presupposition that a god exists, there is nothing intrinsic to the idea of disobedience that requires a negative evaluation. This god, after all, may be an evil creature, in which case disobedience may be evaluated as good or desirable. There is no value judgment in the mere thought of disobedience per se.

Is statement (b) contradictory? Yes, obviously so. Included within the concept of sin is a negative moral evaluation, so the admission of sin entails an admission of evil or wrongdoing. To accept the concept of sin presupposes that one believes in a god and that one believes disobeying this god to be intrinsically wrong.

We see, then, that "sin" and "disobedience to god" do differ; the concept of sin includes the notion of disobedience plus a built-in condemnation of that disobedience. It is this evaluative element that causes guilt.

It must be emphasized that the Christian who accepts the idea of sin cannot evaluate each particular divine rule as good or evil—to do so would require a standard of goodness apart from the will of god. If, however, the standard of goodness exists independently of god's will, the concept of sin is stripped of its force as a psychological sanction. To disobey god, on this basis, may coincide with what is judged to be immoral by an independent standard (since it might be argued that god always chooses the good), but there is no *necessary* connection here between disobedience and immoral action.

The effectiveness of sin as a psychological sanction rests precisely on the fact that for many theists, disobeying god functions as a criterion of immoral action. Acting contrary to god's will is included within the definition of "immoral." It therefore follows, tautologically, that disobeying god is immoral, and following god's rules is considered a necessary prerequisite for being a "good" or "moral" person.

302

Thus, once the concept of sin is accepted, statement (a) is contradictory. With the presupposition of sin, it is absurd to say, "I have disobeyed god, but I have done nothing wrong or evil." Disobedience is already implicitly contained within the meanings of "wrong" and "evil."

This leaves the believer in sin with the following example of circular reasoning: one should not disobey god, because to do so is a sin. And what is sin? A sin is disobeying god.

Although rarely made explicit, this is the basic pattern underlying the concept of sin and psychological sanctions in general. The circularity is necessitated by the nature of a rule-based meta-ethics. The moral is defined in terms of obedience to rules; and, for Christianity, the concept of sin serves as a guilt-inducer to motivate this obedience.

The essential role that sin plays in Christianity has been summarized eloquently by C. S. Lewis, a popular Protestant writer. In the following passage, note the connections made, first, between sin and disobeying God; and second, between sin and a sense of guilt.

> A recovery of the old sense of sin is essential to Christianity. Christ takes it for granted that men are bad. Until we really feel this assumption of His to be true, though we are part of the world he came to save, we are not part of the audience to whom His words are addressed. . . . And when men attempt to be Christians without this preliminary consciousness of sin, the result is almost bound to be a certain resentment against God as to one who is always making impossible demands and always inexplicably angry. . . . The worst we have done to God is to leave Him alone—why can't He return the compliment? Why not live and let live? What call has He, of all beings, to be "angry"? It's easy for Him to be good!
>
> Now at the moment when a man feels real guilt— moments too rare in our lives—all these blasphemies vanish away.[2]

This passage is from *The Problem of Pain*, which carries the following subtitle: "The intellectual problem raised by human suffering, examined with sympathy and realism."

If nothing else, Lewis provides us with an insight into the Christian idea of sympathy; and, to his credit, Lewis does accomplish one of his goals. He illustrates quite vividly, even if unintentionally, a primary cause of human suffering: the idea of sin itself. Lewis has the candor to admit what other Christians prefer to ignore: that Christianity thrives on guilt. Guilt, not love, is the fundamental emotion that Christianity seeks to induce—and this is symptomatic of a viciousness in Christianity that few people care to acknowledge. For all of its alleged concern for the "poor in spirit," Christianity does its best to perpetuate spiritual impoverishment.

In summary, religious morality may be described as the *denaturalization* of values. It divorces the pursuit of values from their natural consequences and relies instead on sanctions, both physical and psychological, to motivate obedience to its moral rules. In Christianity, hell is the most prominent physical sanction; and sin, the psychological equivalent of hell, is the most common psychological sanction.

With its emphasis on obedience, enforced through the inculcation of fear and guilt, Christianity has transformed morality into something that is generally considered ominous and distasteful. With its emphasis on punishment and reward in an afterlife, Christianity is largely responsible for the notion that morality is impractical, and has little or nothing to do with man's life and happiness on earth.

The religious concern with obedience, duty and guilt stands in stark contrast to the rational conception of morality, where man is of central concern, where man's life is the standard of value, and where moral principles function for human welfare. Any link between religion and morality is not only unjustified, it is enormously harmful. The religious view of morality is still widely accepted; children are raised by it, and men attempt to live by it—with the result that millions of people practice, in the name of morality, what amounts to emotional and intellectual suicide.

THE SINS OF CHRISTIANITY

Having sketched the basic meta-ethical distinction between rational morality and religious morality, we shall now explore the specific consequences of religious morality as they are manifested in Christianity.

II

The Conflicting Virtues

Several chapters of this book were devoted to the philosophical conflict between reason and faith, because this constitutes the major epistemological issue dividing atheism from theism. But the conflict between reason and faith extends beyond the philosophical realm into the world of human action and emotion. One's view of reason and its role in human existence will profoundly influence one's approach to ethics, and this is nowhere more evident than in the battle between reason and faith.

Reason is the faculty that enables man to identify and integrate the facts of reality. But man's reason does not function automatically; it requires the choice to exert mental effort, to actively focus one's mind. This is the virtue of rationality. Rationality is the commitment to reason, to mental awareness, to the sustained use of one's mind. A rational man's foremost concern is with facts, with what is true, and he is unwilling to sacrifice the judgment of his mind to the demands or desires of other people.

Intellectually, every man is an island unto himself; no man can assume the responsibility of thinking for another. The virtue of rationality thus entails intellectual independence and the willingness to assume responsibility for one's beliefs, choices and actions.

In direct contrast to the virtue of rationality and its corollaries, stands the primary virtue of religious morality: *obedience*. This, in concrete terms, is the meaning of faith. Translated into action, faith means acting without critical deliberation, acting without regard for the natural consequences of one's actions, acting because it is demanded of one by an authority.

305

Faith requires knowledge only of one's duty and how to obey; beyond this point, it is a simple matter of conformity.

If there is a uniform theme throughout the Bible, it is that God must be obeyed, period. If God commands worship, man must worship. If God commands love, man must love. If God commands tap dancing, man must tap dance. If God commands murder, man must murder.

While the content of Christian ethics has varied throughout history, this principle has remained unchanged: God is the master, man is the slave—and the fundamental characteristic of a slave is that he is not permitted, under the threat of force, to act according to his own judgment. But the Christian God far surpasses the capabilities of any human slavemaster, for he can monitor, not only the actions of men, but their thoughts and feelings as well. The Christian God can, and does, command how man should think and feel.

It is commonly said of totalitarian power seekers that they wish to "play God." This comment has a double edge, and it is far more insightful than most people realize.

The word "faith" has a benevolent sound to many people. They think of the man of faith as a man of inner strength and compassion, such as the early Christians who, rejecting violence, were willing to die for their convictions. Yet it must be remembered that, whereas faith may have inspired acts of courage, it has also inspired moral atrocities. The Christian Inquisitor burning a heretic at the stake was as much a man of faith as the Christian martyr.

Whether their consequences are beneficial or harmful, acts of faith are united by their submission to an authoritative moral code. God demanded of the early Christians that they refuse to submit to state decrees, and they sacrificed themselves in obedience to his will. God demanded of the medieval Christians that they eradicate heresy, and they sacrificed others in obedience to his will. Men praise the former as acts of courage and condemn the latter as moral atrocities, but the underlying principles in each case are identical: *passive obedience to moral rules.*

When a politician asks people to have faith in their govern-

306

ment, it is clear that he is calling for obedience and the suspension of criticism. And it should be equally clear that when a theologian speaks of faith in God, he means that divine rules are to be obeyed without question. The man who seeks truth calls on reason; the man who seeks conformity calls on faith. A morality of independence relies on reason; a morality of obedience relies on faith.

Whether the consequences of an act of faith are good or bad, those consequences are considered by the man of faith to be essentially *irrelevant* to the moral worth of his action. Within the framework of religious morality, the natural effects of one's actions are regarded as secondary to the issue of obedience. By focusing on divine commands, rewards and punishments, religious morality, and Christianity in particular, demands the evaluation of an action divorced from its consequences—and herein lies the primary danger. A morality of conformity, a morality divorced from consequences—this idea has sanctioned more bloodshed and devastation than any comparable notion in ethical theory. Millions of persons have been slaughtered, mutilated and tortured in the name of religious morality, in the name of obedience to a "higher," "nobler" realm.

In personal terms, obedience is a convenient escape from individual responsibility. If a man functions only as an agent of God's will, then it is God, not the man, who bears responsibility. The Christian who refuses credit for a courageous or benevolent action because he claims to have been merely obeying God's will is typically regarded as admirable. Yet, on the reverse side of the same coin, we have the Christian who refuses to accept responsibility for a moral outrage because he too was obeying God's will. Both Christians, by representing themselves as tools for divine use, seek to disown personal responsibility for their actions by shifting the responsibility onto God. Christian humility, therefore, which is commonly viewed as a harmless trait, is actually the manifestation of a wider principle which, when accepted, has taken a considerable toll in human lives.

Only if one understands the central role of conformity in

307

religious morality, can one appreciate fully the ruthless consistency of primary Christian virtues—such as humility, self-sacrifice and a sense of sin—which, without exception, are geared to the destruction of man's inner sense of dignity, efficacy and personal worth. It is not accidental that Christianity regards pride as a major sin. A man of self-esteem is an unlikely candidate for the master-slave relationship that Christianity offers him. A man lacking in self-esteem, however, a man ridden with guilt and self-doubt, will frequently prefer the apparent security of Christianity over independence and find comfort in the thought that, for the price of total submissiveness, God will love and protect him.

In exchange for obedience, Christianity promises salvation in an afterlife; but in order to elicit obedience through this promise, Christianity must convince men that they *need* salvation, that there is something to be "saved" *from*. Christianity has nothing to offer a happy man living in a natural, intelligible universe. If Christianity is to gain a motivational foothold, it must declare war on earthly pleasure and happiness, and this, historically, has been its precise course of action. In the eyes of Christianity, man is sinful and helpless in the face of God, and is potential fuel for the flames of hell. *Just as Christianity must destroy reason before it can introduce faith, so it must destroy happiness before it can introduce salvation.*

It is not accidental that Christianity is profoundly anti-pleasure, especially in the area of sex; this bias serves a specific function. Pleasure is the fuel of life, and sexual pleasure is the most intense form of pleasure that man can experience. To deny oneself pleasure, or to convince oneself that pleasure is evil, is to produce frustration and anxiety and thereby become potential material for salvation.

Christianity cannot erase man's need for pleasure, nor can it eradicate the various sources of pleasure. What it can do, however, and what it has been extremely effective in accomplishing, is to inculcate guilt in connection with pleasure. The pursuit of pleasure, when accompanied by guilt, becomes a means of perpetuating chronic guilt, and this serves to reinforce one's dependence on God.

This condemnation of Christianity as anti-pleasure will undoubtedly be viewed by some readers as outdated. Some contemporary theologians, after all, have attempted to reverse the otherworldly trend of Christianity to a concern for earthly well-being and happiness. From a historical perspective, however, this concern occupies only a fraction of Christianity's history. A theologian, if he wishes, can preach a philosophy of life without reference to sin, salvation, obedience and the supernatural, but such a philosophy has nothing to do with the Bible and Christian theism.

Moreover, to the extent that modern theologians endorse pro-life attitudes, they are merely riding the current of public change. No one is foolish enough to claim, for example, that Christianity has been a primary force in effecting a more open and benevolent attitude toward sex in American society; on the contrary, Christianity has constituted the major obstacle in this area. Most Christian theologians who pass themselves off as radical reformers are decades, if not centuries, behind non-Christian writers; they are little more than politicians of the spirit who cater to public opinion.

When the Christian "reformer" comes forward to declare that sex is not evil and that sex outside of marriage may, after all, be permissible—and when he calls on Christian churches to spearhead his new movement—one must wonder if it ever occurs to him that he is nineteen centuries too late.[3] If such theologians were truly concerned with man's happiness on earth, they would begin by repudiating, totally and unequivocally, Christianity itself.

It cannot be emphasized too strongly that *Christianity has a vested interest in human misery*. This central theme manifests itself again and again in Christian doctrines, and most Christian doctrines are unintelligible unless viewed in this context. The spectacular success of Christianity has been a topic of heated debate among scholars, and it is certainly true that definite historical factors influenced that success. I suggest, however, that much of Christianity's success can be accounted for in another way: Christianity, perhaps more than any religion before or since, capitalized on human suffering; and it was enormously successful in insuring its own existence through the perpetuation of human suffering.

Of course, Christianity, with some exceptions,[4] has never explicitly advocated human misery; it prefers to speak instead of *sacrifices* in this life so that benefits may be garnered in the life to come. One invests in this life, so to speak, and collects interest in the next. Fortunately for Christianity, the dead cannot return to demand a refund.

Through inculcating the notion that sacrifice is a virtue, Christianity has succeeded in convincing many people that misery incurred through sacrifice is a mark of virtue. Pain becomes the insignia of morality—and, conversely, pleasure becomes the insignia of immorality. Christianity, therefore, does not say, "Go forth and be miserable." Rather, it says, "Go forth and practice the virtue of self-sacrifice." In practical terms, these commands are identical.

The preceding overview of Christian ethics is intended to set a context for the remainder of this chapter, where we shall examine some ethical precepts of the New Testament. The theme here, to repeat, is that Christian morality, like all religious moral codes, defines morality in terms of obedience; and most of its precepts serve the purpose, directly or indirectly, of promoting obedience. It is Christianity's obsession with conformity that leads to its various doctrines—doctrines that can only be described as profoundly anti-life. Christianity has found it necessary, out of self-preservation, to oppose the virtues of rational morality; reason, pride, self-assertiveness, self-esteem—these are the enemies of conformity and, therefore, of Christian faith.

Since the foremost aim of Christian ethics, psychologically speaking, is to cultivate a mentality of obedience, Christian ethics, to the extent that one adopts it, will cause and contribute to a variety of psychological problems. It encourages intellectual passivity, fear that one's thoughts and emotions may be sinful, guilt at the thought of sexual assertiveness, and the pervading feeling that one is basically helpless, unimportant and evil. These are serious charges which, if true, constitute an overwhelming moral case against Christianity.

Several volumes could be written about Christian ethics; indeed, many have been written in an effort to determine the content of Christian ethics. There are numerous disagreements among Christian scholars in this area. For example, the doctrine of original sin is a venerable Christian belief that enjoys widespread acceptance even today, and it is definitely contained in the New Testament. But it is a teaching of Paul, not Jesus. Some liberal theologians, therefore, reject it as an essential element of Christian ethics, claiming that Paul, like any interpreter, may have been mistaken. More traditional Christians, on the other hand, maintain that anything in the New Testament, whether uttered by Jesus, Paul or some other apostle, must be accepted as essential to Christianity—and this includes the doctrine of original sin.

Although I find the position of the modern liberal on this issue—as in many others—rather ludicrous, I will avoid this controversy for the remainder of this chapter. Rather than treat the New Testament as a whole, I shall confine this discussion to the ethics of Jesus as reported in the Gospels. While it is generally true that Paul emphasizes sin and human depravity much more than Jesus, and while it is probably true that Paul was more influential than Jesus in many areas, I think it is also true that the teachings of Jesus are not as benevolent as is commonly supposed. Even restricting ourselves to Jesus, it is possible to substantiate the charges against Christian ethics made earlier in this chapter.

III

The Ethics of Jesus

It is fashionable today to hail Jesus as an outstanding moralist. Even atheists who disagree with theoretical aspects of Christianity often regard Jesus as a creative reformer in the sphere of ethics. In evaluating his ethics, however, there are considerable problems in ascertaining what the historical Jesus actually taught. It is clear that the early Christians were expecting his imminent return, and they saw no reason to compile written accounts of his life for future generations. But as time passed, as the memory of Jesus dimmed, and as disillusionment spread, it became necessary to preserve the faith through written stories of Jesus' life—stories that "documented" his miraculous powers in an effort to distinguish him from the many other "messiahs" common in those days.

According to most biblical scholars, written stories of Jesus did not begin to appear until around forty years after his death. Later compiled into the Gospels, these accounts were laden with interpolations and mythology, such as the story of the virgin birth. But it was the biblical Jesus, not the historical Jesus who exerted influence, and it is the biblical Jesus to whom people refer as a great moralist. Therefore, we shall accept the New Testament account fairly uncritically, and we shall disregard the question of to what extent, if any, the biblical Jesus corresponds to its historical counterpart. We shall examine the major tenets of Jesus as recorded in the Gospels—especially Matthew, Mark and Luke which, because of their similar structure and content, are referred to as the synoptic Gospels.

Even taking the Gospels at face value does not solve all problems of interpretation. The teachings of Jesus are unsystematic, and many of them, particularly those related in parable form, are notoriously obscure. This unclarity has resulted in a wide spectrum of opinion among Christian scholars as to what Jesus really meant. Despite these divergent interpretations, however, it is interesting to observe that Christian theologians unanimously agree that Jesus was the greatest moral teacher in history. Considering the widespread disagreement over the content of Jesus' teaching, this unanimity of praise is highly suspicious.

Many Christians feel that Jesus, regardless of what he said, must have been the greatest moralist because he was, they believe, the "Son of God" (however this phrase may be interpreted). Few Christians reserve judgment, read the Gospels and, on the basis of an objective evaluation, conclude that Jesus was outstanding. Instead, believing as they do that Jesus was a divine figure, they assume beforehand that whatever he said must be vitally important, because to believe otherwise would be to cast doubt on his divinity. And this is tantamount to blasphemy.

It must be remembered that the sword of heresy looms as a constant threat over the heads of Christians, and this applies equally well to liberal Protestants. While liberals are perfectly willing to concede that the Bible contains many errors, and while they may go so far as to concede that Jesus was no more than a man, they are unwilling to admit that Jesus advocated principles which, by any reasonable standard of human decency, must be judged as morally repugnant. To overtly disown or condemn the teachings of Jesus—this is the line that no Christian, fundamentalist or liberal, dares to cross, because to cross it would be to define oneself out of Christianity. It is the limit of heresy for even the most liberal of liberals.

To avoid disclaiming the teachings of Jesus, theologians continue to do what they have done for centuries: they *interpret*. Passages unfavorable to Jesus are reinterpreted in a more favorable light, or they are dismissed as unauthentic interpolations. Anything will do as long as it permits the theologian to profess agreement with the ethics of Jesus; the minute he ceases to conform in this respect, he is no longer a theologian, nor can he continue to pass himself off as a Christian.

Because of the theological obligation to endorse the precepts of Jesus, Christian theologians have a strong tendency to read their own moral convictions into the ethics of Jesus. Jesus is made to say what theologians think he *should* have said. Many contemporary theologians find the notion of eternal torment distasteful, so, of course, Jesus could have never taught such a doctrine. Similarly, some theologians prefer to underplay the otherworldly aspects of Christianity, so Jesus becomes, not a prophet concerned primarily with an afterlife, but a social reformer interested in earthly life and happiness. As Walter Kaufmann notes:

Most Christians gerrymander the Gospels and carve an idealized self-portrait out of the texts: Pierre van Paassen's Jesus is a socialist, Fosdick's is a liberal, while the ethic of Reinhold Niebuhr's Jesus agrees, not surprisingly, with Niebuhr's own.[5]

A typical example of this theological gerrymandering is found in *Christian Ethics* by Georgia Harkness:

> ... there is a verse at the end of the parable of the pounds as it is given in Luke which is generally omitted when the story is read. In Luke 19:27 appear the words: "But as for these enemies of mine, who did not want me to reign over them, bring them here and slay them before me." Why do we omit it? Because it does not sound like Jesus! It simply does not seem like the words of one who could say on the cross, "Father, forgive them; for they know not what they do." And even though the textual accuracy of Luke 19:27 is less disputed than of Luke 23:34, we still believe it is the latter in which the real Jesus speaks.[6]

In the course of taking an unprejudiced look at Jesus as portrayed in the Gospels, we shall briefly consider the following questions:

(a) What were the central purpose, theme and scope of Jesus' mission?

(b) To what extent were the moral precepts of Jesus original?

(c) How are the major precepts of Jesus to be evaluated from ethical and psychological perspectives?

(a) The Jesus of the Gospels does not regard himself primarily as a moralist, nor was he so regarded throughout most of Christianity's history; rather, his basic mission was to preach the

314

coming of God's kingdom, and his basic precept was that men must devote themselves totally to God if they wish to enter the heavenly kingdom. "Repent, for the kingdom of heaven is at hand"—these words, according to Matthew, 4.17, inaugurated the crusade of Jesus. And later in Matthew 22.37-38, Jesus says: "You shall love the Lord your God with all your heart, and with all your soul, and with all your mind. This is the great and first commandment." Otherworldliness, total devotion (*i.e.*, obedience), and mandatory love thus emerge as Jesus' basic themes.

The otherworldly focus of Jesus permeated all his teaching. "Truly, I say to you," he told his followers, "there are some standing here who will not taste death before they see the kingdom of God come with power" (Mark 9.1). Since God was soon to usher in his heavenly kingdom, earthly matters were unimportant: "Sell all that you have and distribute to the poor, and you will have treasure in heaven; and come, follow me" (Luke 18.22).

It has been suggested, most notably by Albert Schweitzer, that the teachings of Jesus must be understood as an "interim ethic"—a set of moral precepts to be followed in the interim before the establishment of God's kingdom, which Jesus believed would occur within the lifetime of his followers. As the eminent historian Frederick Conybeare wrote in *The Origins of Christianity*:

> . . . much of the teaching of the gospel was uttered in view of an impending catastrophe and liquidation of this world's affairs, out of which, at a wave of the divine wand, a new and blessed condition was to emerge, just as the phoenix arises, renewed and immortal, out of its own ashes. Jesus felt himself to be the harbinger of a new and divine constitution . . . to be suddenly imposed by divine power and interference. Hence the precepts to follow him; to forsake parents, wife, children, and home; even to neglect the most sacred of all ancient duties—that of burying one's own father.[7]

315

Although many theologians are understandably reluctant to accept this view—since acceptance would entail that Jesus was mistaken concerning the immediacy of God's kingdom—there is strong evidence in its favor. Aside from the many New Testament references indicating that God's rule was near, the precepts of Jesus, almost without exception, are accompanied by the promise of a divine reward. Be humble, counsels Jesus, "and your Father who sees in secret will reward you." Be kind to the poor and disabled, and you "will be repaid at the resurrection of the just." Even the much heralded Sermon on the Mount (regardless of which of the conflicting versions one accepts) is saturated with divine sanctions: "Blessed are the poor in spirit, for theirs is the kingdom of heaven." "Blessed are the pure in heart, for they shall see God." On the reverse side of supernatural sanctions, of course, was the threat of punishment for those who will not listen and obey: "if any one will not receive you or listen to your words," Jesus told his disciples, "shake off the dust from your feet as you leave that house or town. Truly, I say to you, it shall be more tolerable on the day of judgment for the land of Sodom and Gomorrah than for that town" (Matthew 10. 14-15).

Another predominate factor in the mission of Jesus was his narrow sectarianism; Jesus came not to save the world, but to save only a small part of it—namely, the Jews, the "elect," God's "chosen people." Jesus preached in behalf of those whom he believed "thou gavest me." (See Mark 4. 10-12; 13.22, 27; John 6.37, 44, 65; 17.2, 6.) Jesus was a Jew, and he conceived of himself as the Jewish messiah: "Think not that I have come to abolish the law and the prophets; I have come not to abolish them but to fulfil them" (Matthew 5. 17). "Go nowhere among the Gentiles," Jesus instructed his disciples, "and enter no town of the Samaritans, but go rather to the lost sheep of the house of Israel" (Matthew 10. 5-6). When a Canaanite woman begged Jesus to cast a "demon" from her daughter, Jesus replied, "I was sent only to the lost sheep of the house of Israel." It was only when the woman pleaded further that "even the dogs eat the crumbs that fall from their master's table," that Jesus marveled at her great "faith" and agreed to heal her daughter (Matthew 15. 22-28).

Whether or not theologians agree that the precepts of Jesus were intended only for the Jews during the "interim," there can be no doubt but that those precepts are strictly otherworldly in emphasis. Jesus does not prescribe standards of behavior on the basis that they will contribute to man's happiness and well-being on earth. He issues commands, or rules, backed by the brute sanctions of heaven and hell, with the specific choice of sanction determined by how well one obeys. "It is a plain matter," notes Richard Robinson, "of promises and threats."

(b) Perhaps the most widespread delusion about the moral precepts of Jesus is that they are strikingly unusual and original. Nothing could be further from the truth. As one Christian writer has observed, "Point for point, there is nothing in the teaching of Jesus which cannot be found in the Old Testament or in the rabbinical teaching."[8] According to the famous ex-priest and historian Joseph McCabe:

> The sentiments attributed to Christ are . . . already found in the Old Testament. . . . They were familiar in the Jewish schools, and to all the Pharisees, long before the time of Christ, as they were familiar in all the civilizations of the earth—Egyptian, Babylonian, and Persian, Greek and Hindu.[9]

It is interesting to note that in many cases Jesus did not lay claim to the originality now credited to him. The famous Golden Rule is a case in point. Advocated by Confucius 500 years before Jesus, it was also promulgated by Hillel, a Pharisee and older contemporary of Jesus. Quoting the Jewish Talmud:

> And Hillel said: What thou dost not like, do thou not to thy neighbor. That is the whole law; all the rest is explanation. (Sabbath, 31.1)

317

In Matthew 7. 12, Jesus says: "So whatever you wish that men would do to you, do so to them; *for this is the law and the prophets.*" (Emphasis added.) Jesus freely admits that this precept is imbedded in Jewish tradition, thus contradicting the many theologians who prefer to credit him with the formulation.

A similar example is found in Matthew 22.39—"You shall love your neighbor as yourself"—which Christians like also to attribute to the moral creativity of Jesus. Unfortunately for them, however, we encounter the identical words in Leviticus 19.18: ". . . you shall love your neighbor as yourself."

In those instances where Jesus appears to revise or reject older Jewish precepts, he frequently misrepresents the content of the Judaic law. For example, in Matthew 5. 21-22, we read:

> You have heard that it was said to the men of old, "You shall not kill; and whoever kills shall be liable to judgment."
>
> But I say to you that every one who is angry with his brother shall be liable to judgment. . . .

This prohibition against anger was not new to the Jewish tradition; we find the same maxim in Leviticus 19.17: "You shall not hate your brother in your heart. . . ." Again, in warning against "lustful" thoughts, Jesus says:

> You have heard that it was said, "You shall not commit adultery." But I say to you that every one who looks at a woman lustfully has already committed adultery with her in his heart. (Matthew 5.27-28)

A novel idea? Hardly. Exodus 20.17: ". . . you shall not covet your neighbor's wife." Proverbs 6.25-26: "Do not desire her beauty in your heart, and do not let her capture you with her eyelashes; for a harlot may be hired for a loaf of bread, but an adultress stalks a man's very life." And, according to the Talmud, "Whosoever regardeth even the little finger of a woman hath already sinned in his heart" (Berachot 24.1). These and many similar examples illustrate that Jesus did not deviate from traditional Judaism as much as the Gospel writers would sometimes like us to believe.

As mentioned previously, Jesus did not view himself as a moral innovator, nor were his moral precepts notable for their originality. The Jesus of the Gospels is portrayed as a divine prophet and miracle worker, not as a philosopher. Jesus distinguished himself, not by the content of his moral code, but by his conception of himself and his divinely appointed mission. For instance, after the Sermon of the Mount, Matthew 7.28-29 reports that "when Jesus finished these sayings, the crowds were astonished at his teaching"—why?—"for he taught them as one who had *authority*, and not as their scribes."

Jesus represented himself as a divine or semi-divine figure, and he underwrote his precepts with the authority of God. "I seek not my own will," he proclaimed, "but the will of him who sent me. . . . the works which the Father has granted me to accomplish, these very works which I am doing, bear me witness that the Father has sent me" (John 5. 30,36). Jesus was not accused of blasphemy for his moral precepts; rather it was his claim of messiahship that led to the animosity between himself and the Jewish establishment, as represented by the Pharisees.

If we ignore what Jesus said about himself and consider only what he said about morality, he emerges as predominately status quo. This poses a problem for Christian liberals. Strip Jesus of his divinity—as many liberals wish to do—and, at best, he becomes a mediocre preacher who held mistaken beliefs about practically everything, including himself; and, at worst, he becomes a pretentious fraud.

This last remark will undoubtedly seem harsh to many people. Am I not being overly critical of Jesus who, after all, lived in a particular historical context? Perhaps he was trying only to render aid and comfort to an oppressed people. Perhaps he was, despite the biblical references to eternal damnation, a

319

kind and compassionate man. Surely he was sincere in his beliefs and displayed courage by his willingness to die for his convictions. Perhaps it is unfair to pass unequivocal judgment on him from the sparse information provided in the Gospels.

Some of these comments may apply to the historical Jesus, and some may not—it is difficult to say with certainty—but they are irrelevant to the issue under consideration. We are evaluating the biblical Jesus, not the historical Jesus, and the precepts of this Jesus, intermingled with threats of gnashing teeth and eternal torment, contain a strong current of harshness and cruelty. We shall now discuss these percepts in more detail.

(c) On those rare occasions when a philosopher severely criticizes the ethics of Jesus—such as in Richard Robinson's *An Atheist's Values*—many theologians tend to pass over such criticism as superficial and unsympathetic. According to these theologians, who are usually liberal Protestants, we must understand Jesus as a human being with human frailties; and it is unfair, they claim, to subject the teachings of this man, who admittedly was not a philosopher, to the rigor of philosophic scrutiny.

This rejoinder of the Christian, or any similar position, is a concession rather than a reply. If we do not accept Jesus as a supernatural figure, what has he to offer us? Why should anyone bother to read the New Testament except, perhaps, for its historical interest? We know how Jesus has traditionally rated as a god, but how does he rate as a man? Does he, as a moral teacher, deserve the enormous respect that he seems to elicit even from disbelievers? The historical impact of Jesus is undisputed, but does he merit such fame? My response to this last question—which indicates my responses to the previous questions—is an unqualified "no."

Considered in themselves, the moral precepts of Jesus are sometimes interesting, sometimes poetic, sometimes benevolent, sometimes confusing, sometimes pernicious, and sometimes devastatingly harmful psychologically. None, however, are especially profound. If not for their tremendous historical impact, most would deserve little more than a philosopher's passing glance.

320

In assessing the ethical significance of Jesus, it is illuminating to contrast him with the ancient Greek philosophers who preceded him by hundreds of years. The differences are so striking that few scholars care to place Jesus on the same level as such intellectual giants as Plato and Aristotle. Whether one agrees with these philosophers or not, they at least argue for their claims; Jesus, on the other hand, issues proclamations backed by the threat of force.

It is not my purpose here to "refute" the moral precepts of Jesus by demonstrating them to be ethically unsound. Since Jesus does not argue for his doctrines, they are, philosophically, nothing more than arbitrary assertions. And one cannot argue with an arbitrary proposition; one either accepts it on faith or ignores it. Christians prefer the former alternative, while I choose the latter. The precepts of Jesus simply do not merit a serious or comprehensive refutation. My sole purpose in this discussion is to examine the effects and wider implications of Jesus' major doctrines, not to lend them the undeserved respect of a counter-argument.

As indicated previously, the major precept of the biblical Jesus is what contemporary theologians like to call total devotion, or commitment, to God. In this context, of course, the terms "devotion" and "commitment" are euphemisms for their less flattering counterparts: obedience and conformity. As with all theologians, when Jesus says "believe" he means "obey." And when Jesus praises men of great "faith," he is praising men who will obey unquestioningly any command they believe to come from God.

When conformity is required, as it is in Christianity, what are the results? To begin with, the sacrifice of truth inevitably follows. One can be committed to conformity or one can be committed to truth, but not both. The pursuit of truth requires the unrestricted use of one's mind—the moral freedom to question, to examine evidence, to consider opposing viewpoints, to criticize, to accept as true only that which can be demonstrated—regardless of whether one's conclusions conform to a particular creed.

The fundamental teaching of Jesus—the demand for conformity—thus gives rise to a fundamental and viciously destructive teaching of Christianity: that some beliefs lie beyond the scope of criticism and that to question them is *sinful*, or morally wrong. By placing a moral restriction on what one is permitted to believe, Christianity declares itself an enemy of truth and of the faculty by which man arrives at truth—reason.

Whatever minor points may be offered in defense of Christianity, they cannot compensate for the monstrous doctrine that one is morally obligated to accept as true religious beliefs that cannot be comprehended or demonstrated. It must be remembered that this teaching is not incidental to Christianity: it lies at the heart of Jesus' mission, and it has played a significant role throughout Christianity's history. It was this belief that "justified" the slaughter of dissenters and heretics in the name of morality, and its philosophical consequence may be described as the inversion—or, more precisely, the *perversion*—of morality.

To be moral, according to Jesus, man must shackle his reason. He must force himself to believe that which he cannot understand. He must suppress, in the name of morality, any doubts that surface in his mind. He must regard as a mark of excellence an unwillingness to subject religious beliefs to critical examination. Less criticism leads to more faith—and faith, Jesus declares, is the hallmark of virtue. Indeed, "unless you turn and become like children, you will never enter the kingdom of heaven" (Matthew 18.3). Children, after all, will believe almost anything.

The psychological impact of this doctrine is devastating. To divorce morality from truth is to turn man's reason against himself. Reason, as the faculty by which man comprehends reality and exercises control over his environment, is the basic requirement of self-esteem. To the extent that a man believes that his mind is a potential enemy, that it may lead to the "evils" of question-asking and criticism, he will feel the need for intellectual passivity—to deliberately sabotage his mind in the name of virtue. Reason becomes a vice, something to be feared, and man finds that his worst enemy is his own capacity to think and question. One can scarcely imagine a more effective way to introduce perpetual conflict into man's consciousness and thereby produce a host of neurotic symptoms.

Another significant teaching of Jesus, closely related to the preceding, is that certain feelings and desires are in themselves sinful. Merely feeling or desiring something can bring divine condemnation upon oneself, regardless of whether one translates the feeling into action: "every one who is angry with his brother shall be liable to judgment"; "every one who looks at a woman lustfully has already committed adultery with her in his heart."

This idea, as we have seen, did not originate with Jesus, but Christianity has given it an unusually heavy emphasis. Even today Christians are warned to "repent" of evil emotions, which often consists of feelings in the realm of sexual desire.

Morally, this doctrine is reprehensible, because it erases the crucial distinction between intent and action. Psychologically, however, it is nothing less than murder. It is a prescription, a demand, for emotional repression, for deliberately obstructing awareness of one's inner emotional state. Psychological health, to a large extent, consists of being in touch with one's feelings, and to believe that one is not morally permitted to experience certain feelings is to declare war on one's emotions. Of course, a psychologically healthy individual does not *act* unthinkingly on the basis of his feelings, but it is essential to self-awareness that he be able to experience what those feelings are.

This general attitude toward emotions runs throughout the teaching of Jesus. His second commandment, the Bible tells us, is that we should "love" our neighbor as ourselves. Aside from the content of this pronouncement, which is rather difficult to make sense of, the entire notion of commanding feelings in and out of existence is ludicrous. Love is an emotional response to values, and if we do not perceive the necessary values in many people, how are we to force the emotion of love? Jesus does not say. He simply threatens damnation for those who disobey.

We are similarly cautioned by Jesus to be meek and humble, and—even if we overlook the fact that meekness and similar

323

passive qualities are the antithesis of self-assertiveness and self-esteem—we must wonder how the promise of reward or the threat of force can significantly alter a man's inner qualities. There is only one possibility: if the threat of force, of eternal damnation, succeeds in breaking a man's spirit—if it robs him of emotional strength and intellectual independence—he will indeed become meek and humble. Perhaps this is what Jesus was aiming for.

The best thing that can be said about Jesus' approach to human emotions is that it is psychologically naive. The worst thing that can be said is that when men attempt to practice what he preaches, they invariably inflict a great deal of psychological misery upon themselves. As Nathaniel Branden has written:

> Desires and emotions as such are involuntary; they are not subject to direct and immediate volitional control; they are the automatic result of subconscious integrations. . . . It is impossible to compute the magnitude of the disaster, the wreckage of human lives, produced by the belief that desires and emotions can be commanded in and out of existence by an act of will.

> To those who accept the validity of Jesus' pronouncements, and their wider implications for undesired or "immoral" emotions in general, his teachings are clearly an injunction to practice repression. Whether or not by intention, that is their effect.[10]

Another important teaching of Jesus is passive non-resistance to evil. "Love your enemies, do good to those who hate you, bless those who curse you, pray for those who abuse you" (Luke 6. 27-28).

> Do not resist one who is evil. But if any one strikes you on the right cheek, turn to him the other also; and if any one would sue you and take your coat, let

him have your cloak as well; and if any one forces you to go one mile, go with him two miles. (Matthew 5. 39-41)

My first response to these precepts is: Why? For what possible reason should one offer oneself as a sacrificial animal in this way? Such questions, however, do not apply to Jesus, because he is interested only in obedience, not in presenting rational arguments. In fact, when viewed in this context, these commands begin to make sense. We are not to judge others, Jesus says, which is merely another facet of suspending one's critical faculties. We are to tolerate injustice, we are to refrain from passing value judgments of other people—such precepts require the obliteration of one's capacity to distinguish the good from the evil; they require the kind of intellectual and moral passiveness that generates a mentality of obedience. The man who is incapable of passing independent value judgments will be the least critical when given orders. And he will be unlikely to evaluate the moral worth of the man, or the supposed god, from whence those orders come.

In short, there is nothing virtuous in the virtues recommended by Jesus. The only thing close to an ethical precept with merit is the Golden Rule, which is a rough approximation of a fairness ethic, but even this is issued in the form of a command. Generally, Jesus commands us to have faith in God and in himself as a messenger from God—which means the sacrifice of reason—and we are reminded that God will reward those who obey and punish those who disobey. Also, we are told that God is monitoring us at every moment, and that he has complete knowledge of our innermost thoughts and feelings. If the notion of an omnipresent voyeurist does not create a high level of nervous tension and anxiety, not to mention guilt, nothing will.

It is an interesting exercise to ask oneself the following question about each precept attributed to Jesus in the New Testament: What does this precept have to offer a confident, efficacious and happy man? In the vast majority of cases, the answer will be: nothing—absolutely nothing. As Jesus himself put it, "Those who are well have no need of a physician, but those who are sick; I came not to call the righteous, but sinners" (Mark 2.17). In order to fit within the framework of Jesus' mission, one must view oneself fundamentally as a "sinner"—as evil and worthless in the sight of God. In order to accomplish this, it is precisely the qualities of confidence, efficacy and happiness that must be surrendered: "Woe to you that laugh now, for you shall mourn and weep" (Luke 6.25). "For every one who exalts himself will be humbled, and he who humbles himself will be exalted" (Luke 14.11).

What remains after the qualities essential to a rewarding life are surrendered? Nothing—except a man without reason, without passion, without self-esteem. A man, in other words, that will find *anything* preferable to life on earth. Such a man may claim that Christianity has given him hope of happiness in an afterlife, but all that Christianity has really given him is an elaborate excuse, draped in a banner of morality, to continue his blind stumbling through life on earth.

Human misery is a sad spectacle. But it is sadder still when disguised as moral righteousness.

Notes

Chapter 1

1. A. E. Taylor, *Does God Exist?* (New York: The Macmillan Co., 1947), pp. 158-159.

2. Vincent P. Miceli, S. J., *The Gods of Atheism* (New Rochelle: Arlington House, 1971), p. 19.

3. Plato, *Laws*, translated by Benjamin Jowett, Great Books of the Western World (Chicago: Encyclopedia Britannica, Inc., 1952), Vol. 7, pp. 769-770.

4. Thomas Aquinas, *Summa Theologica*, translated by Fathers of the English Dominican Province, revised by Daniel J. Sullivan, Great Books of the Western World (Chicago: Encyclopedia Britannica, Inc., 1952), Second Part, Pt. II, Q. 10, A. 3.

5. Ibid., Q. 11, A. 3.

6. Quoted in Frank Swancara, *The Separation of Religion and Government* (New York: Truth Seeker Co., 1950), p. 140.

7. Taylor, *Does God Exist?* p. 1.

8. John Hick, *Philosophy of Religion* (Englewood Cliffs: Prentice-Hall, Inc., 1963), p. 4.

9. Paul Edwards, "Some Notes on Anthropomorphic Theology," *Religious Experience and Truth*, edited by Sidney Hook (New York: New York University Press, 1961), pp. 241-242.

10. Thomas H. Huxley, "Agnosticism," *Collected Essays* (New York: D. Appleton and Co., 1894), Vol. V, pp. 237-238.

11. See George F. Thomas, *Philosophy and Religious Belief* (New York: Charles Schribner's Sons, 1970), pp. 181-182.

12. Thomas H. Huxley, "Agnosticism and Christianity," *Collected Essays*, Vol. V, p. 311.

13. Ibid., pp. 310-311.

14. Ibid., p. 311.

15. *New Catholic Encyclopedia* (New York: McGraw-Hill, 1967), Vol. 1, p. 205.

16. Jacques Maritain, *The Range of Reason* (New York: Charles Schribner's Sons), p. 97.

17. Ibid.

18. Ibid., p. 98.

19. *New Catholic Encyclopedia*, Vol, 1, p. 1,000.

20. Ignace Lepp, *Atheism in Our Time* (Toronto: The Macmillan Co., 1964), p. 14.

21. Joseph Lewis, *Atheism and Other Addresses* (New York: The Freethought Press Association, Inc., 1960).

22. Robert J. Kreyche, *God and Reality* (New York: Holt, Rinehart and Winston, Inc., 1965), p. 3.

23. David Trueblood, *Philosophy of Religion* (New York: Harper and Row, 1959), p. 84.

24. Fulton J. Sheen, *Way to Happiness* (Greenwich: Fawcett Publications, Inc., 1954), p. 84.

25. John Courtney Murray, S. J., *Theological Studies* (March, 1962). Quoted in Martin E. Marty, *Varieties of Unbelief* (New York: Doubleday and Co., Inc., 1966), pp. 11-12. The italics are by Marty.

26. H. C. Rümke, *The Psychology of Unbelief*, translated by M. H. C. Willems (New York: Sheed and Warn, 1962), p. 13.

27. Thomas S. Szasz, *Ideology and Insanity: Essays on the Psychiatric Dehumanization of Man* (New York: Doubleday and Co., Inc., 1970), p. 36.

28. *Webster's New World Dictionary*, College Edition (Cleveland and New York: The World Publishing Co., 1957), p. 489.

Chapter 2

1. James F. Ross, *Introduction to the Philosophy of Religion* (Toronto: The Macmillan Co., 1969), p. 11.

2. William T. Blackstone, *The Problem of Religious Knowledge* (Englewood Cliffs: Prentice-Hall, Inc., 1963), p. 2.

3. Alfred Jules Ayer, *Language, Truth and Logic* (New York: Dover Publications, 1946), p. 115.

4. Two of the best works available on this subject are: Blackstone, *Problem of Religious Knowledge*, and Frederick Ferré, *Language, Logic and God* (New York: Harper Torchbooks, 1969).

5. Antony Flew, *God and Philosophy* (New York: Harcourt, Brace and World, Inc., 1966), p. 15.

6. Paul Tillich, *Systematic Theology* (Chicago: University of Chicago Press, 1967 [contains three volumes published from 1951-1963]), Vol. I, pp. 236-237.

7. Ibid., p. 238.

8. Paul Tillich, *The Shaking of the Foundations* (New York: Charles Schribner's Sons, 1948), p. 57.

9. Ibid.

10. Paul Tillich, *Dynamics of Faith* (New York: Harper Torchbooks, 1958), pp. 45-46.

11. Walter Kaufmann, *The Faith of a Heretic* (New York: Anchor Books, 1963), p. 90.

12. Tillich, *Systematic Theology*, Vol. II, p. 7.

13. John A. T. Robinson, *Honest to God* (Philadelphia: The Westminster Press, 1963), p. 29.

14. Ibid., pp. 47-48.

15. E. L. Mascall, *The Secularization of Christianity* (New York: Holt, Rinehart and Winston, 1965), p. 111.

16. Ibid., p. 118.

17. Augustine, *Sermo LII*, vi. 16. Quoted in *Catholicism*, edited by George Brantl (New York: Washington Square Press, Inc., 1962), p. 36.

18. Leslie D. Weatherhead, *The Christian Agnostic* (Nashville: Abingdon Press, 1965), p. 39.

19. Thomas McPherson, "Religion as the Inexpressible," *New Essays in Philosophical Theology*, edited by Antony Flew and Alasdair MacIntyre (New York: The Macmillan Co., 1955), pp. 132-133.

20. Quoted in *Varieties of Mystic Experience*, edited by Elmer O'Brien, S. J. (New York: The New American Library, 1964), p. 81.

21. Ludwig Feuerbach, *The Essence of Christianity*, translated by George Eliot, p. 14. (First printed 1854. Reprinted by Harper Torchbooks, New York, 1957.)

22. Nathaniel Branden, *The Objectivist Newsletter*, Vol. 2, no. 1 (Jan. 1963), p. 3.

23. Ibid.

Chapter 3

1. *1968 National Catholic Almanac*, edited by Felician A. Foy, O. F. M. (Paterson: St. Anthony's Guild, 1968), p. 360.

2. Thomas, *Philosophy and Religious Belief*, pp. 180-181.

3. John Hospers, *An Introduction to Philosophical Analysis*, 2nd ed., rev. (Englewood Cliffs: Prentice-Hall, Inc., 1967), p. 482.

4. Feuerbach, *Essence of Christianity*, p. 15.

5. Aquinas, *Summa Theologica*, First Part, Q. 3, Preface.

6. F. C. Copleston, *Aquinas* (Harmondsworth: Penguin Books, Ltd., 1955), p. 132.

7. Flew, *God and Philosophy*, p. 30. Cf. Antony Flew, "Theology and Falsification," *New Essays in Philosophical Theology*, pp. 96-99.

8. Ferré, *Language, Logic and God*, p. 68.

9. For a detailed discussion of analogy, see R. P. Phillips, *Modern Thomistic Philosophy* (Westminster: The Newman Press, 1950), Vol. II, pp. 166-173. Cf. F. C. Copleston, *A History of Philosophy* (New York: Image Books, 1962), Vol. II, Part II, pp. 70-78.

10. Thomas, *Philosophy and Religious Belief*, p. 189.

11. D. J. B. Hawkins, *The Essentials of Theism* (New York: Sheed and Ward, 1950), p. 95.

12. See, Hick, *Philosophy of Religion*, pp. 79-80.

13. Blackstone, *The Problem of Religious Knowledge*, p. 66.

14. Hawkins, *Essentials of Theism*, p. 96.

15. Aquinas, *Summa Theologica*, First Part, Q. 13, A. 11.

16. Phillips, *Modern Thomistic Philosophy*, p. 306.

17. For an explanation of the Thomistic distinction between essence and

existence, see: Knut Tranoy, "Thomas Aquinas," *A Critical History of Western Philosophy*, edited by D. J. O'Connor (New York: The Free Press of Glencoe, 1964), pp. 106-107.

18. Copleston, *Aquinas*, p. 141.

19. Etienne Gilson, *The Christian Philosophy of St. Thomas Aquinas* (New York: Random House, 1956), p. 107.

20. Kreyche, *God and Reality*, p. 18.

21. Copleston, *Aquinas*, p. 141.

22. Aquinas, *Summa Theologica*, First Part, Q. 12, A. 7.

23. Ibid., First Part, Q. 12, A. 1.

24. According to Aquinas, ". . . since power is said in reference to possible things, this phrase, 'God can do all things,' is rightly understood to mean that God can do all things that are possible. . . ." Therefore, "whatever implies contradiction does not come within the scope of omnipotence because it cannot have the aspect of possibility. Hence it is better to say that such things cannot be done, than that God cannot do them." (*Summa Theologica*, First Part, Q. 25, A. 3.) As Hawkins puts it: "It is no limitation upon the power of the Almighty to say that God cannot produce the meaningless." (*Essentials of Theism*, p. 99.) For a technical discussion of omnipotence, see James F. Ross, *Philosophical Theology* (Indianapolis and New York: The Bobbs-Merrill Co., Inc., 1969), pp. 195-221.

25. John Stuart Mill, *Theism*, edited by Richard Taylor, pp. 33-34. (First printed 1874. Reprinted by The Bobbs-Merrill Co., Inc., Indianapolis and New York, 1957.)

26. Kreyche, *God and Reality*, p. 68.

27. Hawkins, *Essentials of Theism*, p. 122.

28. See Nathaniel Branden, *The Psychology of Self-Esteem* (Los Angeles: Nash Publishing Co., 1969), pp. 26-33.

29. Thomas Paine, *Age of Reason*, Part I, pp. 18-19. (First printed 1794. Reprinted by The Freethought Press Association, New York, 1954.)

30. Aquinas, *Summa Theologica*, Supplement to the Third Part, Q. 99, A. 1.

31. Weatherhead, *The Christian Agnostic*, p. 97.

32. John McTaggart, *Some Dogmas of Religion* (London: Edward Arnold, 1906), pp. 209-210.

33. Wallace Matson, *The Existence of God* (Ithaca: Cornell University Press, 1965), pp. 142-143. For another excellent discussion of the problem of evil, see: C. E. M. Joad, *God and Evil* (London: Faber and Faber Limited, 1943), especially chapters 2 and 3.

34. John Hick, *Evil and the God of Love* (New York: Harper and Row, 1966), pp. 370-371.

35. Gilson, *The Christian Philosophy of St. Thomas Aquinas*, p. 17.

36. Richard Taylor, "Faith," *Religious Experience and Truth*, p. 169.

Chapter 4

1. William Barrett, *Irrational Man* (Garden City: Anchor Books, 1962), pp. 92-93.

2. Quoted in Barrett, ibid., pp. 94-95.

3. Tertullian, *The Prescriptions Against the Heretics*, quoted in *Classical Statements on Faith and Reason*, edited by L. Miller (New York: Random House, 1970), pp. 3-10.

4. Quoted in Walter Kaufmann, *Critique of Religion and Philosophy*, pp. 305-307. (First printed 1958. Reprinted by Harper Torchbooks, New York, 1972.)

5. Nathaniel Branden, "Mental Health versus Mysticism," *The Virtue of Selfishness* by Ayn Rand (New York: The New American Library, 1964), p. 37.

6. Richard Robinson, *An Atheist's Values* (Oxford: The Clarendon Press, 1964), pp. 119-120.

7. Ross, *Introduction to the Philosophy of Religion*, pp. 84-85.

8. Ayn Rand, *The Virtue of Selfishness*, p. 13.

9. John Locke, *Concerning Human Understanding*, Great Books of the Western World (Chicago: Encyclopedia Britannica, Inc., 1952), Vol. 35, p. 381.

10. Aquinas, *Summa Theologica*, Second Part, Pt. II, Q. 2, A. 4.

11. Gilson, *The Christian Philosophy of St. Thomas Aquinas*, p. 17.

12. Augustine, *The Confessions*, Great Books of the Western World (Chicago: Encyclopedia Britannica, Inc., 1952), Vol. 18, p. 36.

13. Augustine, *The City of God*, Great Books of the Western World (Chicago: Encyclopedia Britannica, Inc., 1952), Vol. 18, pp. 562-564.

14. Pascal, *Pensées* (New York: E. P. Dutton and Co., Inc., 1958), p. 78.

15. Robinson, *Honest to God*, pp. 101-102.

16. Ibid., p. 103.

17. Henry M. Morris, *Studies in the Bible and Science* (Grand Rapids: Baker Book House, 1966), p. 7.

18. Floyd E. Hamilton, *The Basis of the Christian Faith* (New York: Harper and Row, 1964, 1964), p. 14.

19. Kaufmann, *Critique of Religion and Philosophy*, p. 310.

20. See Andrew Dickson White, *A History of the Warfare of Science with Theology in Christiandom*, Vol. 1, pp. 144-170. (First printed 1896. Reprinted by Dover Publications, New York, 1960.)

21. *New Catholic Encyclopedia*, Vol. 6, p. 254.

22. Rudolph Bultmann, "The Study of the Synoptic Gospels," *Form Criticism*, p. 28. (First printed 1934. Reprinted by Harper Torchbooks, New York, 1962.)

23. William Robert Miller, ed., *The New Christianity* (New York: Dell Publishing Co., Inc., 1967), p. 249.

24. Kaufmann, *The Faith of a Heretic*, p. 100.

25. Aquinas, *Summa Theologica*, Supplement to the Third Part, Q. 97.

26. Rudolph Bultmann and Karl Jaspers, *Myth and Christianity*, translated by Norbert Guterman (New York: The Noonday Press, 1958), pp. 60-61.

27. Kaufmann, *Critique of Religion and Philosophy*, p. 180.

28. Kaufmann, *The Faith of a Heretic*, p. 104. Kaufmann's attack on theology is similar to that of Nietzsche who, in *The Anti-Christ*, wrote: "The way in which a theologian, no matter whether in Berlin or in Rome, interprets a 'word of the Scriptures', or an experience, a victory of his country's army for example, under the higher illumination of the psalms of David, is always so *audacious* as to make a philologist run up every wall in sight" (pp. 169-170). According to Nietzsche, "Whoever has theologian blood in his veins has a wrong and dishonest attitude towards all things from the very first." He even went so far as to declare that, "What a theologian feels to be true *must* be false: this provides almost a criterion of truth" (p. 120). (First published 1895. Reprinted by Penguin Books, Ltd., Harmondsworth, 1968, translated by R. J. Hollingdale.)

Chapter 5

1. Mortimer J. Adler, *The Difference of Man and the Difference it Makes* (New York: Holt, Rinehart and Winston, 1967), p. 143.

2. G. K. Chesterton, Introduction to *God and Intelligence in Modern Philosophy* by Fulton J. Sheen, p. 7. (First printed 1925. Reprinted by Image Books, New York, 1958.)

3. Trueblood, *Philosophy of Religion*, p. 53.

4. Ibid., p. 49.

5. Arthur F. Smethurst, *Modern Science and Christian Beliefs* (New York: Abingdon Press, 1955), p. 14.

6. Ibid., p. 12.

7. Morris, *Studies in the Bible and Science*, pp. 108-109.

8. D. W. Hamlyn, *The Theory of Knowledge* (New York: Doubleday and Co., 1970), p. 50.

9. Francis H. Parker, "Realistic Epistemology," *The Return to Reason*,

edited by John Wild (Chicago: Henry Regnery Co., 1953), p. 152. Parker himself attempts a reconciliation of reason and faith in *Reason and Faith Revisited* (Milwaukee: Marquette University Press, 1971).

10. Celestine N. Bittle, *Reality and the Mind* (New York: The Bruce Publishing Co., 1936), pp. 47-48. Bittle is a Thomist, and he typifies the paradox in which Thomists find themselves regarding faith and skepticism. Because of their Aristotelian background and respect for logic, Thomists have written some excellent critiques of skepticism; and, in many respects, they display a high regard for reason. Thus, according to Bittle, "objective evidence, not faith, is the ultimate criterion of truth in the order of natural knowledge" (p. 315). This is fine as far as it goes, but note the phrase "natural knowledge." This indicates a contrast with supernatural knowledge, and it is here that reason gives way to faith. "Concerning *supernatural* truths," writes Bittle, "it is indeed correct to say that a revelation is required in order to be certain of them" (p. 315). Thomists are not overt skeptics, but they rely on an undercurrent of skepticism in order to divorce the realm of reason from the realm of faith. This is discussed in more detail in the following chapter.

See also: Celestine N. Bittle, *The Science of Correct Thinking*, rev. (Milwaukee: The Bruce Publishing Co., 1937), pp. 291-292. Here Bittle defends inductive reasoning by basing the belief in the uniformity of nature on the belief in God, thus effectively denying that the belief in the uniformity of nature can be grounded in reason.

11. Thomas Reid, *Essays on the Intellectual Powers of Man* (Cambridge: The M. I. T. Press, 1969), p. 744.

12. Ibid., p. 748.

13. Ibid., p. 739.

14. J. L. Austin, "Other Minds," *Philosophical Papers*, edited by J. O. Urmson and G. J. Warnock (London: Oxford University Press, 1961), p. 66.

15. Ibid.

16. Hamlyn, *The Theory of Knowledge*, p. 49.

17. Ayn Rand, *Introduction to Objectivist Epistemology* (New York: The Objectivist, Inc., 1967), p. 70. A series of lectures on "Objectivism's Theory of Knowledge" was presented by Leonard Peikoff under the auspices of the Nathaniel Branden Institute in New York City, and these

lectures were distributed via tape transcript throughout the United States. However, to my knowledge, these lectures have not been available since the dissolution of N. B. I. in 1968.

18. Ibid., pp. 45-46.

19. Rand, *The Virtue of Selfishness*, p. 14.

20. Rand, *Introduction to Objectivist Epistemology*, p. 14. This brief excerpt cannot do justice to Rand's treatment of axiomatic concepts, so the reader is urged to read Rand's monograph in its entirety.

21. Nathaniel Branden, "The Stolen Concept," *The Objectivist Newsletter*, Vol. 2, No. 1 (Jan. 1963), p. 4.

22. Ibid., p. 2.

23. James W. Cornman and Keith Lehrer, *Philosophical Problems and Arguments* (New York: The Macmillan Co., 1968), p. 111.

24. Smethurst, *Modern Science and Christian Beliefs*, p. 10.

25. Hamlyn, *Theory of Knowledge*, p. 51.

26. Lionel Ruby, *Logic: An Introduction* (Chicago: J. B. Lippincott Co., 1950), p. 262.

27. Hospers, *Introduction to Philosophical Analysis*, p. 222.

28. Brand Blanshard, *The Nature of Thought* (London: George Allen and Unwin Ltd., 1939), Vol. II, pp. 413-414.

29. Quoted in *Meaning and Knowledge: Systematic Readings in Epistemology*, edited by Ernest Nagel and Richard B. Brandt (New York: Harcourt, Brace and World, Inc., 1965), p. 397.

30. See pp. 40-41 and pp. 259-260.

31. This approach to certainty is presented in "Objectivism's Theory of Knowledge," a series of recorded lectures by Leonard Peikoff.

32. There are a number of excellent defenses of sense perception, among which I particularly recommend the following: Maurice Mandelbaum, *Philosophy, Science and Sense Perception* (Baltimore: The Johns Hopkins

Press, 1964), Chapter 3; C. W. K. Mundle, *Perception: Facts and Theories* (London: Oxford University Press, 1971); J. L. Austin, *Sense and Sensibilia*, edited by G. J. Warnock (London: Oxford University Press, 1962); P. Coffey, *Epistemology*, Vol. II. (First printed 1917. Reprinted by Peter Smith, Gloucester, Mass., 1958); D. M. Armstrong, *Perception and the Physical World* (London: Routledge and Kegan Paul, 1961).

Chapter 6

1. John Hick, *Faith and Knowledge* (Ithaca: Cornell University Press, 1957), pp. xi-xii.

2. *1968 National Catholic Almanac*, p. 372.

3. Edward V. Stanford, *Foundations of Christian Belief* (Westminster: The Newman Press, 1960), p. 3.

4. Ibid.

5. J. Roland Ramirez, "Faith, Philosophy, and Philosophical Unbelief," *The Christian Intellectual*, edited by Samuel Hazo (Pittsburgh: Duquesne University Press, 1963), pp. 45-46.

6. Brantl, *"Sermo LII"* in *Catholicism*, pp. 169-172.

7. Blanshard, *Nature of Thought*, Vol. II, p. 217.

8. Ibid., pp. 220-221.

9. Robinson, *Honest to God*, p. 98.

10. Aquinas, *Summa Theologica*, Second Part, Pt. II, Q. 2, A. 9.

11. S. M. Thompson, *A Modern Philosophy of Religion*, quoted in Hick, *Faith and Knowledge*, pp. 45-46.

12. Weatherhead, *The Christian Agnostic*, p. 97.

13. Pascal, *Pensées*, pp. 66-67.

14. Ibid., p. 68.

15. Flew, *God and Philosophy*, p. 185.

16. William James, "The Will to Believe," *Selected Papers*, p. 100. (First printed 1896. Reprinted by J. M. Dent and Sons, London and Toronto, 1917.)

17. William James, "The Sentiment of Rationality," *Selected Essays*, pp. 151-152. (First printed 1879. Reprinted by J. M. Dent and Sons, London and Toronto, 1917.)

18. James, "The Will to Believe," p. 108.

19. Ibid., p. 120.

20. Ibid., p. 122.

21. Ibid., p. 110.

22. Ibid., pp. 106-107.

23. Hick, *Faith and Knowledge*, p. 56.

24. James, "The Sentiment of Rationality," p. 153.

25. Quoted in Kaufmann, *Critique of Religion and Philosophy*, p. 119.

26. Ibid.

Chapter 7

1. Wilbur F. Tillett, "The Divine Element in the Bible," *The Abingdon Bible Commentary*, edited by F. C. Eiselen *et al.* (New York: Abingdon Press, 1929), p. 27.

2. Decrees of the Vatican Council, *De Ecclesia Christi*, iv. Quoted in John Baillie, *The Idea of Revelation in Recent Thought* (New York: Columbia University Press, 1956), p. 112.

3. For a more detailed account of the liberal approach to the Bible, see: Baillie, *The Idea of Revelation in Recent Thought*.

4. Robert G. Ingersoll, "Mistakes of Moses," *44 Complete Lectures* (Chicago: Regan Publishing Corp.), p. 8.

5. For a brief history of biblical criticism, see: Samuel Terrien, "History

of the Interpretation of the Bible," *The Interpreter's Bible* (New York: Abingdon Press, 1952), Vol. I, pp. 127-141.

6. Thomas Hobbes, *Leviathan,* edited by Michael Oakeshott (London: Collier-Macmillan Ltd., 1962), p. 272.

7. J. M. Robertson, *A History of Freethought* (London: Watts and Co., 1936), Vol. II, p. 615.

8. Hobbes, *Leviathan,* p. 51.

9. Benedict Spinoza, *A Theologico-Political Treatise,* translated by R. H. M. Elwes (New York: Dover Publications, 1951), p. 8.

10. Ibid., p. 111.

11. Ibid., p. 92.

12. Ibid., p. 11.

13. Paine, *Age of Reason,* Part I, p. 6.

14. Ibid., Part II, p. 176.

15. Ibid., p. 181.

16. Ibid., pp. 76-77.

17. Ibid., p. 151.

18. Ibid., p. 78.

19. Ibid., p. 144.

20. Ibid., p. 147.

21. Alfred Loisy, *The Origins of the New Testament,* translated by L. P. Jacks, pp. 10-11. (First printed 1936. Reprinted in English translation by University Books, New Hyde Park, N.Y., 1962.)

22. Ibid., p. 25.

23. Ibid., pp. 27-28.

24. For a comprehensive and scholarly discussion of the New Testament, see: Robert M. Grant, *A Historical Introduction to the New Testament* (New York: Harper and Row, 1963). Opponents of Christianity have also written thorough critiques of the Bible, and among the best of these are two works by Joseph Wheless: *Is it God's Word?* (New York: Alfred A. Knopf, 1926); and *Forgery in Christianity* (New York: Alfred A. Knopf, 1930).

25. Samuel Terrien, *The Interpreter's Bible*, Vol. 5, p. 218.

26. Phillips, *Modern Thomistic Philosophy*, pp. 355-356.

27. Hospers, *An Introduction to Philosophical Analysis*, pp. 454-455.

28. Loisy, *Origins of the New Testament*, p. 80.

29. Archibald Robertson, *The Origins of Christianity* (New York: International Publishers, 1954), p. 82.

30. David Hume, *An Inquiry Concerning Human Understanding, Essential Works of David Hume*, edited by Ralph Cohen (New York: Bantam Books, 1965), p. 139.

31. Flew, *God and Philosophy*, p. 146.

32. Hume, *Concerning Human Understanding*, p. 139.

33. Ibid., p. 129.

34. Paine, *Age of Reason*, Part I, pp. 63-64.

Chapter 8

1. Stephen Toulmin, *The Place of Reason in Ethics* (London: Cambridge University Press, 1961), p. 214.

2. Corliss Lamont, *The Philosophy of Humanism* 5th ed., rev. (New York: Frederick Ungar Publishing Co., 1965), p. 124.

3. Flew, *God and Philosophy*, p. 193.

4. Antony Flew, *An Introduction to Western Philosophy* (Indianapolis

and New York: The Bobbs-Merrill Co., Inc., 1971), p. 181.

5. Ibid., p. 183.

6. Ibid., p. 182.

7. Flew, *God and Philosophy*, p. 69.

Chapter 9

1. Paul Edwards, "The Cosmological Argument," *The Cosmological Arguments*, edited by Donald R. Burrill (New York: Anchor Books, 1967), pp. 101-102.

2. Hospers, *An Introduction to Philosophical Analysis*, p. 431.

3. David M. Brooks, *The Necessity of Atheism* (New York: Freethought Press Association, 1933), pp. 102-103.

4. Nathaniel Branden, *The Objectivist Newsletter*, Vol. 1, No. 5 (May 1962), p. 19.

5. Mill, *Theism*, p. 13.

6. Chapman Cohen, *Materialism Restated*, 2nd ed., rev. (London: Pioneer Press, 1938), p. 138.

7. Copleston, *Aquinas*, p. 122.

8. Aquinas, *Summa Theologica*, First Part, Q. 2, A. 3.

9. Copleston, *Aquinas*, pp. 122-123.

10. Anthony Kenny, *The Five Ways* (New York: Schocken Books, 1969), p. 44.

11. Phillips, *Modern Thomistic Philosophy*, p. 284.

12. Ross, *Introduction to the Philosophy of Religion*, p. 30.

13. Flew, *God and Philosophy*, p. 88.

14. Bertrand Russell and F. C. Copleston, "A Debate on the Existence of

God," *The Existence of God,* edited by John Hick (New York: The Macmillan Co., 1964), pp. 168-169.

15. Ibid., p. 189.

16. Ibid., p. 175.

17. Some philosophers object to the contingency argument on the basis that necessity and contingency, properly considered, apply to propositions, not to beings. Thus, they claim, while it makes sense to speak of a proposition as necessarily or contingently true, it makes no sense whatever to speak of a being as necessary or contingent. A full discussion of this issue, however, as well as a thorough critique of the contingency argument, would eventually resolve itself into a discussion of "logical possibility"— and this issue is far too complex for the present discussion. In briefest essence, when I say that everything (except the products of volitional choice) exists necessarily, I mean that, given the natural forces of causality, no alternatives are, *in fact,* possible. And where there are no alternatives, we have necessity.

18. Copleston, *Aquinas,* p. 128.

19. Arthur Koestler, *The Ghost in the Machine* (New York: The Macmillan Co., 1967), pp. 197-198.

20. Trueblood, *The Philosophy of Religion,* p. 105.

21. John W. Robbins, "Conservatism versus Objectivism," *The Intercollegiate Review,* Vol. 6, no. 1-2 (Winter 1969-1970), p. 44.

22. Adolf Grünbaum, *Philosophical Problems of Space and Time* (New York: Alfred A. Knopf, 1963), p. 262.

23. E. A. Milne, *Sir James Jeans: A Biography* (Cambridge: The Cambridge University Press, 1952), p. 165.

24. L. D. Landau and E. M. Lifshitz, *Statistical Physics* (London: Pergamon Press Ltd., 1958), p. 29.

Chapter 10

1. Aquinas, *Summa Theologica,* First Part, Q. 2, A. 3.

2. See John Herman Randall, Jr., *Aristotle* (New York: Columbia University Press, 1962), pp. 225-238.

3. H. W. B. Joseph, *An Introduction to Logic*, 2d ed., rev. (Oxford: Clarendon Press, 1967), p. 408.

4. William Paley, *Natural Theology*, 1802. Quoted in Burrill, *The Cosmological Arguments*, pp. 166-167.

5. Ibid., p. 170.

6. W. T. Stace, *Religion and the Modern Mind* (Philadelphia: J. B. Lippincott Co., 1952), p. 88.

7. Matson, *Existence of God*, p. 129.

8. Ibid., p. 130.

9. Ibid.

10. Ibid., p. 104.

11. Lecomte du Noüy, *Human Destiny* (New York: Longmans, Green and Co., 1947), p. 28.

12. Stace, *Religion and the Modern Mind*, p. 86.

Chapter 11

1. Branden, *The Psychology of Self-Esteem*, p. 3.

2. Lamont, *The Philosophy of Humanism*, p. 170.

3. Rand, *The Virtue of Selfishness*, p. 2.

4. For an excellent discussion of this entire issue, see Walter G. Everett, *Moral Values* (New York: Henry Holt and Co., 1918), pp. 1-35.

5. Rand, *The Virtue of Selfishness*, p. 5. For an elaboration and specific formulation of the connection between values and life, see Branden, *The Psychology of Self-Esteem*, pp. 60-69.

6. Branden, *The Psychology of Self-Esteem*, p. 61.

7. Rand, *The Virtue of Selfishness*, p. 15.

8. Ibid., p. 16.

9. A number of fairly recent books on ethics are a welcome relief from the analytic trend. See, for example, Henry Veatch, *Rational Man* (Bloomington: Indiana University Press, 1966), and *For an Ontology of Morals* (Evanston: Northwestern University Press, 1971). Cf. Mortimer Adler, *The Time of Our Lives* (New York: Holt, Rinehart and Winston, 1970), and Robert G. Olson, *The Morality of Self-Interest* (New York: Harcourt, Brace and World, Inc., 1965).

10. Some philosophers deny that there is a sharp distinction to be drawn between normative ethics and meta-ethics, as these labels are usually conceived. Thus, according to Georg Henrik Von Wright, "There is also a philosophical pursuit deserving the name 'ethics', which shares with a common conception of 'meta-ethics' the feature of being a *conceptual investigation* and with a common conception of 'normative ethics' the feature of aiming at *directing our lives.*" *The Varieties of Goodness* (London: Routledge and Kegan Paul Ltd., 1963), p. 6. Cf. Veatch, *Rational Man*, pp. 17-23.

11. Portions of this discussion are taken from an article of mine that appeared in the December 1972 issue of *Invictus* magazine (No. 24).

12. This approach to "free will" is sometimes called the agency theory of volition. For further elaboration of the relation between volition and causality, see Nathaniel Branden, *The Psychology of Self-Esteem*, pp. 54-59. A general discussion of agency theory is contained in Richard Taylor, *Action and Purpose* (Englewood Cliffs: Prentice-Hall, 1966). Also excellent in this regard is Georg Henrik Von Wright, *Explanation and Understanding* (Ithaca: Cornell University Press, 1971).

13. Von Wright, *The Varieties of Goodness*, p. 161. For an interesting discussion and justification of the practical syllogism, see Nicholas Rescher, *Introduction to Value Theory* (Englewood Cliffs: Prentice-Hall, 1969), pp. 28-48. A distinction between "standards" and "rules," although different from mine, may be found in Paul W. Taylor, *Normative Discourse* (Englewood Cliffs: Prentice-Hall, 1961), pp. 5-47.

14. Ayn Rand, "Causality Versus Duty," *The Objectivist*, Vol. 9, No. 7 (July, 1970), p. 4.

15. I do not wish to suggest that human goals themselves are immune to rational evaluation, but a discussion of this rather complex issue lies beyond the scope of the present discussion. My point here is one of primacy. In other words, does morality serve man, or must man serve morality? I would defend the former, whereas religious moral codes characteristically defend the latter.

Chapter 12

1. Nietzche, *The Anti-Christ*, p. 166.

2. C. S. Lewis, *The Problem of Pain* (New York: The Macmillan Co., 1962), pp. 57-58.

3. Some modern Christians, including Catholics, insist that Christianity is in no way anti-sex. See, for example, John L. Thomas, *Catholic Viewpoint on Marriage and the Family*, rev. ed. (Garden City: Image Books, 1965), p. 110. However, for anyone who doubts the appalling record of Christianity in the area of sex, I strongly suggest a careful reading of G. Rattray Taylor, *Sex in History* (New York: The Vanguard Press, Inc., 1954). A reading of various Church Fathers, such as Augustine, will also prove instructive.

4. The exceptions are the various ascetic practices of early Christian sects, which are still recalled by Catholics in glowing terms. "For about two centuries," writes the historian W. E. H. Lecky, "the hideous maceration of the body was regarded as the highest proof of excellence." *History of European Morals from Augustus to Charlemagne*, Vol. 2, p. 107. (First printed 1869. Reprinted by George Braziller, New York, 1955.) Lecky provides a detailed account of these various gruesome practices.

5. Kaufmann, *The Faith of a Heretic*, p. 216.

6. Georgia Harkness, *Christian Ethics* (New York: Abingdon Press, 1957), p. 30.

7. Frederick C. Conybeare, *The Origins of Christianity*, pp. 153-154. (First printed 1909. Reprinted by University Books, Evanston and New York, 1958.)

8. Harkness, *Christian Ethics*, p. 48.

9. Joseph McCabe, *The Sources of the Morality of the Gospels* (London: Watts and Co., 1914), p. 209.

10. Nathaniel Branden, *The Disowned Self* (Los Angeles: Nash Publishing Co., 1971), p. 108.

Selected Reading
List

Blackstone, William T. *The Problem of Religious Knowledge*. Englewood Cliffs: Prentice-Hall, Inc., 1963 (Paperback).

Blanshard, Paul. *American Freedom and Catholic Power*. 2d ed., rev. Boston: Beacon Press, 1958 (Paperback).

Branden, Nathaniel. *The Psychology of Self-Esteem*. Los Angeles: Nash Publishing Corp., 1969.

Burrill, Donald R., ed. *The Cosmological Arguments*. New York: Doubleday and Co., Anchor Books, 1967 (Paperback).

Ducasse, C. J. *A Philosophical Scrutiny of Religion*. New York: The Ronald Press Co., 1953.

Ferré, Frederick. *Language, Logic and God*. 1961. New York: Harper and Row, Harper Torchbooks, 1969 (Paperback).

Flew, Antony. *God and Philosophy*. New York: Harcourt, Brace and World, Inc., 1966.

——, and MacIntyre, Alasdair, eds. *New Essays in Philosophical Theology*. New York: The Macmillan Co., 1955 (Paperback).

Hick, John, ed. *The Existence of God*. New York: The Macmillan Co., 1964 (Paperback).

——. *Philosophy of Religion*. Englewood Cliffs: Prentice-Hall, Inc., 1963 (Paperback).

347

Hook, Sidney, ed. *Religious Experience and Truth.* New York: New York University Press, 1961.

Hospers, John. *An Introduction to Philosophical Analysis.* 2d ed., rev. (Chapters 21 and 22.) Englewood Cliffs: Prentice-Hall, Inc., 1967.

Hume, David. *Dialogues Concerning Natural Religion.* Edited by Henry D. Aiken. New York: Hafner Publishing Co., 1966 (Paperback).

Huxley, Thomas H. *Collected Essays.* Volume V. New York: D. Appleton and Co., 1894.

Ingersoll, Robert G. *Ingersoll's Greatest Lectures.* New York: The Freethought Press Association, 1944.

Joad, C. E. M. *God and Evil.* London: Faber and Faber Ltd., 1942.

Kaufmann, Walter. *Critique of Religion and Philosophy.* 1958. New York: Harper and Row, Harper Torchbooks, 1972 (Paperback).

——. *The Faith of a Heretic.* 1961. New York: Doubleday and Co., Anchor Books, 1963 (Paperback).

Kenny, Anthony. *The Five Ways.* New York: Schocken Books, 1969.

Lamont, Corliss. *The Philosophy of Humanism.* 5th ed., rev. New York: Frederick Ungar Publishing Co., 1965 (Paperback).

Lewis, Joseph. *Atheism and Other Addresses.* New York: The Freethought Press Association, 1941.

Matson, Wallace I. *The Existence of God.* Ithaca: Cornell University Press, 1965.

McCabe, Joseph. *The Story of Religious Controversy.* Edited by E. Haldeman-Julius. Boston: The Stratford Co., 1929.

McTaggart, John. *Some Dogmas of Religion.* London: Edward Arnold, 1906.

Mencken, H. L. *Treatise on the Gods.* New York: Alfred A. Knopf, 1930.

Nietzsche, Friedrich. *Twilight of the Idols and The Anti-Christ.* Translated by R. J. Hollingdale. Harmondsworth, England: Penguin Books, Ltd., 1968 (Paperback).

Paine, Thomas. *Age of Reason.* 1794. *The Complete Works of Thomas Paine.* Volume 1. New York: The Freethought Press Association, 1954.

Rand, Ayn. *For the New Intellectual.* New York: Random House, 1961.

——. *The Virtue of Selfishness.* New York: The New American Library, 1964.

Robertson, Archibald. *The Origins of Christianity.* (Rev.) New York: International Publishers, 1954.

Robertson, J. M. *A History of Freethought.* 2 volumes. London: Watts and Co., 1936.

Robinson, Richard. *An Atheist's Values.* Oxford: The Clarendon Press, 1964.

Russell, Bertrand. *Why I Am Not a Christian.* Edited by Paul Edwards. 1957. New York: Simon and Schuster, 1966 (Paperback).

Smith, Homer W. *Man and His Gods.* Boston: Little, Brown and Co., 1955.

Taylor, G. Rattray. *Sex in History*. 1954. New York: The Vanguard Press, Inc., 1970.

Thrower, James. *A Short History of Western Atheism*. London: Pemberton Books, 1971.

Wells, Donald A. *God, Man, and the Thinker*. 1962. New York: Dell Publishing Co., 1967 (Paperback).

White, Andrew Dickson. *A History of the Warfare of Science With Theology in Christendom*. 2 volumes. 1896. New York: Dover Publications, 1960 (Paperback).

Index

Religious authority, appeal to 173-177
Religious morality 291-292, 297-305
conflicts with reason 305-311
virtue of 305
Revelation 193-218 (see also Bible; God; Miracles)
Robbins, John 254
Robertson, Archibald 216
Robertson, J. M. 198
Robinson, John A. T. 34-35, 36
Robinson, Richard 101, 109-110, 180-181, 317, 320
Ross, James F. 29, 101, 246
Ruby, Lionel 143
Rümke, H. C. 23
Russell, Bertrand 145, 248-249

Santayana, George 188
Schweitzer, Albert 315
Science
faith and 146-147
religion and 89-90, 113-115
Sense perception: skepticism and 147-162
Sex and Christianity 308-309
Sheen, Fulton J. 23
Sin, concept of 301-304
Skepticism
essential to Christianity 127-130
faith and 125-130, 140-147
reason and 134-140
sense perception and 147-162
universal 130-134
Smethurst, A. F. 129, 141
Solipsism 145
Spinoza, Baruch (or Benedict) 198-200
Stace, W. T. 265, 271
Stanford, Edward V. 170-171
Stratonician presumption 232-233
Sufficient reason, principle of 252
Supernatural being (see also God)
concept of 228-234
cosmological arguments for (see

Cosmology, arguments of)
defined 37-39
existence of 221-223, 224-226
proof, conditions of 223-224
Szasz, Thomas, S. 23

Taylor, A. E. 3, 5
Taylor, Richard 90
Teleological argument 258-262
Tertullian 99-100
Theism (see also Atheism, God; Supernatural being)
agnosticism and 9-10
atheism and 89
defined 7-8, 16
on the defense 27-28
rational 226
Theist
agnostic 10, 13
rational 227
Theology
affirmative 55-60
and Christian God 51-60
compared with philosophy 119
natural 221-234
negative 51-54
Thomas, George F. 10, 48, 57
Thomism (see Aquinas, Thomas)
Thompson, S. M. 181
Tillett, Wilbur F. 194-195
Tillich, Paul 33-35, 49
Toulmin, Stephen 224-225
Transcendence 37-39
Trueblood, David E. 128-129, 254

Unknowable (see also God; Supernatural being)
existence of 42-46, 50-51
reason and 107

Value judgments (see Meta-ethics)
Voluntarist theories of faith 181-189
Von Wright, George Henrik 294

Weatherhead, Leslie D. 42, 79, 182